Praise for Kriste

Why Can't I Ju.

Kristen Milstead provides a social psychological analysis of narcissistic abuse using the empathetic voice of a survivor. Survivors who read this book will be able to trust the "light-bulb" moments this rare perspective offers.

—Bree Bonchay, LCSW, Author of *I Am Free: Healing Stories About Surviving Toxic Relationships with Narcissists and Sociopaths* and Founder of World Narcissistic Abuse Awareness Day (WNAAD)

Kristen has a straightforward way of explaining the complex topic of narcissistic abuse. Her book shares both insights from her personal experiences and a clear and compassionate framework for understanding the complex ways that ostensibly loving relationships can morph into something utterly corrosive and dangerous.

—Dan Partland, Emmy-Award Winning Director of *#UNFIT: The Psychology of Donald Trump*

In *Why Can't I Just Leave?* author Kristen Milstead provides you with the answers you need to understand why you're stuck in a relationship with a narcissist, sociopath, or other exploiter so you can finally make your escape.

—Donna Andersen, Author of Lovefraud.com and *Red Flags of Love Fraud: 10 Signs You're Dating a Sociopath*

The truth is often hard to face. Getting free from an emotionally abusive relationship and facing *that* truth will be the hardest thing you will ever do. This book is packed with been-in-the-trenches wisdom and the key to your freedom.

—Tracy A. Malone, Founder of
Narcissist Abuse Support,
Author, and Coach

With the courageous use of her own intimate relationship, Kristen Milstead provides both an exploration and explanation of every aspect of "pathological love relationships." Descriptions of personal experiences and those of others, psychological theory, and detailed behavioral observations guide the reader through the journey from the beginning of a relationship with a partner whose concepts of reality, relationships, and ethics are based wholly on satisfying their emotional needs to how to extricate oneself from the grasp of the partner's malignantly fantastical world. Every aspect is covered in both practical and theoretical detail, as well as by example.

—David M. Reiss, M.D., Psychiatrist
(Private Practice—San Diego, Boston, NYC),
and Co-Author, *The Dangerous Case of Donald Trump*

Testimonials about Kristen Milstead's e-book, *Taking Your Life Back after a Relationship with a Narcissist*, and her website, https://www.fairytaleshadows.com:

I have read articles and books about narcissism for twenty years. You are the most accurate and insightful of any author. Thank you for your wisdom and being able to reach victims' minds and hearts.

—Cindy

You are such an exceptional writer and so giving with your wise and compassionate heart to help others involved with narcissists. This article is outstanding and one I'm going to share with my therapist. In fact, she liked your *Taking Your Life Back* booklet so much she asked me for two copies!

—Vicki

This is simply a "thank you" for what you do. Your resources and willingness to describe and analyze your abuse are excellent. So many resources are just too academic. Your "voice" is a pleasant blend of academic information and personal revelations.

—Sam

Kristen, I wanted to thank you so much for your free booklet. It was actually one of the most important resources I've read on narcissism and really helped me leave my narc. I struggled to understand why it was so hard, but the booklet helped me understand and work through those issues. I think it's good enough to sell, truly! I hope you are reaching lots of people with this really helpful resource of yours and thank you again. I wish more women knew about it. I see so many people struggling with leaving, and it is hard, but your ideas and exercises really did help.

—Lara

I showed your website to my therapist, and we've been talking about the situations around abuse in our sessions. I don't even remember how I stumbled across your website, but I thank the universe every day that I did. Reading your articles gave me enough space to have that out-of-body experience enough breath to be a witness to my own behavior. To snap out of the charm parade long enough to say—hold on a second. I guess, in a way, you were part of that day—the day I finally got away.

—Rachel

Thank you so much for writing these articles. It's been three years now that I've started to do research on narcissism, yet I stayed so confused. A few weeks ago, I stumbled on your site and everything I've read could be my words or thoughts. Everything you write resonates so well. A week ago, I started no-contact. Thank you, thank you, thank you.

—Sarah

Your articles are so helpful because you describe how we are feeling. Most describe characteristics of the narcissist. I am so thankful I found your site.

—Stacy

One of the things I love so much—coming from someone that has experienced this—is that for victims of emotional abuse, what you write comes from the most authentic place. You are not just writing an article about narcissism because it is a topic many are writing about—you are writing about it because you have a new and intelligent perspective to add. It comes through in your writing. This type of writing is so important because it not only helps you move beyond your pain, but it reaches your hand out to others and tell us it's going to be okay.

—Jessica

I wanted to express my deep appreciation and a heartfelt thank-you for your blog. It helped me get through some incredibly trying, seemingly hopeless times. Your courage is incredible, and your ability to transcend your own pain and loss through this blog has helped me in my own dark journey, as I'm sure it's done for so many others. I'm so very grateful!

—Claire

You've been instrumental to my being able to verbalize the chaos that twirls around in my head. You don't know this, but I forward the posts that resonate to my psychologist to better explain what I'm feeling.

—Valerie

Excellent! I've read most of these articles and passed them to a friend or two who also are recovering from this situation. Your articles are A++! Highly recommend reading all these to anyone who's recovering or researching their relationship/s.

—Kathleen

I love the understanding and support of your articles and do thank you so much for all you do to let us know we are not crazy or alone.

—Nicole

Thank you, Kristen! The knowledge, understanding, empathy, and solidarity you provide towards all your readers and followers become their guiding light towards a beautiful, narc-free life!

—Renee

I found your online blog, and I think it's an incredibly well-written and accurate set of writing that perfectly describes what I went through over the space of ten years. It really helped me process some things. Thank you.

—Kim

Kristen as a grateful follower of your content, I feel compelled to reach out and say THANK YOU. Really, the information you have published has been of the highest quality. I appreciate how well you are able to articulate and put into words your own experiences and share with the world what NPD abuse patterns look like and how to heal from it. Being one who has listened to and read a bit on the topic, I want you to know that for me personally, your work certainly stands out as some of the highest quality I have yet read. Your work has spoken to me and resonated with me powerfully, and I want you to know that. You are shining a light of hope and understanding, helping others like myself shed the scales of chaos, confusion, pain, hurt, trauma bonding, and so on … so that we can be empowered, know we're not alone, understand there is a path of healing, and that not all people are like this. Forgive me for the length of my message, but I wanted to convey my sincerest thanks to you and encourage you to keep up the good work. It is making a difference.

—Matt

You are quickly establishing yourself as having some of the best content out there on narcissistic personality disorder. Thanks for your contributions and willingness to be such a powerful messenger, blaring the clarion call of truth regarding such a damaging and poisonous disorder, helping those of us who have found ourselves in such an entangled web of pain and confusion. Thank you.

—Dan

Kristen, you will never know the positive healthy impact your blog has made in my life. My narcissist left in May 2017 after four years. I identify with everything you are doing to help those of us who have experienced what you have also. Just sending out a huge THANK YOU for all your help. Please don't stop. YOU have made a much-needed difference in my life.

—Mary

I am not kidding when I say that yesterday I read your sixty-five-page book with wonder and recognition and again today, taking more care to absorb its contents more thoroughly. In my thirty-five years of being married to a narcissist, I often thought desperately to myself that there was no one in the world with whom I could identify. But maybe, sadly, his type is more common than I thought. It would certainly seem that way after reading your powerful book. Thank you for writing it so simply that even this "bear with little brain" can understand and get excited about each paragraph as it unfolds its familiar story. Imagine his shock, like I truly blind-sided him when I announced I was going to apply for a divorce.

—Jennifer

I just sent you a message through your website, but I wanted to connect on here as well. You've made the difference in my life where I was actually suicidal at certain points in my recovery because of the destruction he did to my psyche. You set me free. Forever love and gratitude to you.

—Miranda

I want you to know what your articles and perspective has done for me. I've identified the fact my abuser was a narcissist and I needed to move on, through other outlets, but until I came across your site and your perspective, I couldn't actually go no-contact with full conviction. I felt like you were with the same person I was with. You presented the information so well, and you weren't asking me to take a class or workshop if I wanted to actually succeed in moving on. You saved my life. I left him and moved to another city, but he still infiltrated my life until I came across your site. I'm forever indebted to you. Thank you, thank you. You validated me and my experience fully. So much gratitude.

—Crystal

This, by far, is the best description of the relationship between a "normal" person and a narcissist. I will read the rest in sections because so much applies to my ex-narcissist's behavior and as I continue recovery, I am always finding new things that fit this man perfectly. Although I am not interested in another relationship with anybody, this is valuable information to know when interacting on any level with another person. I have also recommended your page to a couple of my friends who went through the same hell as me. I am also hoping your wisdom will help one of my friends currently in a very rocky relationship with a narcissist. Thank you for sharing with the world!

—Katherine

I just want to say thank you so much for your beautiful writings and let you know that your words help me more than you were ever know. I feel lost and confused, and it's a horrible journey, and I just want to get to the other side. Your words and writings make me feel less afraid and alone. I am on several forums already, but this particular site and I guess the way you express your experience of what you went through resonates with me.

—Bella

I appreciate your work in trying to educate people about this problem, as I feel no one on the outside can fully grasp the true reality of it. Your courage is amazing! The eloquence and simplicity with which you are able to describe what happens in a narcissistic relationship is epic! Although I have little faith in myself anymore and have a long road to recovery, your words give me the conviction to stay with it.

—Rory

I'm supporting a friend through a long, long break-up with her narcissistic and psychopathic ex. At times, it's been really hard to help; jumping in is a natural urge I've had to fight against, as sitting back and watching relapse after relapse has been incredibly hard. We've both found your website a real help. Your writing is so practical and accessible. We can both relate. So, just a big thanks, really. I know it's a long road, but I hope we've turned a corner now.

—Tim

Kristen, I am so thankful to you for all your write ups. Six months of reading them again and again, and I understood where I stand. There is no pain now, and I am blossoming into someone happier each day and releasing what all I had given up for that man. God bless you.

—Etka

Don't know what I would do without your site. That is all I can say right now. You are my lifeline. So much gratitude.

—Taryn

Please keep writing your articles; they are so important and helpful in my recovery. You understand it all so well. Many thanks.

—Jacqui

I'm very thankful for your blog. First and foremost, I'm not crazy! Thank you for that. At the moment, what I'm reading on here is helping to guide me as I assess my narcissist husband and understand what I've been going through. Having the information that your blog provides is priceless, for many reasons. The fact that I'm not crazy is good to know. The fact that there is a real term to describe my husband and terms/definitions describing what he's done to me has made me cry from relief. I now have help to guide me through this horrible period of life, along with providing hope for my future. Thank you for that.

—Kelly

It was your site that finally set off the biggest and final lightbulb for me. After many articles and videos that kept resonating with me, I still felt disbelief. There was something really profound to your posts: everything that didn't make sense made too much sense. I believe the information on your site gives such a good wide spectrum view of all types. It even brought me full circle to having met many … unfortunately … and starting in childhood. Thank you again for helping so many and myself included!

—Lisa

WHY CAN'T I JUST LEAVE?

A GUIDE TO WAKING UP AND WALKING OUT OF A PATHOLOGICAL LOVE RELATIONSHIP

KRISTEN MILSTEAD, PH.D.

AUTHOR ACADEMY elite

Published by Author Academy Elite
PO Box 43, Powell, OH 43065
www.AuthorAcademyElite.com

Identifiers:
Library of Congress Control Number: 2021910770
ISBN: 978-1-64746-827-9 (paperback)
ISBN: 978-1-64746-828-6 (hardback)
ISBN: 978-1-64746-829-3 (e-book)

Available in paperback, hardback, e-book, and audiobook.

Some of the concepts in this book have been previously discussed in articles on my website, www.fairytaleshadows.com. This material is referenced for the purposes of synthesizing and expanding it to provide the new and original content in this book.

This book is dedicated to everyone who has ever lost themselves in a pathological love relationship and felt the despair of drowning in plain sight.

Nothing changes instantaneously; in a gradually heating bathtub you'd be boiled to death before you knew it.

—Margaret Atwood, *The Handmaid's Tale*

To know and not to know, to be conscious of complete truthfulness while telling carefully constructed lies, to hold simultaneously two opinions which cancelled out, knowing them to be contradictory and believing in both of them . . . that was the ultimate subtlety: consciously to induce unconsciousness, and then, once again, to become unconscious of the act of hypnosis you had just performed.

—George Orwell, *1984*

A man will often try to hold out beyond the limits of his endurance because he continues to believe that his tormentors have some basic morality, that they will finally realize the enormity of their crimes and will leave him alone. This is a delusion. The only way to strengthen one's defences against an organized attack on the mind and will is to understand better what the enemy is trying to do and to outwit him.

—Joost A.M. Meerloo, *The Rape of the Mind*

Table of Contents

Question One: What's Wrong with My Partner?

Question Two: Is My Partner "Good" or "Bad?"

Question Three: Why Can't I Just Leave?

Question Four:
Where Did I Go?

Question Five:

How Do I Get Out of Here?

Author's Note

This book is about psychological manipulation as a form of abuse in relationships. People who are otherwise rational, intelligent, and educated can find themselves, under the right conditions, doing things they wouldn't ordinarily do. Over the past few years, I heard from doctors, attorneys, business owners, teachers, people running for political office, and even mental health professionals who told me they have been victimized. Their ages vary, their gender identities and sexual orientations vary, and their racial identities vary; they are Christian, Muslim, and Jewish, and they live all over the world. When we fail to acknowledge that psychological manipulation is abuse and can happen to anyone, we help ensure it stays an invisible problem. This invisibility makes it easy for predatory people to continue to victimize others and makes it more difficult for survivors to get the recovery assistance they need.

In this book, I include some of my personal experiences in a pathological love relationship. I chose to include these experiences alongside the more objective parts of the book as an example of one cohesive set of events that can occur in a relationship with a pathological partner to demonstrate how a relationship like this one becomes a trap that closes around a person's mind. I thought many times of removing the parts of the book containing my story, worried that they may be a distraction from what I had hoped to accomplish. However, my editor convinced me to leave them in, suggesting that their authenticity was one of the most significant factors contributing to the weight of everything else in the book. I'll take her word for it and let readers be the judge of that.

I am aware that some of my actions may make me appear naïve at best. I'm less concerned about how I'm perceived than that some people will read those parts of the book, and no other possibilities will occur to them. Sadly, they will have missed the point of this work. However, if I can inspire those of you who recognize your journey and feelings of hopelessness in my experiences, then my vulnerability will have served its purpose. Although I've included them here for illustrative purposes, please note that my experiences are mine alone and do not necessarily represent all pathological love relationships.

The events I share about my life were reconstructed or, in the case of some of the dialogue, taken directly from emails, text messages, my journal entries, and narrative writing I did during or right after the relationship ended. I changed names, locations, and identifying details not central to the events that transpired to protect the privacy of individuals who played a role in what happened. To best highlight the themes in the book, I selected certain parts of my experience. Although this is probably obvious, it should be said that they do not characterize the complexity of the relationship dynamic, nor are they fully demonstrative of the intensity or degree of chaos and abuse that occurred for the nearly four years the relationship lasted.

Also, I am a sociologist, and I wrote this book through that lens. I focused on the social forces that create power imbalances and condition behavior. I became interested in how, over time, these repetitive unequal dynamics change someone who is in a relationship with a pathological partner. As I am not a medical professional, please also note that the information, descriptions, and suggestions offered in this book should not replace or substitute advice given to you by one. If you need medical, health, psychological, or psychiatric care, assistance, or consultation, please seek a licensed medical professional for care and assistance. Before taking any of the actions suggested in this book, please evaluate your safety and develop a crisis plan as needed. Appendix C at the end of this book may assist you with finding resources and agencies that can help you with this task.

This book is the one I needed when I was trying to leave my relationship. I didn't know I needed it, but I did. It is my greatest honor to humbly share the research and information in it with you now. Understanding why a relationship with a pathological partner creates an invisible prison around us can be the first step to empowering ourselves and breaking free.

Foreword

It is 2021, and pathological love relationships have only slowly come into the public's awareness. It seems incomprehensible that these relationships haven't warranted more concern or attention, as they put people unknowingly in close, sustained contact with pathological individuals who have some of the most dangerous disorders in the *Diagnostic and Statistical Manual of Psychiatric Disorders, Fifth Edition* (DSM-5), such as psychopathy, antisocial personality disorder, and narcissistic personality disorder. What these relationships can do to survivors of them is likely the epitome of true harm and trauma.

Millions of dollars are spent every year on researching the psychopathic mind, but not one dollar has been spent on researching the impact of their behavior on those with whom psychopaths interact in their everyday lives, particularly, in their romantic relationships. There are no billboard campaigns or grant funds, no celebrity spokesperson or fund-raisers, no government prevention programs or fliers or tele-thons to distribute information about what psychopathy or these other dangerous disorders can look like in everyday life or the warning signs that someone might be in a pathological love relationship. The most dangerous people on the planet come with no warning.

For thirty years, I have worked as a therapist with survivors of pathological love relationships who experience extreme trauma, and in 2008, my book *Women Who Love Psychopaths—Inside the Relationships of Inevitable Harm with Psychopaths, Sociopaths & Narcissists* was the first book to detail the relationship dynamics, trauma response, and survivor profile of these victims. Only thirteen years have passed since the publication of the first edition of *Women Who Love Psychopaths* and The Institute for Relational Harm Reduction & Public Pathology Education began warning others about pathological love relationships. Today, there are more than eleven million Google results for terms like "narcissistic abuse," and millions of survivors of these relationships have formed a grassroots movement. Much like the domestic violence movement, survivors of pathological love relationships have been the engine and the wheels that have taken this machine forward.

This explosion in available information speaks volumes about the prevalence of these relationships; being a victim of one of the "danger zone" pathological personalities is not that rare. Survivors have expressed and described their own experiences, also giving a voice to millions of others in the United States alone who have had similar experiences. The absence of available information in the past isn't an indicator that the problem didn't exist. As the #MeToo movement has proven, past silence about or obliviousness to an issue doesn't mean it is a new phenomenon. Its emergence in public discourse is simply a sign that it's a movement whose time has come.

And this movement's time has come.

If you are reading this book, you are likely curious if you are or have been in a pathological love relationship. You also may have noticed that it is quite difficult to find therapists, resources, programs, and help, despite eleven million pages on Google. This emerging field of public awareness, research, and counseling is in the initial stages of providing the necessary training for the widespread availability of those resources. Until it becomes more readily available, survivors find most of their answers in books.

As one of the pioneers in this new wilderness, I can tell you that not all books are created equal. My personal goal decades ago was to bring these inevitably harmful relationships into the spotlight so that we could study how they were different from other dysfunctional relationships that were harmful yet did not lead to the totalism of the survivor's destruction the way pathological love relationships do. We, like you, were tired of others assuming it was simply a "bad breakup" and asking why survivors did not just move along and "get over it." What we found was a consistent "fingerprint" left behind for identification by a devious, destructive, and disordered partner. That fingerprint showed some of the most atypical, yet complex trauma I had ever seen splayed on survivor after survivor. It has taken our agency thirty years to unearth what makes that trauma different than that of the trauma experienced by survivors of other negative events—even other abusive situations. Our research has been able to pinpoint why your relationship was so "dramatic and erratic" and why you were targeted—and to identify the hallmark symptom of pathological love relationships: cognitive dissonance.

Kristen Milstead has done an excellent, and more importantly, *accurate* job of explaining these relationships of "inevitable harm." While she is a survivor, her book is more than a tell-all book of "My Life with a Narcissist," which you can find in abundance anywhere. Her Ph.D. in Sociology lends a brilliant and professional view for survivors to understand the human interaction patterns behind these relationships that have left survivors either paralyzed from cognitive dissonance and intrusive thoughts or wildly oscillating between loving and loathing, craving and repulsion, and wanting and not wanting.

You have waited a long time for this direly important information that can help you understand and heal. In fact, it is accurate information and education about pathological relationships that has been at the forefront of what helps survivors know what to seek help *for*. As I always say, "You won't heal what you don't identify."

Kristen's book is a one stop shop for understanding the pathology behind your partner, your relationship dynamics, why you were targeted, the symptoms of your trauma, and steps you can take toward leaving you partner.

Who could ask for more?

Sandra L. Brown, M.A.
Founder of The Institute for Relational Harm
Reduction & Public Pathology Education and
Current President of The Association for NPD/
Psychopathy Survivor Treatment, Research & Education

QUESTION ZERO:

Why Am I Reading This Book?

My brain was continuing to ruminate and be obsessed about the end of this relationship. I couldn't eat, I couldn't sleep, I was having difficulties concentrating on my daily activities. I found all this was not normal as I had gone through much more difficult situations than that in my life. One day, just by chance, I went online looking for a description of a sociopath . . .

—*Erin,* survey respondent

1

You Chose This Book for a Reason

We stood in a crowded bar, but that didn't stop Amir from waving to the bartender impatiently for a fresh rum and Coke. I watched him flirt with the young woman on the other side of him, a woman he'd met at the hotel pool earlier. He had invited her to meet us after dinner, as if we hadn't spent the past eighteen months in a passionate relationship together with him whispering to me daily I was the love of his life.

Unsure of what to do, I looked around the spacious lobby of the resort, which was tucked garishly among several others along the powdery sand of the Jamaican shoreline. The bar was centered between tall, white, marble columns. Plush, blue couches and a black grand piano hovered at the perimeters of the room, where beautiful, tanned people draped themselves over the furniture, talking to one another about their beautiful lives. I sat in shock, unable to fathom the stake that had been driven through mine.

Amir had finished at least twice as many drinks at the bar as I'd had on top of several rum and Cokes at dinner, and when he stood up, he fell. The crowd in the room gasped and went silent as he ambled to his feet, the knees of his suit pants dusty. Two staff members rushed over, but Amir waved them away and held his arms out to show everyone he was okay. He turned to me, glaring as if I'd had something to do with his fall. After saying something to the woman next to him, he growled in my ear that he was going back to our room.

"Are you coming?" he said.

I froze, contemplating the trap before me. If I followed Amir back to the room, his drunken contempt for me would take over. We would be alone with nothing to stop him from unleashing it on me. Yet if I stayed without him at the bar too long, he'd accuse me of going back to another man's room.

Maybe he would pass out.

I looked down and shook my head, and I could see him staring out of the corner of his eye before he tore off into the night.

Then, it was as if I had willed it to happen. A man appeared beside me. He was in his early thirties with dark blonde hair, dressed in a brown, checked sport coat and a button-down shirt.

"I can't talk to you," I said before he had said a word.

"What?" His eyebrows creased in confusion.

"I mean, I have a boyfriend."

"Oh," he said, relaxing. "Well, he's a very lucky man."

"Uh—thanks," I said, my eyes darting around the room. The lobby had several entrances, and my eyes flicked back and forth between all of them. Each time my eyes fell upon the one Amir had walked through, his shape materialized for an instant, then disintegrated. I felt faint.

"Did he come here with you?"

"Yes, he did. And if he sees me talking to you, he's going to be really upset." I blurted it before I could even stop myself. My heart hammered in my chest now.

The man's eyes creased again with concern. As soon as I saw it, I lost my composure, and I started to cry. "I'm sorry. I have to go."

"Wait. Wait, are you okay?" He touched the underside of my arm, where I had a bruise in the shape of a thumbprint.

No. I'm not okay.

The enormity of it all crushed me, pushing me away from myself. It was a dream, yet it wasn't. I wasn't sure exactly how I had ended up there. Yet every excruciating detail had been its own slicing blade, and dozens of tiny cuts were draining me out.

About a week before Amir and I had left for Jamaica, his secrets had been eating me alive, and I finally decided I had to know the truth.

He had stormed out of the apartment we shared when I asked him why he lied to me about a social media app he claimed he didn't use. I'd found out about his lie by accident when I found his profile and asked him about it. It was one small lie, and according to him, a petty thing to ask him about—and it might have been in isolation. Yet it was a lie stacked on top of eighteen months of competing sets of facts and forceful half-truths and his insistence that I'd just heard him wrong, or I was starting arguments over nothing. Either way, I was going crazy, or there was something I didn't know.

Then, after his dramatic exit, his rage escalated in a barrage of texts meant to punish me for questioning him. One of them was a blunt declaration that he was still dating not one but two of his ex-girlfriends: Sandi and Julia. A few minutes later, he retracted it, telling me he'd said it only to hurt me. But I had wondered whether it was true after all, so I'd decided to ask the women.

I found Sandi on Facebook and sent her a message. She and I had met before a few times on good terms, so I thought she might tell me the truth. "Are you and Amir still dating? Or sleeping together or whatever?" I asked her. "I just want to know the truth. I won't be mad at you—he is the one who owes me loyalty."

"I'm not going to lie to you," she responded. "He tried to start something with me, but I never slept with him. I can assure you of that."

Sandi's response hacked its way into my life, slashing one of those clean dividing lines between then and now. Her words gave shape to a man I didn't know, a man who was the opposite of the one Amir had spent over a year showing me. The Amir I knew had been slowly revealed over time through thousands of hours spent together and conversations in which what she told me was just not in character. That man I knew was loyal and passionate and affectionate. He was relatively inexperienced and innocent when it came to relationships, and almost all his past girlfriends had betrayed him. And he loved me. Very, very much. He said so multiple times a day. He lost his temper frequently, and he was jealous of every man I knew and even some of my friends, but he wasn't unfaithful. Not the man I knew.

Yet hadn't he just said himself in a text that he wasn't *that man I knew after all?*

Before I could finish processing what she'd said, Sandi then gave me even more truth than I had asked for. "I'm going to be completely honest with you. You can't trust Amir. It's just not who he is. He is always going to try things with other girls. He got engaged on purpose when I was dating him. He had no problem cheating on her and me."

I had to reread the last sentence.

He got engaged on purpose when I was dating him.

My hands shook as I typed back to her. "He told me about an engagement that was made between him and someone when he was a baby and that he didn't get a say at the time, but he said he hadn't wanted it, so it had been broken off, and it was over."

"Haha . . . no, not at all what happened. He went to Pakistan three years ago for his sister's wedding when we were dating and essentially forced his parents into arranging the marriage, then

he tried to come back and keep the engagement a secret while we were still dating. He is still with his fiancé—he hasn't broken that off—so there is always a chance he will run off."

Blood seemed to whoosh out of me, and a rush of cold air surrounded me. I felt myself slip outside of my body as if I was watching myself. "How do you know he hasn't broken it off?"

"As far as I've been told, it hasn't been broken off. It's a hard thing to do since he asked for the marriage, and why would he do that since she's forced to wait for him?"

Why would he do that? All the reasons why he might break it off flooded into my mind at once.

Maybe because he said so many times that wasn't the life he wanted. Then, I wondered why he made a point of going to the trouble of making me believe the engagement was some artifact of the past and starting a relationship with me if it wasn't true?

Maybe because we live together, signed a lease, and moved into a new apartment. Why do all those couple things, like get a joint bank account with someone, if you're planning to marry someone else?

Maybe because he's mentioned the two of us getting married like a million times, and he can't marry two people at the same time?

I couldn't make the facts Sandi had given me and the events I'd experienced over the past eighteen months come together in my head in a way that didn't leave jagged edges sticking out.

"I thought he might have changed dating you, but if he hasn't, he's not worth your time," she said. "You seem like a smart woman, but he is so manipulative. He's just bad news. And over the summer, he has admitted to everyone multiple times that he was just using you for your money. You can do better. You will be much happier without him." I couldn't even remember a situation between us where my money could have been an important factor. We shared all the bills. He didn't have access to any of my personal financial accounts.

However, I suddenly remembered I had recently decided to put his name on my life insurance policy after he claimed I didn't love him and didn't want to be with him. I couldn't even remember at that moment how the life insurance had come up anymore, but it was an act I had done to prove to him that the opposite of what he had said was true.

As I sat on the bed Amir and I shared texting with Sandi, I heard the front door open and close as Amir arrived home. I stepped into the living room to confront him and saw him lying on the couch staring at his phone, the light from its display reflected off his face. He didn't even glance up at me.

Anger boiled over inside me, and I stalked over to the couch, ripped the phone out of his hands, and tossed it onto the sofa beside him. He looked up at me, surprised.

"You wanted the engagement! You asked for it! And you're still engaged!" I screamed.

His mouth opened and closed, but he said nothing.

"Sandi told me," I said. "You lied to me! Why would you do that? Why?"

I expected him to deny it. Maybe he would try to disqualify what Sandi said by giving his account again of how badly she'd mistreated him or deflect and accuse me of trying to start an argument. Perhaps, he would even angrily storm out the door again.

Instead, he looked up at me coldly and sneered. "I don't have to tell you anything. How does it feel to be used?"

I took a step backward in shock, unable to say anything in response.

When I told him our relationship was over, Amir coldly told me he wouldn't move out because his name was on the lease as well. I told him I would move out instead, and he responded that after I did, he would abandon the apartment and move in with some of his family members who lived outside the United States. He wouldn't think twice about leaving me with trying to salvage my credit by paying rent on two apartments.

The next day, however, he gave me a proposition. I'd learned about the engagement just days before we were to leave on a trip to Jamaica. If I agreed to go on the trip with him anyway, he said, he would move out when we returned. Seeing no option but to hope he would keep his word, I agreed to go.

My gut told me there was still more. I'd learned some things from Sandi, but what about Julia, the other ex-girlfriend he'd mentioned in his outburst? I reached out to Julia via Facebook Messenger with a feeling of dread, letting her know what Amir had said and asking her for any information she had.

"Do you have time to call me?" she responded.

I was at work when I received her message. What on earth did she have to tell me? "I have about a half-hour at noon."

Her message came back almost instantaneously. "I don't think that will be long enough."

My heart pounded as I took the elevator up to the roof of the building and listened to her story over the phone. For two hours, she explained how she and Amir had continued their relationship the entire time he and I had been together. He had also proposed to her many times, which she verified by sending me his text messages.

Afraid of how Amir would react if he knew what else I'd learned, I intended to keep from him indefinitely that I knew about Julia, or at the very least make sure he didn't find out until after he moved out. Yet that didn't go as planned. He found out I knew on our first full day in Jamaica and exploded in a rage, becoming a man I had never seen before. I thought about the life insurance and wondered if he planned to kill me.

The days in Jamaica after that passed by, but they were not days so much as seconds bleeding out under which I endured his terrorism. During that time, it was as if I existed with a presence like that of a faint, wispy cloud that drifts until the wind blows it apart into nothingness. Sometimes I had wondered if I was there at all.

Amir befriended others quickly as if nothing was happening behind closed doors and invited them to sit with us at dinner, imposing them upon me almost cruelly to observe my silent pain. He laughed easily with them, entertaining them with stories of living in Washington, D.C., or traveling to Vegas, asking me to chime in occasionally to confirm a tale. He danced wildly to the music pumping out of the speakers at the beach, encouraging me to join in. I half-heartedly participated in volleyball games in the pool while he dived after each ball competitively as if a win meant anything more than a smattering of applause by onlookers. Sometimes, he even flirted with women at the bars, smirking at me, daring me to say something. There was an implicit threat behind the imposition of this guise of normalcy/not normalcy he had thrust upon me. I had done my best to play along while the blazing sun beat mercilessly down on our skin, and the tops of my arms reddened, the pain of the burn not penetrating my numbness.

I had spent seven days trapped on an island with a man who had terrorized and abused me in every way you could hurt a person. I would not leave the same woman I had been when I arrived. Now, here I was, standing at the bar in the lobby with the man who had asked me what was wrong. What should I say to him? He was still holding my arm, looking at the bruise, and I knew I could never explain.

"Yes . . . look, he cheated on me. I'm only here with him because he said he wouldn't move out of our apartment unless I came here, and if he sees me talking to you, he might do worse than this."

As I had heard my voice, robotically speaking, what I'd said made little sense even to me. What boyfriend would cheat on his girlfriend, then say he wouldn't let her leave the relationship unless she went on vacation with him, of all things? And then, why go on vacation with her only to turn it into a nightmare? And cheating wasn't even half of it. Not really. And then, how could I even explain how I got here with a man like that anyway? Everything was all twisted.

Without even thinking about what I was doing, I blurted out to him random bits and pieces of what had happened. My tears started to dry up as I talked. Words came pouring out that I couldn't stop, and I let out some of what I'd been so careful to hold in. It was as if I could prove to myself I hadn't imagined it by saying it out loud. I wasn't crazy.

The man listened quietly, then with his eyes still full of concern, he said something I'll never forget: "He sounds like a psychopath."

It Wasn't Supposed to Be Like This

Being in a pathological love relationship is one of the most exhilarating, devastating, heart-pounding, confusing, frightening, and painful experiences anyone could, I dare say, ever experience.

One moment, your partner pulls you into the most passionate love affair you have ever known. The next moment, he or she casts you aside with no explanation, often leaving you in the depths of despair and with damage to your physical health, emotional well-being, bank account, or all three.[1] It throws both your emotions and ability to reason into turmoil as you struggle to make sense of what has happened to you. Your entire life becomes consumed with the puzzle of why it all happened.

You likely cannot explain to yourself, much less anyone else, why you can call a relationship both exhilarating and devastating or why you may miss someone who punishes you with a sudden breakup or silent treatment.

If you're reading this, then something terrible has happened to you. I know this because it also happened to me.

I wish I could say that trip to Jamaica was the last interaction between Amir and me. It wasn't. No label exists to explain what it was, but it took me over two years to finally break away from him. *Over two years.*

It doesn't mean I didn't try. There were significant reasons I couldn't see and accept the truth during those two years.

This book is about what it means to both see and not see at the same time. It's a guide to help you understand why we try to leave and fail until that day when we try to escape and finally succeed. This book will help you learn everything that happens in between so you can get out sooner.

I would guess that, as you read this, you're in one of four places emotionally (or maybe you're like I was and alternate between one or more of them):

1. You only recently found out that something was wrong, that your partner appears to have a problem. You may be reading other books or articles but have difficulty believing what they describe applies to your situation, despite the remarkable similarities.

2. You're pretty sure your partner has a problem, but you may have trouble believing it's serious. Sometimes, you might even think the problem isn't actually a problem or that you might be the problem. In any case, you feel torn about leaving or staying. You're so confused about everything that's happened, and you aren't sure you want to give up.

3. You *know* your partner has a problem, and you no longer want to be in the relationship, but you feel powerless to do anything about it. You feel stuck in the relationship for some reason. A part of you may be holding out hope that things will go back to the way they were at the beginning of the relationship, although you know deep down that will almost surely never happen. You don't even understand anymore what is keeping you there.

4. You know your partner (or ex-partner) has a problem. The two of you keep breaking up, but you can't

> seem to stay out of the relationship. You have so many unanswered questions that keep you hanging onto the past and keep you stuck in a loop where you feel as if you'll never be free of what ties you to your partner. You may feel despair most or all the time.

Maybe you're unsure if you should read this book, about whether it applies to your circumstances. I wrote this book for everyone who has a voice inside them telling them to pick it up, even if they're unsure why.

I'm going to assume that if you could have, you would have already left the relationship—or you would at least already know for sure if you wanted to or not.

You're reading this book for a reason—even if you don't know what it is yet.

There are also reasons you may be unsure if this book is for you, even if you identified with the descriptions above.

Hidden Pictures

In the early 1990s, a new form of bizarre art swept the nation. Books titled *Magic Eye* filled with page after page of the colorful artwork dominated *The New York Times*. Thumbing through a *Magic Eye* book, one would see colorful two-dimensional computer-generated patterns repeated across each page.

However, what made the artwork so popular was the hidden image beyond the pattern. This image appeared three-dimensional when some viewers stared at the picture in just the right way. The creators of these images explained that these three-dimensional images appear because the computer algorithm that generates the pattern tricks our brains into perceiving depth, as if there is *space between the lines of the pattern.*[2] The pictures are sort of like the cubes we're taught how to draw in elementary school out of two overlapping squares.

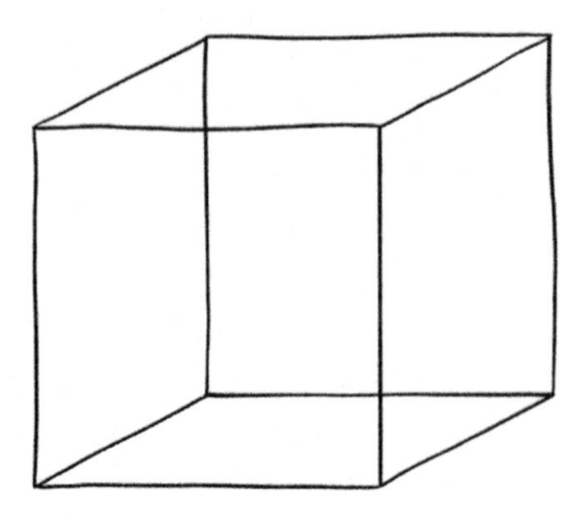

Figure 1.1: Two-Dimensional Box

After the computer algorithm tricks us into seeing depth in the picture, it hides an image under the colorful, repeating pattern. When you first look at the picture, however, all you see is the pattern. It's only through intense staring that some people can eventually see the three-dimensional hidden image.

Can a person's life look like it has a specific pattern but be hiding a completely different picture inside of it no one can see? Not even, or maybe especially, that person?

Can the mind be tricked into believing a reality but be hiding another one underneath?

If you were being abused, you'd know it. Right?

You don't need to come up with the answer to that question yet. However, I'd like you to use the exercise below to think about what your relationship is like right now.

Pathological Love Relationship Checklist

Take a few moments to read the following list of items below. Do any of them pertain to your situation? Put a checkmark beside the ones that feel true for you. Go with your gut feeling. Do not stop to think too hard about each one.

_____ 1. Your intuition tells you that something is off, that there are things about your partner right under the surface you don't know.

_____ 2. You hear conflicting stories about your partner that make little sense.

_____ 3. You catch your partner in lies, even lies that make no sense to tell.

_____ 4. You see your partner acting friendly with people they told you had wronged them in the past or with whom they claim they are not on good terms.

_____ 5. Your partner gets upset about little things you do that seem illogical. The anger is fierce or seems to come out of nowhere.

_____ 6. You do or say things that make you feel guilty or question yourself or have uncomfortable emotions in response to your partner's behavior you have never felt in your past relationships.

_____ 7. Your partner frequently or relentlessly accuses you of cheating without cause.

_____ 8. When you try to communicate with your partner about something that's bothering you, the conversation devolves into nonsense. They somehow turn the conversation back around on you and insist your reasonable questions or statements of concern are the causes of arguments.

_____ 9. When you first met your partner, the relationship accelerated quickly, and you felt you had found a soulmate.

_____ 10. Your partner's actions rarely match their words.

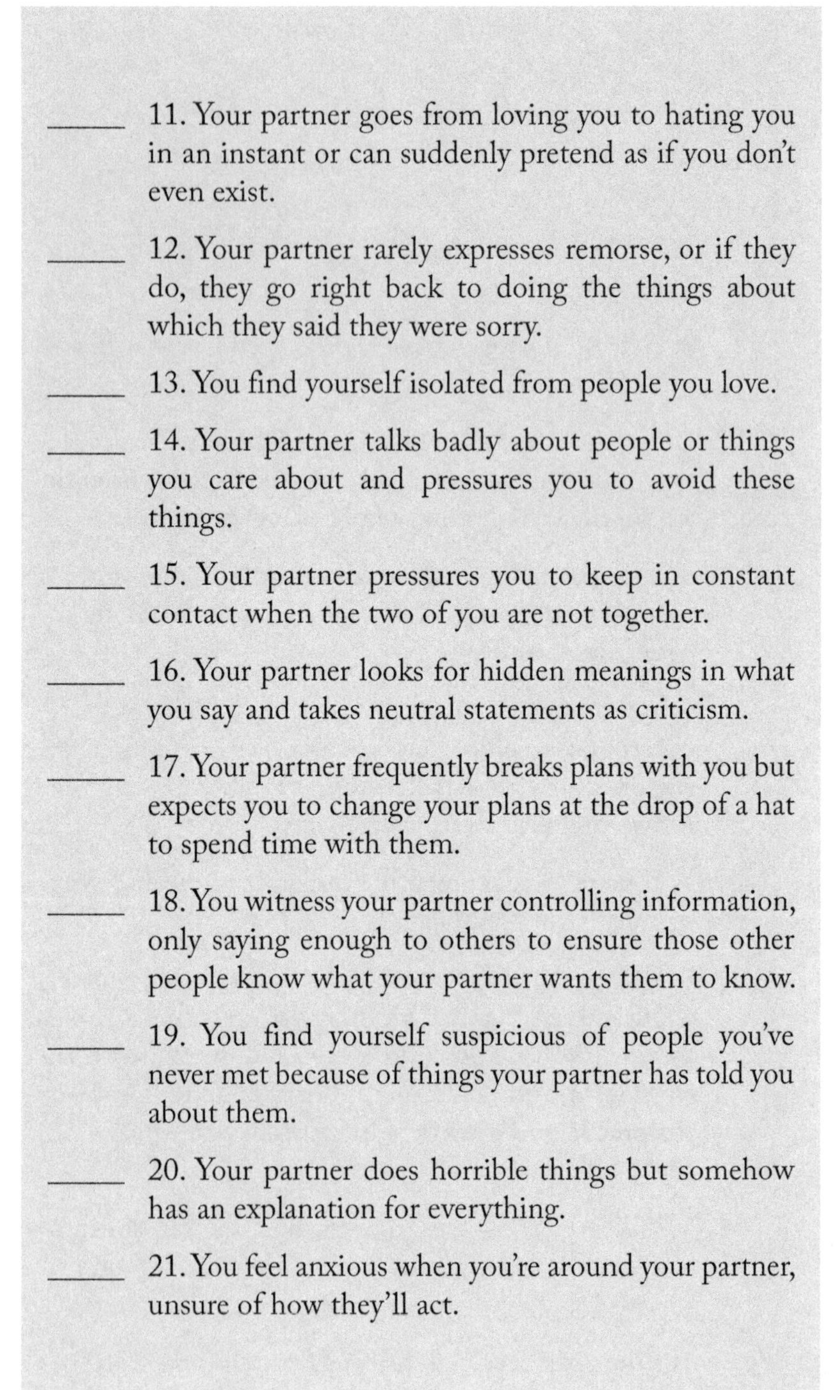

_____ 11. Your partner goes from loving you to hating you in an instant or can suddenly pretend as if you don't even exist.

_____ 12. Your partner rarely expresses remorse, or if they do, they go right back to doing the things about which they said they were sorry.

_____ 13. You find yourself isolated from people you love.

_____ 14. Your partner talks badly about people or things you care about and pressures you to avoid these things.

_____ 15. Your partner pressures you to keep in constant contact when the two of you are not together.

_____ 16. Your partner looks for hidden meanings in what you say and takes neutral statements as criticism.

_____ 17. Your partner frequently breaks plans with you but expects you to change your plans at the drop of a hat to spend time with them.

_____ 18. You witness your partner controlling information, only saying enough to others to ensure those other people know what your partner wants them to know.

_____ 19. You find yourself suspicious of people you've never met because of things your partner has told you about them.

_____ 20. Your partner does horrible things but somehow has an explanation for everything.

_____ 21. You feel anxious when you're around your partner, unsure of how they'll act.

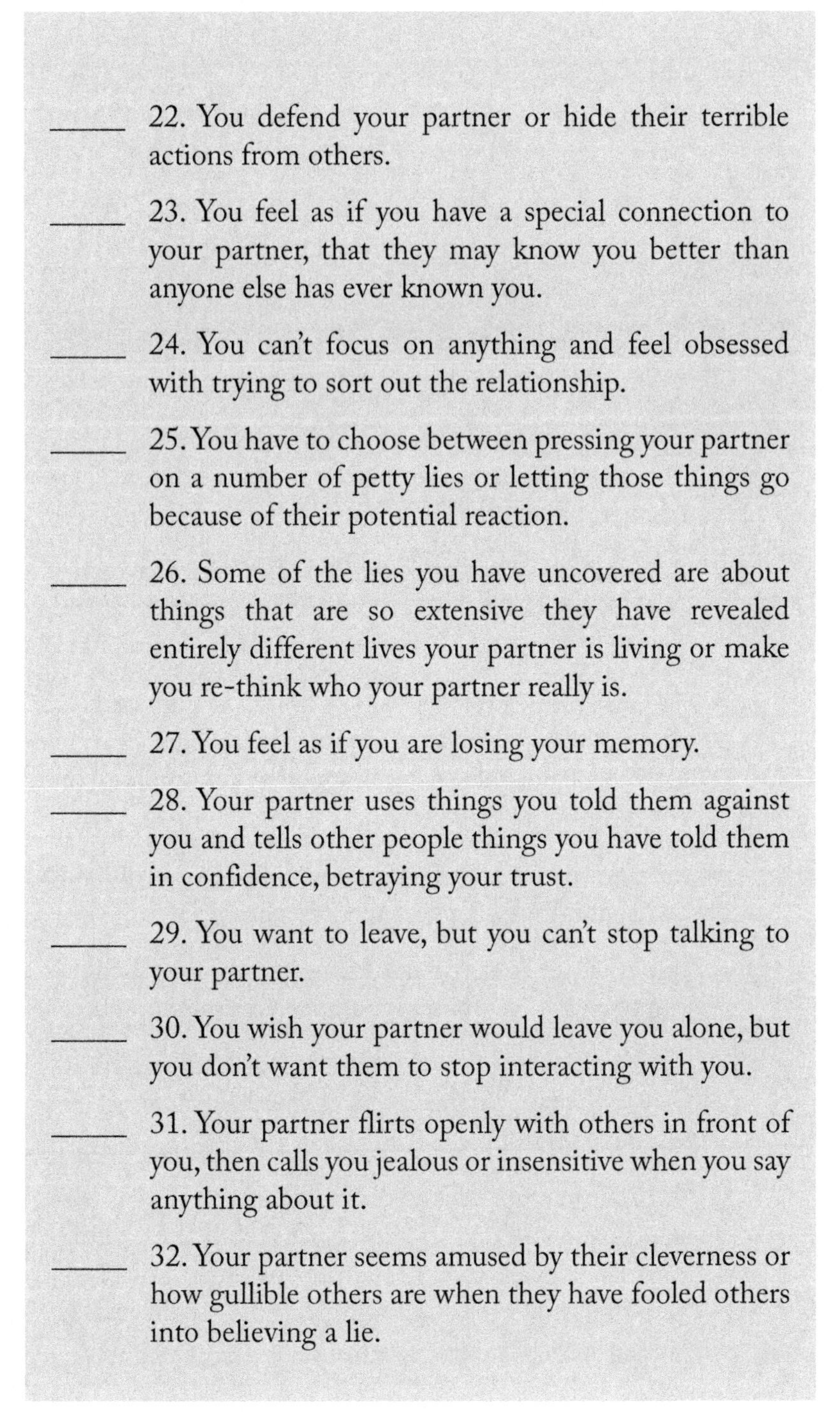

_____ 22. You defend your partner or hide their terrible actions from others.

_____ 23. You feel as if you have a special connection to your partner, that they may know you better than anyone else has ever known you.

_____ 24. You can't focus on anything and feel obsessed with trying to sort out the relationship.

_____ 25. You have to choose between pressing your partner on a number of petty lies or letting those things go because of their potential reaction.

_____ 26. Some of the lies you have uncovered are about things that are so extensive they have revealed entirely different lives your partner is living or make you re-think who your partner really is.

_____ 27. You feel as if you are losing your memory.

_____ 28. Your partner uses things you told them against you and tells other people things you have told them in confidence, betraying your trust.

_____ 29. You want to leave, but you can't stop talking to your partner.

_____ 30. You wish your partner would leave you alone, but you don't want them to stop interacting with you.

_____ 31. Your partner flirts openly with others in front of you, then calls you jealous or insensitive when you say anything about it.

_____ 32. Your partner seems amused by their cleverness or how gullible others are when they have fooled others into believing a lie.

_____ 33. You can't imagine a future in which you and your partner are not together.

_____ 34. Your partner invades your privacy and uses things they find that mean nothing at all to "prove" stories in their mind that you are a cheater or a liar.

_____ 35. Your partner spends long periods in the bathroom, making up excuses about what they're doing there.

_____ 36. You frequently dissociate or withdraw or even become physically ill.

_____ 37. You are verbally abused (perhaps in a covert or underhanded way), then called too sensitive if you protest.

_____ 38. After episodes in which your partner verbally abuses you or storms out, your partner may pretend as if those episodes never happened, not apologizing for their behavior.

_____ 39. Your life is full of chaos and drama, and you don't understand why it never seems to end.

_____ 40. You feel as if you are losing yourself in the relationship, and you don't recognize yourself anymore.

_____ 41. You live by a set of double standards in which it's okay for your partner to do something but not for you to do the same thing.

_____ 42. Your partner tries to control where you go or with whom you interact. If they don't forbid these things directly, they punish you when you don't comply by verbally abusing you or threatening to cheat, hurt you, or leave the relationship.

_____ 43. You find yourself apologizing even though you're not sure what you did wrong.

_____ 44. You often feel like your partner is competing with you or jealous of you and wants to sabotage you.

_____ 45. You find yourself playing detective, and you've never been a jealous person in the past.

_____ 46. You are full of questions and never get any real answers.

_____ 47. You often feel as if your partner is two different people, and you are continually trying to figure out how someone who loves you could act the way they do.

_____ 48. Their first reaction to being confronted about the harmful effects of their behavior is often smug anger or even indifference, rather than empathy or remorse.

_____ 49. At the beginning of the relationship, they told you they had never loved anyone the way they love you.

_____ 50. They react with anger when they believe you have kept something hidden from them, even when you didn't intend to, or when you have not included them in a decision or activity.

_____ 51. You are not "allowed" to have natural human reactions and emotions to abnormal events. When you express an emotion or react, your partner tries anything to end the conversation.

_____ 52. Your partner claims you're ungrateful for the things they have done for you, and your lack of gratitude is a cause of their behavior toward you.

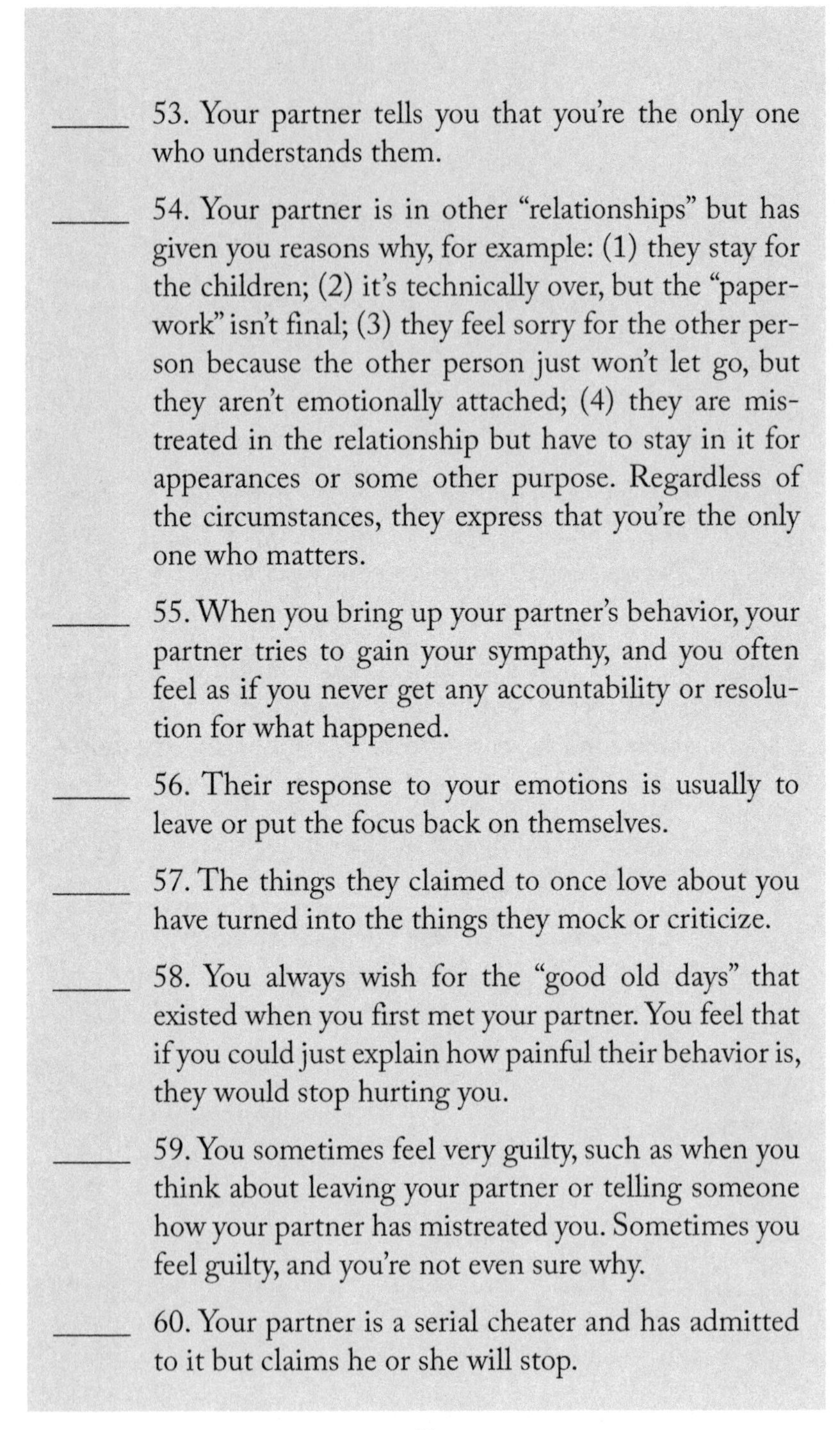

_____ 53. Your partner tells you that you're the only one who understands them.

_____ 54. Your partner is in other "relationships" but has given you reasons why, for example: (1) they stay for the children; (2) it's technically over, but the "paperwork" isn't final; (3) they feel sorry for the other person because the other person just won't let go, but they aren't emotionally attached; (4) they are mistreated in the relationship but have to stay in it for appearances or some other purpose. Regardless of the circumstances, they express that you're the only one who matters.

_____ 55. When you bring up your partner's behavior, your partner tries to gain your sympathy, and you often feel as if you never get any accountability or resolution for what happened.

_____ 56. Their response to your emotions is usually to leave or put the focus back on themselves.

_____ 57. The things they claimed to once love about you have turned into the things they mock or criticize.

_____ 58. You always wish for the "good old days" that existed when you first met your partner. You feel that if you could just explain how painful their behavior is, they would stop hurting you.

_____ 59. You sometimes feel very guilty, such as when you think about leaving your partner or telling someone how your partner has mistreated you. Sometimes you feel guilty, and you're not even sure why.

_____ 60. Your partner is a serial cheater and has admitted to it but claims he or she will stop.

_____ 61. Your partner uses past relationships (mistreatment by exes) as an excuse for their behavior.

_____ 62. Sometimes when you're expressing strong feelings or crying, your partner shows no emotion at all or seems annoyed. Other times, it appears as if your partner is amused by your pain.

_____ 63. Your partner disappears for days or weeks at a time and becomes unreachable, and you have no idea where they are.

_____ 64. When your partner leaves, you desperately miss them and don't understand why.

_____ 65. Your life feels as if it is at a standstill. You don't have any hobbies or other interests anymore. Your entire life revolves around your partner.

_____ 66. Your mind feels like there is a fog in it, and you feel as if you're going crazy sometimes.

_____ 67. Your partner promises to change, then does the very same things they did that broke your trust before. They can never give you a satisfactory answer as to why they keep doing those things.

_____ 68. Your partner tells you something, but later when they repeat it, it seems different. This subtle change has happened many times, and you can't tell if they really said something different, or you remembered it wrong.

_____ 69. You feel split in two—you know you need to get out of this relationship, but something keeps you in it.

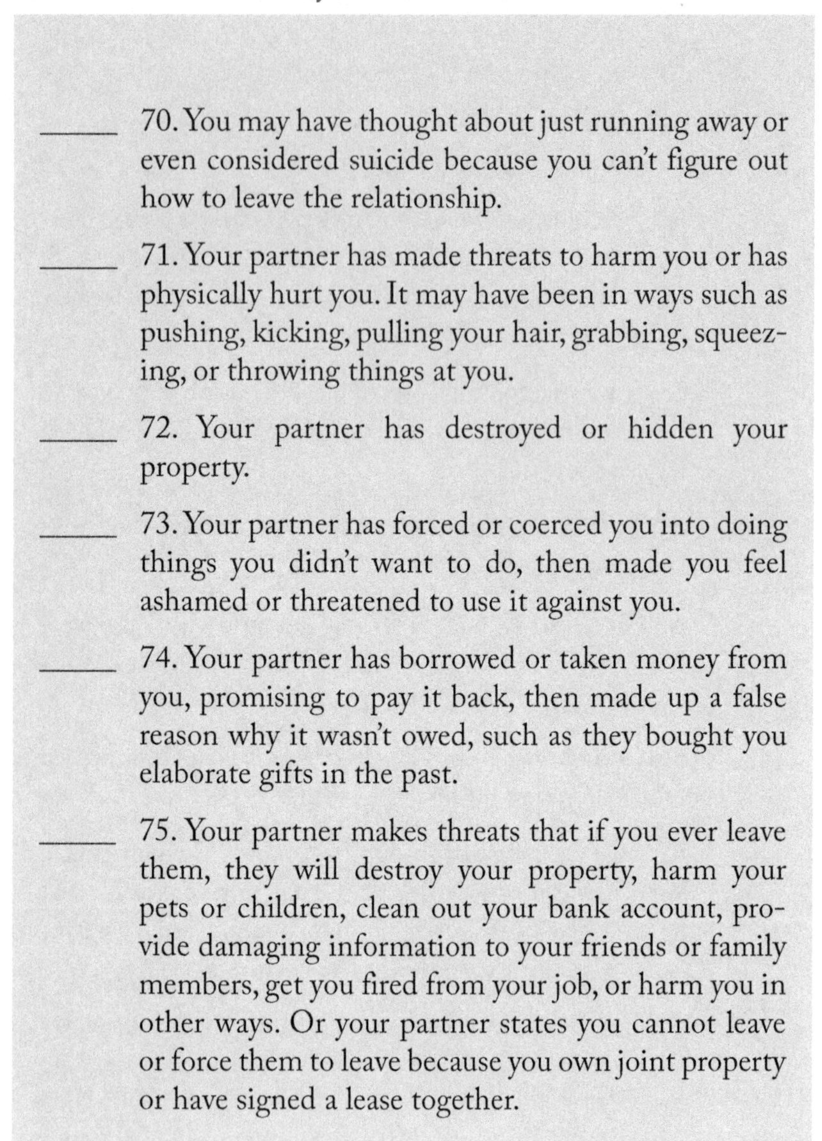

_____ 70. You may have thought about just running away or even considered suicide because you can't figure out how to leave the relationship.

_____ 71. Your partner has made threats to harm you or has physically hurt you. It may have been in ways such as pushing, kicking, pulling your hair, grabbing, squeezing, or throwing things at you.

_____ 72. Your partner has destroyed or hidden your property.

_____ 73. Your partner has forced or coerced you into doing things you didn't want to do, then made you feel ashamed or threatened to use it against you.

_____ 74. Your partner has borrowed or taken money from you, promising to pay it back, then made up a false reason why it wasn't owed, such as they bought you elaborate gifts in the past.

_____ 75. Your partner makes threats that if you ever leave them, they will destroy your property, harm your pets or children, clean out your bank account, provide damaging information to your friends or family members, get you fired from your job, or harm you in other ways. Or your partner states you cannot leave or force them to leave because you own joint property or have signed a lease together.

How did answering those questions make you feel?

There is no magic number of items you need to check to determine if your partner is abusive or that you're in a pathological love relationship.

Instead, think about your reaction to the items on the checklist as you filled it out. Was it easy to fill out? Did you hesitate to check some of the items even though you felt as if you should? Did you think of times when one of them was valid but didn't want to add a check because you thought of reasons not to?

For instance, maybe your partner promised to change, or your partner did something later that "balanced it out." Maybe your partner hasn't done it in a long time. Perhaps you feel as if the only reason it happened was because of something you did. Maybe you felt guilty about checking off an item or just thought you were checking off too many of them. Maybe there was an item that felt too painful to check.

Throughout my relationship with my ex-boyfriend, I could never make sense of his actions. He certainly never provided a rational explanation, and I ended up turning to the Internet in desperation, trying to find out if something like what I had experienced had ever happened to anyone else.

It had. In future chapters of this book, you'll read stories from other survivors whose experiences probably also look a lot like yours in many ways, just as they did mine.

As I read through an article, I would think: *That is precisely what's happening. But I'd better read another article just in case this isn't really what's going on.*

I'd find another survivor's story with an uncanny resemblance to mine, even down to the exact phrases and words said by the survivor's partner in the story that my ex-boyfriend had used. It was as if someone had wrenched open my brain, seen my memories, and poured some of them out onto the screen.

Still, I'd think, *I'd better read another article.*

One after the other, the articles drilled into my sleep-state, trying to pry open my eyes. However, no matter how many articles I read that explained in excruciating detail exactly what I was going through, it was *never enough.*

What I know now is that I was not searching for validation of my experience. My brain recognized immediately that the articles described exactly what I had experienced. I had already confirmed that other people had faced these things.

I kept reading because I needed more validation of my judgment. What did *my* experiences mean? How should I interpret them?

I had lost my ability to decide authoritatively for myself what was true and what wasn't. Even though I objectively recognized my experiences intellectually, I still wanted an outside source to confirm it was okay for me to trust my internal voice.

Yet the only one who could validate my judgment was me.

I was being *psychologically manipulated* and couldn't fully acknowledge and process the truth in those articles in one sitting. Or two. Or ten.

But deep down, some part of me was awake, listening.

So, about that checklist above.

If you felt confused or concerned about the consequences of checking off items or hesitant about checking anything off for some reason, this itself is a vital warning sign. There is a strong possibility you are being psychologically manipulated.

This is a bold claim and probably not one you are comfortable with me making. I wouldn't be either. The term "psychological manipulation" may cause you to pause because of the stereotype that says only weak-minded or stupid people can be psychologically manipulated. You, however, are not these things, and you can know this to be true because your partner valued you enough to enter a relationship with you.

There's a lot more to say about that in Chapter 13, but for now, it's important to keep in mind that there's nothing special about how psychological manipulation works that makes certain people impervious to it. *Anyone* can be psychologically manipulated. Corporations spend billions of dollars a year on advertising because it works. Casinos in Las Vegas use psychological tricks to get patrons to gamble billions of dollars a year. Those tricks are all things we don't notice, but they range from what fragrance they pump into the air to the fact that there are no clocks or windows. They include how often the slot machines pay out and that the roulette table has a sign displaying every number that has come up recently, even though that has no bearing on what numbers will come up next.

We'll talk about psychological manipulation a lot in this book; however, for now, just hold onto the idea that your confusion is a warning sign. As you read the rest of this book, remember how compelling that confusion is as an indicator that you're in a pathological love relationship. In Chapter 2, you'll read a brief description of what we know about psychological disorders that help explain why people do the things in the checklist. Understanding why people with impaired consciences behave as they do is important. However, this book will not help or encourage you to type your partner into a category. Since we're focusing on *you* and not your partner, I'm going to try to help you stay out of dead ends that sometimes work in your partner's favor. If we're not careful, getting lost in categorization can become a trap.

If you weren't confused as you completed the checklist but it was easy to complete because almost every item applied, you probably know why you picked up the book. You just need to figure out how to purge the poison. If it was easy to fill out and you didn't check many items, well, I would encourage you to fill it out again another time to see if your responses change.

When you are in the type of relationship I write about in this book, you may have the urge to blame yourself or protect your partner. You may have supporters who have been able to help you figure out what's going on in your life. However, the only one who can eventually give you trust in yourself back is you. Ultimately, only you can determine why you picked up this book and whether you should use it to help you leave your relationship.

How This Book Is Organized

To prepare for writing this book, I conducted a survey of women and men who identified themselves as survivors of current or past pathological love relationships.[3] Specifically, I asked questions to learn more about their partners' behavior, how it had changed over time, and how it had impacted their lives. I also asked questions to learn about the current status of their relationships.

The survey showed that survivors had strikingly similar experiences in their pathological love relationships with their partners. What was even more striking was that the thoughts and emotions in response to the experiences were also similar. In some cases, the survivors even used similar language when expressing themselves in deeply personal ways about their individual situations. Finally, there were significant differences in the survey between how survivors who had left their relationships and survivors who were still in them each talked about their relationships.

By putting the responses to the survey questions in the context of social science research on other types of high-control situations, I discovered a framework to explain how survivors in psychological love relationships process the relationships. There are five critical questions survivors at various stages in their relationships ask themselves in one form or another. The questions appear to follow a sequence that corresponds to the events that transpire in the relationship:

1. What's Wrong with My Partner?

Something terrible happens—or many things happen over time—that leads us to have a sudden realization that our partners are not who we believed them to be. Doubt creeps in that something is not right; however, our partners usually, but not always, step in to correct their image initially. This question sets off the psychological turning point in which we never view the relationship in the same way again.

2. Is My Partner "Good" or "Bad?"

Our partners continue to alternate between their abusive behaviors and loving behaviors. Long periods of psychological abuse, chemical bonding, and our early attachment to our partners condition us to adopt one view that denies or excuses the bad behavior even if we know on a different level it can't rationally be explained. We realize we don't actually know who our partner really is and may develop an obsession with trying to figure out our partner's true motivations and character.

3. Why Can't I Just Leave?

Time passes as we're still frozen trying to settle our minds on "the truth" about our partners. We never do. While we are busy doing that, we lose ourselves to our partner's pathological worldview. The longer we stay, the more control we give up. As our partner's behavior becomes even more extreme, so do our desires to both leave and stay, and it feels as if we will split in two with those competing and escalating needs.

4. Where Did I Go?

Our partner's psychological and sometimes physical or financial control of us may become almost absolute as our lives narrow. We no longer know who we are anymore. We can't act on our behalf and may even contemplate terrifying options in desperation to escape the relationship. We feel imprisoned by a psychological dread that is all-encompassing.

5. How Do I Get out of Here?

Leaving our partners is not only a physical act. It is also a psychological one. When survivors ask themselves this question, they have reached a crisis point where the worst possible outcome of leaving cannot be worse than the worst possible outcome of staying. For some, that means contemplating death and seeing nothing left to lose. To ask this question and then to successfully answer it is to break through a prison of the mind that requires not will or assertiveness, as some people outside the relationship wrongly believe. It takes the strength greater than that of a pathological partner who has been feeding off us for months or years until we are almost too weak to recognize ourselves anymore.

We can consider these questions "turning points." They drift into our minds when a rational thought collides with a gut feeling, and something clicks into place. Both our bodies and our minds are in sync. The former sends the thought, but the latter tells us it's *right.* We may get a *prickly sensation.* There could be clamoring like alarm bells in our brains or a lump of dread sitting dead center in our chest. Maybe for a few moments, everything stops spinning—or perhaps it starts. It's likely the questions slide into and out of view—sharp, then fuzzy again. The shift to asking each one, however, brings a desperate need for clarity.

If you're reading this book, you may have already asked yourself some of these questions. When you're in a pathological love relationship, it's easy to get stuck in mental loops thinking about them. Sometimes we may become so plagued with self-doubt and fear we just lose hope and give up trying to answer them. Sometimes the self-doubt leads us to think we should stop thinking about the questions, that if we think too much about them, something will happen. We're not exactly sure what, but something will change. We think maybe there might be something a little subversive about them.

There is.

When we hear ourselves ask these questions, we should know this one thing above all else: they come from our authentic selves. We shouldn't doubt them when they sharpen into awareness, as strange as their content may seem. They are warnings. Our partners try hard to keep us from finding or learning the answers to them. Yet as painful as the questions are, if they weren't opportunities, our partners wouldn't care if we asked them or not.

Underneath these five questions, a set of secondary questions swirls around them like tangled vines:

- Is my partner really pathological?
- Can my partner change?
- Does my partner mean to hurt me?
- Does my partner love me?
- What if the problem is me?
- How will I survive without my partner?

These questions do not come from our authentic selves. They loop in and out of one another as potential traps, arising as counterarguments to distract us from exploring the other ones.

We will examine them all.

I'll warn you that I cannot provide you with definitive answers to some of the questions. Some of the questions are so individualized that I cannot answer them generally in a book for everyone. They are not for outsiders to answer—you must think about the question and find the answer for yourself. Some of the other questions are not worth answering at all.

One of my goals for this book is to help you sort out which question is which. With that in mind, I can help you with the following:

- Why we ask these questions in the first place
- Why we have so much trouble figuring out the answers
- Whether a question is worth exploring
- What the range of possible answers or solutions might be
- What we *can* trust, what's essential in determining the answers, and where *not* to look for the answers and why

At a minimum, there is one question you will close this book knowing the answer to, and it's on the cover. If it isn't clear by now, knowing the reasons you can't leave is the master question that helps to unlock the answers to all the others. Your partner doesn't want you to leave, so if he or she can keep the door closed on that one, all the others will remain closed by default.

One more thing:

You'll notice a special feature throughout the book called **Pathological Love Stories.** Each box with this title contains survivor stories from the survey responses and focuses on one theme. The quotes in these boxes are included as examples that highlight the information in the surrounding text. You will also continue to read my journey in the **My Story** sections, located after the descriptions of each of the five major questions.

You are not alone.

How to Use This Book

I want to be honest. This book will probably be painful to read. Perhaps it already has been.

You may right now or at certain points throughout this introduction have gotten angry or upset. You may have wanted to throw the book across the room. The information may have felt overwhelming or confusing, or you may have felt like rejecting some of it. All of those are valid responses, so if you've made it this far, you should be proud. However, that probably won't be the last time you experience any painful emotions while reading this book.

I should warn you upfront that some of the book's sources are narcissists, and their descriptions may seem harsh and cold. Despite how painful it sometimes was for me, reading their words was one of the most important ways I found to heal from my relationship, as it allowed me to learn what the world was like through their eyes. Though it's not pretty, that point of view allowed me to make progress in my recovery at a rate that might otherwise have taken me years. I judiciously use their words here not to excuse the behavior of low-conscience individuals, but to help you understand it, then use what you learn to get out from under the spell of the one you know.

If something in here gets too intense, please put the book down.

This book is not meant to be read in one sitting or even two or three. You may need to stop and psychologically process what you've read.

I hope you'll decide to keep reading, then decide what you think when you finish.

That voice inside you that told you to pick up the book is counting on you.

When something hits you hard emotionally, that's probably an excellent indicator that something about what you read is resonating with your experiences even if you can't put your finger on why, and a little reflection (in a dose you can manage) might be helpful. As you're reading, if you run across any terms you don't understand, there's a glossary in Appendix B that defines some common terms relevant to pathological love relationships.

I want to tell you a secret—something your partner doesn't want you to know.

You're going to make it out. If I can do it, you can do it. I believe in you.

2

Psychological Manipulation Is Abuse

We are in the middle of a silent epidemic.

Currently, sixty million people in the United States alone will experience a pathological love relationship, according to Sandra L. Brown, M.A., author of a ground-breaking book on the subject, *Women Who Love Psychopaths,* currently on its third edition.[4] Despite the prevalence of these relationships, the harm they cause still has not received the mainstream attention it deserves, likely because, as Brown says, there isn't yet a shared cultural understanding of what a pathological love relationship is.

Brown, who is a pioneer in the field of survivor treatment and founded the Institute for Relational Harm Reduction, explains that a pathological love relationship consists of four elements:

- a partner with a conscience-impaired personality disorder
- a partner with personality traits that attract conscience-impaired individuals
- the dramatic yet predictable relationship dynamic between the two partners
- the traumatic impact of the relationship on the partner of the conscience-impaired individual

A pathological love relationship, by definition, leads to inevitable harm for the partner of someone with a low-conscience disorder.

The personality disorders she refers to in which low conscience is a factor are called the cluster-B personality disorders in the *Diagnostic and Statistical Manual of Psychiatric Disorders, Fifth Edition*, or *DSM-V*, the manual that classifies all mental health diagnoses.[5] Cluster-B personality disorders include narcissistic personality disorder (NPD), antisocial personality disorder (ASPD), and psychopathy. Brown refers to them generally as the Spectrum of Low-Conscience Disorders.[6] She claims the neurobiology at least partially responsible for causing the personality disorders does not allow the disordered individuals to recognize the damage they cause others, learn from the pain they cause, or change their behavior for reasons that aren't self-serving. She calls these the "Three Inabilities" of pathological individuals that will always lead to suffering for their romantic partners. Put another way, a pathological love relationship, by definition, leads to inevitable harm for the partner of someone with a low-conscience disorder.[7]

According to Brown, the field of pathological love relationships is following a similar trajectory to that of domestic violence more generally. The former began in the early 2000s as a grassroots movement, is being slowly picked up by researchers and mental health professionals, and has coalesced around the language of social justice.[8] During the past five years, there has been an exponential growth in the information available about pathological love relationships online, much of which can be found under the keyword search term "narcissistic abuse." Yet the harm caused by pathological love relationships still remains largely invisible to the public.

The concept of narcissistic abuse appears to have first emerged online as "Narcissistic Victim Syndrome" in a *Medical News Today* article in 2004. It describes a specific pattern of emotional and physical symptoms in clients who sought mental health treatment for difficulties coping with their lives. The article described the symptoms as including "no particular physical disease process, yet a variety of physical and/or emotional complaints, including insomnia, weight loss or gain, depression, anxiety, phobias, broken bones, lacerations, or bruises . . . an overwhelming feeling of emptiness or doom." The author, Mary Jo Fay, writes that the clients may "talk about or attempt suicide . . . [are] frequently rather nervous, with a guilt-ridden, anxious look and effect [sic] . . . [are] restless, worried, and/or demonstrate a fake laugh that seems to hide something else. . . . In extreme cases they may describe sudden outbursts of rage with accompanying violence. They may have even been arrested for assault on their spouse."[9]

Yet there was another significant and often-missed pattern in the partners of the clients. The clients described living under extreme conditions in which their partners showed a lack of regard for their autonomy and had an excessive amount of control over them. Their partners behaved with an entitlement to treat them this way and made them feel defective if they objected. Sometimes, the partners used physical abuse or sexual abuse to enforce the unequal dynamic. Most often, what the clients experienced was an ever-changing system of rules, rewards, and psychological punishments. The partners appeared to have little to no remorse for their actions, treating the clients as "objects."[10] This pattern of behavior was recognizable as pathologically narcissistic.

Christine Louis de Canonville, a therapist in the United Kingdom who recognized narcissistic abuse almost a decade ago and has been treating clients and training other therapists since that time, says:

> *When I speak of narcissistic abuse, (abuse that can lead to Narcissistic Victim Syndrome), I am speaking about a form of abuse that is very insidious. What I mean by insidious is that the abuse is covert, cunning and often indirect. This form of abuse is often carried out in a subtle and clandestine manner, because narcissists go to great pains to avoid being observed publicly as being abusive.*[11]

The covert, subtle nature of this type of abuse is why it is often unrecognized, even by victims themselves. The National Domestic Violence Hotline refers to domestic violence on its web page as "a pattern of behaviors used by one partner to maintain power and control over another partner in an intimate relationship."[12] It lists physical abuse, emotional and verbal abuse, sexual abuse, sexual coercion, reproductive coercion, financial abuse, digital abuse, and stalking. Unfortunately, narcissistic abuse appears to be so difficult to recognize that the term doesn't appear anywhere in the online resources available on the Hotline, even though it fits the description of abuse.

If you try to look up a definition of narcissistic abuse online, it often refers to another type of abuse. The headline of one online article reads, "Narcissistic Abuse Is the Scary New Kind of Emotional Abuse You Need to Know About." A writer on *Psychology Today*'s website writes:

> *Narcissistic abuse is generally defined as emo*
> *behaviour on the part of someone with Narcissi*
> *Disorder (NPD), although it may also include p*
> *ual abuse. I want to focus on narcissistic abuse of*
> *nature because it's this type of abuse which can be s*
> *person on the receiving end to identify.*

The article then describes the *symptoms* o abuse, rather than tactics of emotional abuse us petrator, to define it. Using effects on the victim narcissistic abuse is another standard method of de cissistic abuse.[13]

I don't come away from definitions like thes standing what narcissistic abuse is. It isn't precise to narcissistic abuse is another form of emotional abu can narcissistic abuse include physical or sexual abuse emotionally abusive behavior? It also doesn't explain pr how it is abusive or what it means to be "another ty emotional abuse—why call it out as different?

And where is the specific description of the perpetr behavior that is abusive? How would anyone know wha abuser does to someone that is damaging?

Why would we define narcissistic abuse by the effects the victim when the abuser's actions determine every oth type of abuse the Hotline mentions:

- The physical abuser hits, slaps, or pushes
- The verbal abuser insults, criticizes, or calls the victim names
- The sexual abuser insults the victim in sexual ways or with derogatory names or holds the victim down during sex without consent
- The stalker sends unwanted messages, uses social media to track the victim, or damages the victim's property

And so on. None of these types of abuse are defined by
r the victim feels because of the abuse. The effects of abuse
not the abuse itself.

That narcissistic abuse is treated differently from the other
ıes of abuse tells us something interesting about it. Returning
Canonville's description of narcissistic abuse, in only three
ntences, she used the following words to describe it:

- Insidious
- Covert
- Cunning
- Indirect
- Subtle
- Clandestine

It's so insidious, covert, cunning, indirect, subtle, and clandestine that not only do victims have trouble recognizing it—but even people who know it exists do not seem able to characterize it.

But just because something is indirect, subtle, and covert doesn't mean it isn't there.

After my relationship with my ex-boyfriend ended, I obsessively read everything I could get my hands on, searching for answers to what had happened to me. Yet I couldn't find a definition of narcissistic abuse that didn't refer back to itself in some way or end in a description of the effects on the survivor.

For example, a pathological partner engages in narcissistic abuse in a pathological love relationship. As a result, his or her partner becomes a survivor of narcissistic abuse and the pathological relationship. I read about various tactics pathological partners used. Many of them my partner had used; some of them he did not. He also did other things that seemed abnormal that I never saw mentioned anywhere.

Figure 2.1:
What Is Narcissistic Abuse?

I'm the kind of person who has arguments with myself in my head—and sometimes out loud—much to the bewilderment of those around me, I'm sure. When I went through this emotional roller coaster trying to find the answers, I kept running over and over the same argument trying to find the missing piece that wasn't there. My thoughts went something like this:

> **Me:** *So, it's the effects on a person that tell us narcissistic abuse occurred. But . . . what exactly is that abuse? I still don't understand what happened to me. Why did this happen?*

Also, Me: *Yes, you do. Double life. Verbal abuse. Pathological lying. Cheating. Stalking you. Other stuff.*

Me Again: *But what do we call that?*

Me: *Narcissistic abuse.*

Other Me: *But other people are experiencing the same emotional and psychological symptoms you are and seem to have dealt with a relationship partner similar to yours; however, they did not go through all of these things. So, what is the common denominator?*

Me: *The emotional and psychological effects.*

Other Me: *Why are the effects the same if we did not experience the same thing?*

Me: *Because a pathologically narcissistic person did those things.*

Other Me: *That doesn't make sense. The person is not the cause—the acts are the cause. Yet how can that range of random things have the same effect on so many different people? What is the commonality? What is the thing that holds them all together?*

Me: *The narcissistic person.*

Other Me: *Yes, but what is the one thing the narcissist is doing to us that is the same? There must be something.*

Me: *Narcissistic abuse.*

Other Me: *But what is narcissistic abuse then? It's not the individual acts because those aren't always the same. It's not the effects because those came after.*

Me: . . .

The invisibility of narcissistic abuse is where we start our journey. It is the seed of all our confusion within our own pathological love relationships. Though we cannot see the shadowy walls around us, we know they are there. That contradiction is the source from which every question in Chapter 1 springs.

If you were being abused, you'd know it. Right?

Not if our partners can help it.

This book is about turning on the lights. We're going to get out the magnifying glass and inspect the abuse in pathological love relationships. We will examine it, flip it around, and explain what is so unique about it. Using social psychological research and the stories of survivors, I will show you how psychological manipulation erodes our identities and grinds down our ability to act in our own best interest.[14] **Psychological manipulation *is* the primary abusive behavior used in pathological love relationships.**

Narcissistic abuse is not just another type of emotional abuse. It should be distinguished from other types to capture its unique qualities and charms. We must understand how psychological manipulation affects us so we can arm ourselves against it. Our pathological partners use a particular set of techniques to shape our thoughts, behavior, and emotions until we become exactly who they want us to be. The personality they wish to mold is a compliant, obedient, self-doubting one. This manipulation is a primary reason we, as survivors, begin to resemble one another so much that we even have the same thoughts.

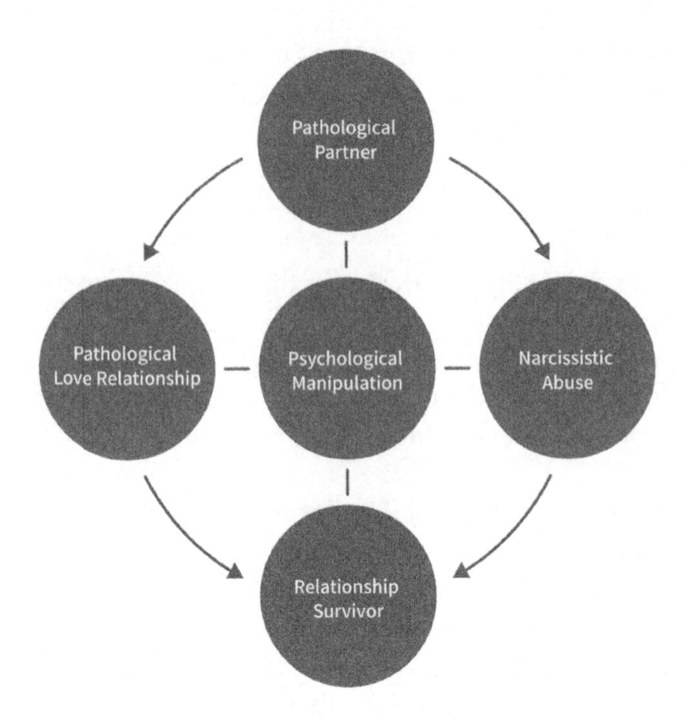

Figure 2.2:
Pathological Love Relationships = Narcissistic Abuse = Psychological Manipulation

Yet if those thoughts, actions, and emotions are not ours, then they are not real.

When we understand how we got here and why we are thinking, feeling, and acting this way, we can start to make decisions that put us on a new path, one that doesn't lead to psychological manipulation. We can choose differently.

Once we see how a magic trick works, it no longer amazes us.

Why Do They Do That?

Throughout the book, I've mostly chosen to use the term "pathological partners," often referred to as narcissists, psychopaths, sociopaths, and malignant narcissists in other resources. I use this term to represent the range of all possible disordered dispositions of low-conscience individuals who are the abusers in relationships characterized by narcissistic abuse.

It's essential to dig into these disorders to learn more about what low-conscience individuals have in common, as it helps shed light on the abuser's behavior and mindset. Low-conscience disorders are usually variants of either NPD or ASPD.[15] The two disorders are distinct, but some narcissists, or those with an NPD diagnosis, also have overlapping characteristics with ASPD.

According to psychoanalyst Otto Kernberg, narcissism exists on a continuum with healthy narcissism at one end and pathological narcissism at the other. Healthy narcissism is the ability to maintain positive self-regard coupled with an investment in the outer experience of others.[16] In contrast, pathological narcissism is exploitative and parasitic. Pathological narcissistic personalities feel "as if they have the right to control others and exploit them without guilt."[17]

Many theories exist on what causes unhealthy narcissism, and a consensus has not been reached. One view is that narcissism develops when someone suffers either abusive and neglectful treatment or overvaluation or both during childhood. Another idea is that narcissism is caused by a brain abnormality in which the frontal cortex and amygdala regulate empathy and emotions differently.[18] Some researchers think it is biosocial and that a combination of these things can cause it. However, they all seem to agree that no matter what causes it, the result is that pathological narcissism manifests itself in someone as an unstable core self protected by a false self. The core self feels worthless and shameful, so the narcissist must continually prop up the false self with fantasies of how great they are to avoid feeling those emotions. They will go to great lengths to keep up that fantasy—sometimes doing outrageous things to maintain it. These actions are the result of the disordered personality.

The *DSM-V* defines a personality disorder as an "enduring pattern of inner experience and behavior that deviates markedly from the expectations of the individual's culture, is pervasive and inflexible, has an onset in adolescence or early adulthood, is stable over time, and leads to distress or impairment."[19] In the *DSM-V*, criteria for diagnosing NPD and ASPD appear twice. When validity problems with the traditional personality disorder criteria had become apparent, new multi-dimensional models of personality disorders were proposed to resolve those issues.[20] However, the American Psychiatric Association (APA) had not decided to accept them as replacements for the traditional categorical criteria by the time the fifth edition of the *DSM* was published. Therefore, the APA decided to include both classification methods for diagnosing personality disorders.[21]

The traditional categorical model of NPD requires someone to have at least five of the following nine criteria:[22]

- An inflated sense of self, accompanied by the belief that they are superior to others, and, therefore, they should be treated as more important
- Unrealistic and pervasive fantasies of being rich, famous, and influential, or of being excessively beautiful, admired, and envied
- A belief that they are extraordinary and can only relate to and be understood by other "special" or high-status people
- A desperate need for excessive attention and admiration
- A sense of entitlement and belief that others should automatically comply with their expectations

- A willingness to exploit others in their interpersonal relationships to get what they want
- A lack of empathy for the circumstances and feelings of others
- Pathological envy of other people or a belief that other people envy them
- An arrogant attitude

The multi-dimensional NPD model examines a narcissist's sense of self and how they interact with the world separately. This model can distinguish between types of narcissists, and three decades of psychological research supports the existence of three major types: classic, vulnerable, and malignant.[23]

The first type, classic, is the type of narcissist many of us think of when we hear the word "narcissist." Their entitlement is overt—they thrive on attention and expect other people to flatter them, feeling invisible when the limelight isn't shining on them. They don't like being criticized and often perceive differences of opinion as criticism. Classic narcissists also feel superior to others and get angry when they don't receive the treatment they think they deserve. If others are in the spotlight, they'll do something to turn the focus back to themselves.

The second type, vulnerable narcissists, don't enjoy the spotlight, but they share their sense of entitlement and feelings of superiority with classic narcissists. They may hide these things better than classic narcissists, however. What makes them "vulnerable" is how they present themselves; their self-importance is covert. Because they don't crave attention themselves, they may find other important people to associate with or attach themselves to important causes or ideas to achieve the status or validation they need.

The third type of narcissist, malignant narcissists, differs from the other two. They have a sadistic streak and try to dominate others through deceit and manipulation and may view their interactions with others as a "game." This third type has many overlapping characteristics with individuals diagnosed with ASPD.

Some mental health professionals believe ASPD is a subset of NPD, which would mean that all those with ASPD are self-entitled and think they're superior.[24] However, others believe they're different personality disorders and that what sets them apart is their lack of interest or concern with social conventions. They don't step all over people because they think they're better than everyone else; they just don't care what anyone else thinks.[25]

Only three of the seven criteria in the traditional categorical ASPD model are needed to receive a diagnosis. Those criteria include:

- Repeated violations of social norms or actions that would result in arrest if caught and a lack of concern about violating these laws and social norms
- Pathological lying or the use of false names or information to con others for personal gain or enjoyment
- Acting in the moment without regard to future consequences
- Physically aggressive behavior toward others (e.g., getting into fights, assaulting others, etc.)
- Lack of concern about the safety of self or others, which they demonstrate with their reckless or dangerous behavior
- Consistent financial, social, or professional irresponsibility or in another area where an obligation or expectation is unmet

- Lack of remorse, as indicated by indifference to or rationalizing hurting, mistreating, or stealing from someone else

The overlap between NPD and ASPD highlights the problems noted in the *DSM-V* with the traditional diagnostic categories. Patients rarely meet the criteria for only one. Some patients may even have criteria from several disorders but don't meet enough to be diagnosed with any of them.

The alternative multi-dimensional model in the *DSM-V* contains dimensions for pathological traits and for something called personality functioning. There are four areas of personality functioning described for each personality disorder: identity, self-direction, empathy, and intimacy. Individuals must have impairments in at least two out of the four and meet the disorder's pathological trait criteria to receive a diagnosis.

Most of the traditional categorical NPD model criteria that focus on how narcissists view themselves and others have somehow been folded into the multi-dimensional model. Yet there is one trait that no longer appears—the one that centered on "exploitative behavior." Instead, exploitation appears as a feature of ASPD. The new NPD model doesn't contain any criteria in which a narcissist harms others directly. The *DSM* seems to indicate that those types of traits are possible but are unnecessary:

> *Trait and personality functioning specifiers may be used to record additional personality features that may be present in narcissistic personality disorder, but are not required for the diagnosis. For example, other traits of Antagonism (e.g., manipulativeness, deceitfulness, callousness) are not diagnostic criteria for NPD but can be specified when more pervasive antagonistic features (e.g., malignant narcissism) are present.*[26]

In other words, in the multi-dimensional NPD model, no combination of the criteria would result in a narcissism diagnosis because a person was manipulative, deceitful, or exploitative. Those behaviors all fall into the category of ASPD. If they do appear with some of the NPD traits, then that could indicate malignant narcissism. However, the line does seem a little clearer—at least on paper.

When it comes to psychopathy and sociopathy, the traditional ASPD model seems to consider them all the same. In the multi-dimensional model, however, psychopathy is noted as a variant of ASPD "marked by a lack of anxiety or fear and by a bold interpersonal style that may mask maladaptive behaviors." Sociopathy is not mentioned.[27]

A thorough description of NPD and ASPD is outside the scope of this book. This brief introduction is designed to provide an overview of the complexity of the scientific and philosophical battles about these terms. For this book, we can assume the behavior of abusers in pathological love relationships is, at the very least, manipulative, exploitative, deceitful, and unremorseful. Sometimes they can shut off their empathy for others, or they may have very little of it to begin with. Beyond that, other traits may vary.

The figure below demonstrates the overlap in these traits among the disorders. The diagnostic categories are in flux, however, and distinguishing the difference between one type of low-conscience individual from another is difficult for even professionals to do.

Table 2.1: Pathological Personality Traits Across Low-Conscience Personality Disorders

		Narcissistic Personality Disorder *Any 5 of the traits indicated with +*	Malignant Narcissist *All of the traits indicated plus at least two more of the indicated with +*	Antisocial Personality Disorder *Any 3 of the traits indicated with +*
Narcissistic Personality Disorder Criteria and Dimensions	**Leadership/Authority**			
	A preoccupation with fantasies of unlimited success, power, brilliance, beauty, or ideal love	+	+	
	Envy of others or a belief that others are envious of him or her	+	+	
	A demonstration of arrogant and haughty behavior or manners	+	+	
	Grandiose Exhibitionism			
	A sense of self-importance	+	+	
	A belief that he or she is special and unique and can only be understood by, or should associate with, other special or high-status people or institutions	+	+	
	A need for excessive admiration	+	+	
	Entitlement/Exploitativeness			
	A sense of entitlement	+	+	
	Interpersonally exploitative behavior	+	+	
	A lack of empathy	+	+	

Antisocial Personality Disorder Criteria and Dimensions				
	Callousness/Manipulativeness			
	Deceitfulness, as indicated by repeated lying, use of aliases, or conning others for personal profit or pleasure		+	+
	Lack of remorse, as indicated by being indifferent or rationalizing having hurt, mistreated, or stolen from another		+	+
	Disinhibition/Impulsiveness			
	Failure to conform to social norms with respect to lawful behaviors, as indicated by repeatedly performing acts that are grounds for arrest			+
	Impulsivity or failure to plan ahead			+
	Reckless disregard for the safety of self or others			+
	Consistent irresponsibility, as indicated by repeated failure to sustain consistent work behavior or honor financial obligations			+
	Hostility			
	Irritability and aggressiveness, as indicated by repeated physical fights or assaults			+

This book refers to "pathological partners" and sometimes "low-conscience individuals" to encompass all abusers who engage in narcissistic abuse. The checklist in Chapter 1 can be used as a wake-up call to help you determine whether your partner is someone who might fit into one of these categories. If you recognized your partner's behavior in the checklist and took a leap of faith when you kept reading, waiting for more answers, this information may provide some of the validation you need to reality-test.

Sandra L. Brown, M.A., whose research concluded that the survivors in her study were in relationships of inevitable harm, asserts that once you recognize your partner has an impaired conscience, knowing the precise disorder or disorders is unnecessary to understanding the harm you've suffered in the pathological relationship or to regaining control of your life.[28]

Once we become aware that there is a reason for our confusion and can accept that reason, having more information about our partner's pathology doesn't make it any easier for us to leave or to have a speedier recovery once the relationship ends.

3

But . . . Is My Partner Really Pathological?

It's easy to get lost in the clinical information and diagnoses, so before we go any further, let's just stop right now and address all that head-on.

As you read through that information in the previous chapter, were you trying to compare the criteria to your partner's behavior to see if they met the diagnosis for NPD or ASPD?

Ask yourself:

- Were you able to come to a definitive conclusion, or do you have doubts?
- What would you do with that information if you could come to a definitive conclusion?

- Does ruminating about it make you feel better or worse?
- Would you stay in the relationship if the answer seems to be "no," even if your partner was hurting you or you knew something was wrong?

Reading information about NPD and ASPD is meant to begin helping you identify what you're experiencing. I encourage you to avoid the temptation to use the diagnoses to figure out whether your partner's level of narcissism is unhealthy or whether he or she qualifies for one of the diagnoses described or to classify your partner's narcissist "type."

Reading about and understanding the diagnostic criteria has significant value that should not be understated. Because the abuse we experience in the relationships is invisible, having the terminology to frame what's been happening to us is not only validating. It's necessary. Without it, we couldn't escape the abuse because we couldn't recognize it. Right now, it's the only frame we have for looking at it. Remember? No one is really talking about the abuse—they're talking about the abuser. So, that's how the breakthrough usually arrives.

Pathological Love Stories

How We Stumbled on Revelation

"My sister said I should Google the meaning of a narcissist. The more I read, the more I identified myself in the scenarios. . . . After reading what narcissistic people do, it all started falling into place. The examples were exactly as he was or what he said."

"His behavior was strange, so I Googled it, and up came narcissistic personality disorder."

"Knew something was wrong early on—but stayed confused for many years. Saw an article on gaslighting on Facebook, which led me to narcissism and explanations/understanding of all his confusing behavior."

"I read an article online about emotional abuse, then took a "walking on eggshells" test, and out of 100 points, I scored a seven. It was devastating. I was shocked, so when I told my sister, she said he was a narcissist, and I began researching the subject. Everything I read was him. I was sitting on the floor, and I can recall how hard it was to accept. I thought I was going to die . . . the stories other women shared . . . it was mind-blowing, to say the least."

"I decided to go 'no contact' after reading an article in a psychology journal about narcissistic psychopaths. I realized as I was reading that it felt like the author had been following me and describing my day-to-day interactions with my ex-husband."

"I read up on the behavior every night educating myself. I was in denial at first, but what I read in it . . . everything was true. It was scary. I thought I was alone until I found a support group."

"I slowly became more baffled and exhausted, which made me start to research narcissism."

"I came across an article on narcissists. I'd never heard of such a thing and was amazed at how they were describing my ex and our relationship perfectly."

"I reconnected with an old friend, and she started helping me process and see things for what they really were, things that I had been questioning myself about. She mentioned the word narcissist, and I Googled the word and couldn't believe that he was right in front of me on the page. I was devasted."

"I began to see some patterns in his behaviors. This eventually led me to ask Google this question: What is wrong with a person who becomes enraged and attacks you when you question them or try to discuss a problem with them? The answer was narcissistic personality disorder. I started learning everything I could about NPD. . . . Then, my second big 'aha!' moment happened when I started watching Leah Remini's Scientology and the Aftermath *TV show. I'm still not sure why, but in the show intro when she said something like, 'If this religion is so perfect and wonderful, then it should be able to withstand a little questioning!' The first time I heard it, I immediately broke down and cried."*

"I finally contacted Women's Aid. . . . I was then put on a group support course to identify exactly the areas of psychological abuse I was subjected to, and listening to stories of other women (of all orientations, ages, and backgrounds) really clarified this for me. The course never used the term 'narcissist,' but it was frequently thrown around by all group members, and it finally cropped up online when I was Googling types of mental abuse. I came across the concept of narcissistic abuse online when looking up types of emotional abuse, and it was a revelation."

"I stumbled across an article via Pinterest. I then did extensive research across the web and compiled three pages of direct examples of her behavior that matched being a narcissist."

See Appendix A.

Finding or seeking out information on terms like "narcissist" gives a shape to our experience and allows us to make sense out of nonsense. For the first time, perhaps ever, we are given some control again, and we realize that what is happening to us is not happening in our heads. It's real.

Understanding the criteria can be enough. The survivors in the "Pathological Love Stories" recognized themselves and their experiences in what they read about how narcissistic people treat others. Reading or hearing that external information helped them to trust their judgment about what they had experienced.

Yet there's a danger in going too far when we stay caught up in an obsession over the narcissist or psychopath label. When we jump from thinking about ourselves and what we've experienced to applying what we read to our partner's thoughts and motivations, we suddenly have to guess at things we can't know for *sure*. This is where we have to be careful because things can get dangerous. It's the gaps where we've filled in the blanks that allow our partners to continue to manipulate us into doubting ourselves.

We can't know what they're really thinking. Their lies are proof of that.

Their actions are the only thing we can trust.

They love it when we get confused about their motivations because it allows them to continue to confuse us. As long as we're wrapped up in their mind games looking for the clues, questioning *what* they are, they can also keep us doubting what they've put us through.

Figure 3.1:
The Diagnosis Mind Mill

Most likely, your partner will never be under the observation of a mental health professional and will never receive an official clinical diagnosis. Most people with these personality disorders don't seek treatment because they don't think anything is wrong. Their actions are ego-syntonic, or compatible with how they see themselves and the rest of the world.[29] Mental health professionals offer treatment to people who want to change and are capable of changing, and individuals with these disorders often believe they are superior to others and are disinterested in "fitting in." It's also important to keep in mind that someone can have personality-disordered traits that affect their empathetic response without having a full-blown diagnosis. So, trying to figure out what "diagnosis" they have is not going to be a good use of time if they don't have one.

However, once you have the mental shift to accept a huge gap exists between how you and your partner each approach the world as the reason for what's happening to you, you can move beyond focusing on these diagnostic categories. Now, you can shift your focus to only two: people who can empathize, feel remorse, and learn from their mistakes (cooperative social actors); and people who can't do these things (pathological social actors).

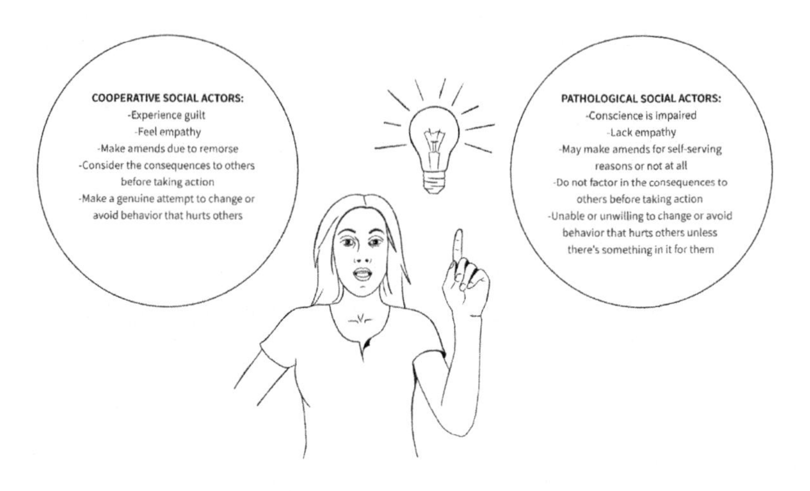

Figure 3.2:
Cooperative Social Actors vs. Pathological Social Actors

To be clear, the distinction between pathological social actors and cooperative social actors is not that non-pathological actors never do things that hurt others or act irresponsibly or do things others would consider immoral. Dr. Martha Stout, who wrote *The Sociopath Next Door*, writes:

> *Even a normal person's conscience does not operate on the same level all of the time. One of the simplest reasons for this changeability is the fundamental circumstances of living inside a fallible, need-driven human body. When our bodies are exhausted, sick, or injured, all of our emotional functions, including conscience, can be temporarily compromised.*[30]

People have lapses in judgment and make mistakes. They sometimes make spontaneous, irrational, or emotional decisions and later wish that they had thought through them a little longer. What distinguishes their actions and intentions from pathological actors is their capacity for empathy and willingness to make genuine attempts to change or avoid doing things they know are hurtful. People who do things that hurt others often feel guilty about it. In contrast, people with an impaired conscience may act callously about the harm they cause or feign regret. But are they genuinely sorry? No. Will they stop doing it? Regardless of what disorder they may have, they see no reason to just as they saw no reason not to do it in the first place. And as Sandra L. Brown, M.A., writes in *Women Who Love Psychopaths*, "While these disorders each have their own unique aspects (and researchers enjoy discussing their differences), what we have found is that most victims don't find the differences all that notable in their own aftermath experiences."[31]

On the other hand, maybe your doubt tips in a different direction. You may have a nagging doubt about the label, not because you don't know how to type your partner but because you wonder if your partner is really any of these things at all. What if your partner is one of the cooperative social actors and is just a jerk? What if you're being too over-zealous?

As discussed in Chapter 1, the topic of narcissistic abuse is exploding in popularity right now and is just now beginning to make its way into mainstream awareness. As a result, the term "narcissist" has become such a buzzword, perhaps you fear that the term is being overused and that you are participating in labeling others unfairly.

Recall that recognizing whether you are a victim of narcissistic abuse is not really about being able to diagnose or label your partner. It's about understanding what is happening to you. Dismissing your own abuse because your partner hasn't received a psychiatric diagnosis would be equivalent to waiting for a court to convict your attacker and compel them to register as a sex offender before defining what happened to you as rape. Our experiences are not real only when our social institutions label those who caused them.

How would we know the difference then between someone who is just a jerk and someone who has a low-conscience disorder?

Jerks may do some of the things in the checklist in Chapter 1. However, usually, it's not midway through the relationship before their actions can make you start feeling desperate, panicked, and worthless. We know pretty early on whether someone's a jerk or not. The difference between a jerk and a pathological person is that a pathological person is inconsistently jerk-like. We should not be confused about whether someone is really a jerk or not. If sometimes the person we thought is a jerk seems god-like, there may be something else going on.

Another major difference between a regular jerk and a pathological partner is that when you tell a jerk how you feel, they'll usually do one of two things: either straighten up their behavior or just move on. Sometimes a jerk doesn't know they're a jerk. Sometimes a jerk will try to get away with whatever they can until someone calls them on it. Sometimes a jerk has an epiphany when they are forced to face their shame and decides that isn't who they want to be. Sometimes a jerk realizes what's at stake when they stand to lose something important and decides to change. Sometimes, when faced with the pain they've caused, a jerk has a shred of guilt and cuts someone loose they've been stringing along.

Pathological social actors, or low-conscience individuals, keep the people they hurt close to them by any means necessary because it benefits them. They shut down their partner's expressions of suffering by projecting the causes of that suffering back onto them. Instead of showing them mercy, they make their partners work harder to earn the love they promised but never delivered. These are acts of cruelty and sadism.

Is your partner pathological?

You owe yourself an honest answer to that question, and you're the only one who can answer it.

QUESTION ONE:

What's Wrong with My Partner?

I always knew he was selfish. I assumed it was because he is an only child. I started to realize a few months in that things didn't quite add up, and I brushed it off as silly things to lie about, so why was I looking for a problem? When the infidelity began (or I became aware of it) and he smirked rather than showing me genuine concern, I knew something was wrong.

—*Shari*, survey respondent

What's wrong with my partner?

You have asked yourself this question already, or you would not be reading this book.

Something is wrong—and not wrong in the way people sometimes mean it when they say there is a problem in the relationship. This is not that. On a gut level, a truth has surfaced that drives something sharp straight through you. There is something about your partner's actions that, no matter how many times you turn them over in your mind . . . well, they just don't make sense.

It wasn't always like this. In fact, when you look back at the beginning of the relationship, it was as if your partner was a completely different person.

Then, everything changed.

Your relationship used to be a fairy tale, everything perfect. Your partner was your soulmate and seemed to anticipate every desire and need you ever had. The two of you had appeared to share so many similar experiences, and it felt like you had a mirror image you had been searching for your entire life. The attention made you feel appreciated like you never had before. Your world expanded to make room for this new person in your life who wrenched vulnerability out of you as you cradled your life around him. You bloomed under the adoring eyes of someone you felt could truly see you.

And then . . . you were ripped out of the fairy tale world and thrust into a nightmare, a funhouse where everything twisted into its mirror opposite. The relationship buried you under its weight, and you watched the world fade away as you slipped deeper inside yourself. The cruelties your partner inflicted on you with such pleasure were things you wouldn't fantasize about in your worst moments as punishment for enemies.

These moments of cruelty are the uncontaminated flashes of insight when you realize something is not normal, and you ask yourself, *What is wrong with my partner?* This first question, spurred by your partner's behavior, sets off the chain reaction that changes the course of your life.

Yet sometimes, it feels as if you never actually realized anything at all, as if it had been a clever magic trick. Your partner showed you the Queen of Hearts, then shuffled it back into the deck while you weren't looking.

It's as if nothing happened. It was all in your head.

Or was it?

My Story

After stepping off the plane in Jamaica, we moved through customs and were ushered outside to a short bus, dusty white but for the orange smears of rust near the bumper. Amir sat first, and I took my seat beside him, soon realizing we had selected the wrong side on which to sit down. The parchment-colored window flaps were rolled up, and the Caribbean sun beat down on my arm mercilessly. Hours on the clock flattened out as I sweltered in the midday heat.

Lush, emerald foliage hugged the two-lane highway as we rode on the shuddering vehicle through the city. A salty breeze smothered us as it made its way in through the windows, hinting at the ocean we could not yet see. Damage from hurricanes-past still lingered, and periodically, we passed a strip of road where trees stooped over like broken men, bark exposed, palm fronds wild like wind-blown hair. But the leaves were green again. Vivid and alive. The grass near these trees, also green, was trodden, as if a fairy tale giant had slogged through to remind everyone who was boss.

The bus snaked up and down mountain curves until we arrived at our destination: a sprawling, all-inclusive resort along the southern coast. Our room at the resort was a pristine model of atmospheric Western romance. Up three stairs in the center of the suite was a king-sized bed with Egyptian cotton sheets and an adjoining two-person Jacuzzi. Off to the side was a living and dining room area and a wet bar we were informed would get refilled daily with soda, beer, and local rum. A dozen roses sat on the table near the door with a note that told us to enjoy our stay and each other.

If not for the circumstances, it would have been the proverbial paradise.

Our trip got started with drinks at one of the bars. Numb, I made small talk with him as if we were at the beginning of our relationship instead of near the horrible end. In the days leading up to the trip, Amir had alternated between coldly treating me as if I didn't exist and apologizing wildly about his outbursts. Begging me for another chance, he insisted there was a reasonable explanation for the whole engagement issue and what he'd said to me when I had told him I knew. He didn't know I also knew he had been proposing to his ex-girlfriend, Julia. A few days before we left, she sent me a recording of a phone call he had made to her while he was at work. He had told her our relationship was over, and he had moved out. He'd also asked her to fly out to where we lived and promised to pay for her hotel. There were other calls, too, calls where he imposed himself on her, jerking off in the middle of their conversation without warning. I asked her not to send me any more.

"You see, I know what he is like, but you are just learning," Julia said. "I know this hurts you to hear it, but this is who he is. He always used to tell me about you—where you work, how much money you have, about the things you do, and I would think about how you seem so much better than he is, and what are you doing with this man? You don't need him. You need to know who he is."

This sounded familiar. It sounded like what Sandi had said. I know what he is like. *What is he like? Why does everyone else know this but me?*

And why does everyone keep mentioning money? *I thought. It's as if I'm a trust-fund baby. Did having a steady income, good credit, and a 401k mean you "have money" to Amir?*

"I didn't ever contact you about him because maybe you are happy with him, and you don't want to know, I thought. I knew you wouldn't believe me if I reached out to you. But I told myself that if you ever contacted me, I would tell you the truth," she said.

My jealousy made my eyes burn. Yet this woman showed me kindness. "Why do you still talk to him if you don't want to be with him anymore?" I asked her.

"I did once love him very much," she said. "I understand now that he is not serious." It didn't really answer my question. Not until down the road would I understand her—how the letting go comes in stages.

She had sent me many messages of encouragement to strengthen my resolve for the trip to Jamaica. She knew the terms. She believed he would try hard to win me over again, and that's why she was going for the shock value. She wanted me to see his other face.

Sitting at the bar, talking to him as if we barely knew one another, it suddenly hit me that I didn't know him. I was there with a stranger. I got cold. I hardly knew how to act. I was floating, and too late, I realized how naïve I had been coming there with him. I understood what Julia had meant, why he had wanted me there. I was isolated, and he had caught me off guard with what he'd done. And I'd thought I could just come to an island with him and be around him without any time apart for seven days straight, that it would all be just lying around on the beach, then we'd go home, and he'd be gone. I could begin figuring out what had just happened and pull my life together. I hadn't really thought about what those long days on the beach would be like. What would it feel like to sit around with my thoughts about what he'd already done while he sat right beside me? I hadn't thought through the range of possible things he might do when he interacted with me or how I could prepare myself for them. There, in Jamaica and out of familiar territory, he could more easily control how I perceived all that had happened, and since I had no idea who he really was, I also had no idea what he would be willing to do.

Yet what choice did I have but to come?

My feelings swung back and forth wildly as the sun slid closer to the ocean, and the clouds turned pink. His fluctuating moods made me edgy, and the rum and Cokes weren't helping. I needed to be pleasant enough to him so he would leave at the end of the week when we returned. I didn't know what he was thinking, but I knew he outmatched me. I would have to swallow my shock and despair to get through the week, and no matter what, I absolutely could not reveal I knew anything about Julia. I had no idea how I would do that. I had no idea how I would do any of it, and he knew that. He didn't have to know about Julia to know I was at a severe disadvantage.

After dinner, we took a walk on the beach. The sound of the sea calmed me.

"The water here is so different than the Atlantic Ocean. It's warm," I said, pulling on his hand until his feet were in the tide.

Then, I pulled him a little farther until the waves crashed against our knees.

He gave me a look. He'd told me he didn't know how to "float." He could swim, he said, but when he got tired, he couldn't tread water.

I pulled off my sundress. "Take off your shirt," I said. The ocean was white under the moon, and as it collided with my body, I shrieked.

The moonlight gleamed on us as we stood alone in the water. I led him deeper into the cold darkness beyond the shore, and he let me, trusting me. As the bottom dropped out from under our feet, I realized I wasn't pretending anymore. I was still in love with him. We held hands and swam together, the warm waves washing over us.

He picked me up in the water and cradled me, smiling at his triumph. I desperately wished this moment we were sharing was real. It is real. No, it isn't. Yes, it is.

The cleansing water covered my tears.

Back in the room, he moved to kiss me, and I couldn't stop him. He looked directly into my eyes and said, "I love you. You're my everything."

Tears sprung involuntarily into my eyes. Times when he'd said that before flashed into my mind. Those words used to mean something, and now they didn't mean anything. No, they *never* meant anything, *I reminded myself.*

"I'm sorry," he whispered. For which wrong was he apologizing? What I knew about or what I didn't? All of it? The tears flowed freely. The way he was looking at me felt real, seemed real. There was no lie in his eyes to be detected. Yet what he said can't possibly be true, *I thought.* I can't be your everything.

The next morning, I woke up in his arms, but anger had replaced some of the tears. How dare he say that to me? He didn't know what I knew. He had all these secrets. All these lies. Yet he still had the nerve to say that to me.

The irritation lingered as we prepared to head down to the pool. All I could think about was the secret I carried. Julia. It took me too long to get ready because I was so distracted. I held the two books in my hand I'd brought with me in my suitcase.

"I don't know which one to take," I mumbled.

He shrugged from his place on the bed, where he was flipping through television channels, waiting for me.

"Take both," he said.

"Hmm . . . good idea. That way, if I'm not happy with one, I can put it down and pick up the other one," I said. "Funny you should come up with that."

He didn't look away from the TV. I shoved the books into the beach bag, and we left the room. As we walked down the path toward the pool, he pulled his shirt off.

"God, I'm so sexy," he said, his eyes flicking around from person to person as we passed them. "I'm the sexiest one here." The fact that that's what he was thinking about after the things he'd done pushed the boil inside me a little higher. Dude, calm down. You're not that sexy, *I wanted to say, just to shut him up. I bit my*

tongue, remembering the goal to have him walk out the door of our apartment at the end of the week.

After a quick breakfast and tour of the grounds, we jumped in the pool and sat at the swim-up bar under a palapa, downing rum. We agreed we'd head out to the beach at 4:30 in the afternoon. As he got drunker, though, he grilled me about men in my life past and present, making wild accusations. The conversation got edgier because of my irritation. I was indignant. How dare he make accusations? This wasn't new. He'd been unreasonably jealous for practically our entire relationship. But now, his accusations took on a whole new meaning. Now that I knew he was living multiple lives, it was like a double hit. I couldn't stop myself from making quips like the one in our room about the books alluding to the idea that I knew something was going on but never saying anything outright. His agitation increased.

At one point, for no reason that seemed apparent beyond his usual insecurities, he asked me with which man in my life I'd had the best sex.

"I know who it was," he said angrily, naming a man from my past.

"What? No, it wasn't. You know it was you."

"You're just saying that. Well, you know who I had the best sex with? It was Julia, okay?"

It was as if he'd uttered, "Abracadabra." A sharp needle of pain slid into the numb haze in my brain. It didn't matter whether he was serious or saying it to hurt me. He'd uttered the magic word, and the dam burst open. The secret I'd been keeping was over.

"Oh, I know all about Julia." I mocked some of the texts I'd seen. "Send me a picture. Show me your tits. I want to snort coke off your ass. *Seriously? You don't even do coke. Or do you?"*

His face contorted first into one of disbelief, then into one of hate.

"I've known for several days," I said. "You see, Julia and I have been talking."

"Good," he said and shrugged.

"Why? Why did you do it?"

He jumped off the barstool and headed for the side of the pool. Cold water splashed up and hit my cheek. Chlorine burned my eyes.

"I don't have to talk about this," he said, splashing and pulling himself out of the pool quickly. I clambered out behind him, grabbing my towel, forgetting my bag.

"Why? Why? Please just tell me why? You were asking her to marry you?" I cried.

"Because I knew it wasn't going to work between us," he snarled as he headed back up the path of the grounds to our suite. It made no sense. Why play these games, then, where he dragged me to Jamaica and begged me for a second chance? But it wasn't just that.

"No . . . why the entire time . . . from day one we were together? Who are you trying to be with? There are three of us?" I cried.

He said nothing as he opened the hotel room door, and I followed quickly behind him before he could shut it and lock me out. He slammed it behind me as I slipped inside. The housekeeping staff had visited the room, and they had made the bed. They had scattered pink rose petals across the floor and the white bed comforter. He crushed them under his feet as he paced the room. I watched him, growing more and more upset at his refusal even to acknowledge what I'd said.

"I know everything," I said, anger creeping into my voice again at his silence. "She told me everything. She gave me screenshots of your conversations going back for months."

"I don't have to explain anything to you," he said.

My hands shook. I was both crumbling and holding at the same time. "You led me to believe you wanted to be with me. And you're telling me you love me, I'm your everything, just last fucking night, and also telling her you love her, that you were going to bring her here. I heard a recording."

He gave a snorting kind of laugh. "Yeah, right. I was never going to bring her here. I never loved her. She was just a booty call." He moved around the room, looking for something, snatching items off the table, the desk, knocking papers onto the floor. I could smell the fruit from the tray left for us on the table by room service before we'd arrived starting to rot. "Both of you were just pieces of meat. I was just biding my time until I could find someone better. You were both just women that I could fuck. I can do better. Fuck both of you. In fact, I'll fuck someone else right here in front of you."

He grabbed something and stormed out of the hotel suite, and I saw him sit in a chair on the porch. I sat frozen, thinking about whether I should get on an airplane and go home. It had been three days since I had discovered all of this. I wasn't sure I had the thousands of dollars available it would take to fly back across the world at a day's notice, break a lease, pay a new deposit, and move all my things in that short of a time without saving more money first. I had just spent a substantial sum three months before to move in with him.

Even if I did leave Jamaica immediately, there wouldn't be enough time to make my own arrangements to be out of the apartment before he got back—assuming he didn't just hop on a plane himself and follow me. And what of his threat to abandon the apartment if I moved out? I still had to figure out how to deal with that if I left.

My mind kept whirling in these circular patterns trying to find an exit. By surprising him that I knew something he'd kept secret from me, I'd flipped his script, and he'd lost control. What did that mean? It means he must realize now that I had come here knowing that, so he's going to think I'm playing a game with him, *I thought. What would he do to get control back? I hated to think.*

The only thing that seemed rational at that moment was just playing out the week and letting him be in charge. Maybe he would be so disgusted with me he would just leave at the end of the week when we got back. Surely, with everything out on the table, he would see there was no point in sticking around. I suddenly realized I needed to act as if I didn't care what he did. Maybe that wouldn't even be too hard. He's in charge—I have no control. He loves me, he hates me, he ignores me. It's all the same. I never even know what I'm going to get from moment to moment, and what I do makes no difference. I might as well just do nothing. If I just act as if I don't care, surely, he will get bored and just leave on his own.

To my surprise, as I sat on the couch, Amir opened the door and stood right in front of me.

"It's 4:30. Are you ready to go to the beach?"

I slowly looked up at him.

"I'm not going," I said.

"You said we were going to the beach at 4:30." His voice sounded oddly calm.

A small part of me hidden away cried out, wanted to go. Please make this all go away. Please let him love you and pretend this didn't happen. I pushed the voice away and looked back down at my phone. "Things have changed."

He continued to stand and look down at me for a few moments, then picked up a chair and threw it across the room. He stormed back out.

I soon learned, however, that he didn't like for me to be out of his sight for too long, so after that, I rarely was. He'd dragged me down to the beach after all. That's where he wanted to go, so that's where we went.

"I'm going to do everything I can to hurt you while we're here," he said, the glint in his eyes a different one than I'd ever seen before. "I know how to make you cry. I know how to trigger your bottom." I stared out at the ocean, where he had held me just the night before. I didn't acknowledge his comments, so he said once again that he would do everything he could to hurt me. I pushed myself away from him inside so there would be no tears. A piece of me stayed behind to make sure no tears actually fell. His words sounded so alien from the man I knew that I couldn't even comprehend he had actually said them and that somehow made

it just slightly easier to bear. I sat, stone-faced, knowing I didn't know the man next to me who laughed cruelly and waggled his fingers in front of my face. He got up and waited for me to follow him to dinner.

I picked at my food in the dining room as he sat across from me, looking everywhere but at me. The tears I had held back welled up in my eyes involuntarily, and one of them fell down my cheek before I could stop it.

He dropped his fork on his plate noisily. "Seriously?"

I swallowed and tried to stop crying. "I . . . I can't help it."

"People are going to look at us."

"Amir, I just . . ."

"You're ruining my dinner. Do you want me to walk out of here?"

His coldness brought more tears to my eyes, and I bowed my head. Shaking his head, he slammed his gold napkin onto the table and stalked away in disgust.

Now, the couple at the next table looked over, where before they hadn't been. I didn't move, not knowing what to do next. A few seconds later, my phone buzzed inside my purse, indicating I had a text.

"Thanks for ruining it," he said. "You ruin fucking everything. I can't even eat in peace."

"I am only here with you, and you want me to stay with you all the time. I am in so much pain I can barely breathe."

"Call 9-1-1."

"You won't even talk to me."

"Well, I'm not going to talk to you. All you do is fucking cry and bitch why I did this or did that. Get your fucking self together. Cuz I don't need this shit in my life."

I wanted to appeal to that other Amir. The one I thought must be in there somewhere and who loved me. I didn't know this one. "I'm trying. But I loved you. Or who I thought you were. I just needed some kindness from you, and maybe I could get myself together. If you'd just explain why you did it all."

"I don't have to explain anything to you."

"All the plans we made meant nothing. They were a lie."

"Yes, they were. Now leave me alone."

I wiped my face with my napkin, pushed my sadness away, and told myself I was a strong woman and that I had to get through this week. I steeled myself for his behavior and came up with the idea that I would use nature to refocus my attention away from him when I needed to. As I had done on the beach when he'd told me he was going to try to hurt me, each time he attacked me, I would stare into the ocean or at the golden sky or think about or imagine how the water or the sun felt. I would not think about what he was saying.

When I got back to the room, however, I was surprised to find Amir in good spirits, as if the conversation we'd just had had never happened. He had showered and was walking around the living area of the suite naked. He hopped and danced around the room as he sometimes did, looking at me and trying to make me laugh.

I lay down on the bed, overwhelmed and exhausted from Amir's emotional outbursts.

"You just don't get it," he said when he realized I wasn't laughing. "You don't understand how much I love you. One day, you'll know. You're going to see me on TV."

I stared up at him, and he pointed at the dark television behind him.

"I'm going to be up there; you're going to see me. My first fight, I'm going to look right into the camera and say it's for you," Amir said. He was a boxer and mixed martial arts fighter who had been in a few local matches and had vague aspirations of being another Floyd Mayweather. "Then, you'll know. Here, you wanted to take a bath tonight in the Jacuzzi, didn't you?"

I said nothing as he walked over to the tub and turned on the water. A few minutes later, he shut off the water and lay beside me. The deep loss flowed through me as if carried by my blood cells. I felt it in my fingertips, and I felt it in my head, making me dizzy. I floated above everything. Amir turned over in bed and looked at me.

"What?" he said.

What? What? The entire world was upside down, and he was asking me, "What?"

"Don't you understand? It's not just what you did to our relationship. It's everything. Everything is gone now. I had relationships with your friends, your brother, and your sister. I care about them. And now I guess I'll never even see them again. We had plans. We had a home together. We bought furniture together. You said those things were lies, but those things were my life."

At that moment, his eyes changed, and the wall dropped. His mouth fell open, and he grabbed me quickly to him and held me. His reaction was so unexpected, so genuine, that I couldn't stop the sobs that slipped out.

After about a minute, he pulled back and looked at me, kissing my cheek.

"Okay, let's stop crying," he whispered. "It'll be okay."

But I couldn't stop. His demeanor shifted as a hardness fell over his face.

"What the fuck are you crying for? I'm being nice to you."

"I can't help it," I said.

He stood up, disgusted. "I should have gone to that woman's room."

Pain seared through me like a hot poker. "What woman?"

"Don't worry about it," he said.

He stalked into the bathroom, and my heart hammered as I understood the implication of what was about to happen. I followed, standing next to him as if my presence could stop it. My hands were shaking, so I absent-mindedly picked up a comb, running it through my hair to give myself something to do. Panic bloomed in my chest.

"Where are you going?" he said. He finished slicking his hair back with the open bottle of gel next to the sink and grabbed his

cologne, watching me in the mirror. "You going to go fuck someone too?"

"No. I'm going to take my bath," I said. The voice that spoke was calm. I didn't know where it came from.

He flexed in the mirror. "I look really sexy right now," he said, smiling at his reflection. "I could get any woman here."

This time, I couldn't stop myself. "Good luck with that," I mumbled.

He turned to me, contempt blowing off him in waves. "I could fuck you in your fucking face right now if I wanted to."

"Are you threatening to rape me?" I didn't know where this detached voice came from.

He turned. "Don't worry. I'll get it somewhere else."

The calm woman vanished, and I fell to the floor in front of him. "Please don't go, Amir."

He stepped around me and walked toward the door. "I'll be back."

After he left, I stayed on the floor, the cold tile numbing my body. I cried until snot ran out of my nose, then it felt like I had no more tears left to cry. I wasn't sure how much time had gone by. Half an hour? An hour?

Finally, I sat up and crawled into the two-person bathtub. The water was ice-cold. I turned on the hot water faucet, shivering with my knees drawn to my chest, running the water until it nearly burned me.

A thought entered my mind as I sat in the tub, knees still drawn to my chest. It was so insidious that cold tentacles of fear slid themselves down my spine. What if he had brought me out here to this island to kill me? He'd been so insistent that we take this trip together. I'd thought it was just a control thing. Julia had thought it was because he wanted to try to win me back. Yet suddenly, the mystery of the two voices that didn't know each other, Sandi and Julia, who had both mentioned to me they had heard from Amir that I "had money," snapped into place. I didn't have money, but he would if I died and he collected on my life insurance policy . . . which I'd added him to just a few months before when he'd insisted I didn't love him and wasn't serious about him.

Is that what taking me on this trip is all about? We were breaking up, and this was his last chance? Maybe he was planning to say I went missing or that I'd drowned. Is that why he kept insisting we go to the beach, even when it was not an appropriate time? Is that why he always wanted me with him? Is that why he was so angry that I cried in public—because I made us stand out? "I'm going to do everything I can to hurt you," he'd said. Maybe he didn't see a reason to hide it anymore.

A part of me just couldn't believe it. No, he wouldn't do that.

But I didn't know the man who had done the things to me he had done that day. I didn't accept it was the same man I loved. I didn't even know what the man I'd seen that day was capable of.

Amir and the stranger with his skin had taken turns that day appearing and disappearing in front of me, and a growing sense of both danger and disbelief surged inside me like a pulse. Anything seemed possible to me at that moment.

While still in the bathtub, the door opened suddenly, and Amir walked in. He was smiling, carrying a coconut.

"Baby, look what I brought you," he said, a spark of excitement replacing the glint of cruelty. "A man was slicing them open with a machete right outside and handing them out."

I didn't really want the coconut, yet I knew I risked facing his wrath if I didn't accept it. I blinked, holding out my hands, and he eagerly handed me the token prize. I took a sip, and the sweet liquid hit my stomach, making me feel nauseous. When I set it down on the edge of the bathtub, his face fell.

"What, you don't want it?"

"No, I do. I'm just savoring it," I said.

When I got out of the bathtub, I ended my first full day in Jamaica by taking screenshots of the text conversations I had had with Sandi and Julia, then I emailed them to myself. I then texted the password to my email account to my mom.

Just in case.

4

The Story All Around Us

As I was growing up, my mom and I were both fans of comedic actress Goldie Hawn. When I was in high school, we went together to see one of her movies, *Deceived,* a movie that didn't turn out to be very funny at all.

In the film, Hawn's character, Adrienne, is swept off her feet by art dealer Jack, and they marry quickly. Fair warning that I'm about to spoil the rest of the film. Then again, maybe you can already see what's coming.

Fast forward several years: Adrienne and Jack have a daughter, and Jack is suddenly accused of selling forged art to a local museum. When he goes on a business trip, we learn from Adrienne's point of view that he has died in a car accident.

As the plot unfolds, Adrienne learns Jack is not really dead and that his name isn't really Jack. When Adrienne finds "Jack" again, he tells her he had taken on the identity of his dead best friend in high school years ago out of grief. He explains that he's innocent, that he's not selling forged art, yet he felt he had no choice but to fake his death because he's being blackmailed. Of course, he also expresses how much he's still in love with her. Never mind the fact that he let her believe he was dead, and she probably never would have seen him again if she hadn't sought him out.

While attempting to help "Jack" find a missing artifact to give to the person blackmailing him, Adrienne learns he has a third identity. She finds the address where he is living under this third identity. Pretending not to know him, she talks to the pregnant woman living there and stumbles on wedding photos of the woman with "Jack." She then sees another picture of her own daughter, a child she had with "Jack" years ago. The pregnant woman comments that it's her husband's dead sister, which we know is the lie Jack has told his new wife.

I remember sitting in the theater and hearing the audience gasp at the end of the film as Jack's final deceptions were uncovered. During the movie, Jack had also behaved like a stereotypical psychopath in a thriller—stalking, kidnapping, and killing. Yet his physical violence is not what I remembered over the years.

What stuck with me was being *with* Adrienne as she peeled away each layer of Jack until nothing remained. Her shock was my shock, reflected to me in her facial expressions. I remembered each incremental moment when Adrienne learned a new fact that conflicted with her idea of what the truth had been. She'd revise her version of reality to keep up. She did this right up until the end, until the moment came when she discovered the entire life she was living was a lie.

Of *Deceived*'s premise, the scriptwriter, Mary Agnes Donoghue, said:

> *You're sitting there at night and look over at your husband or your wife and think: Who is this person? I was fascinated by*

> *the idea of having a safe middle-class existence, predictable, and then certain events take place that let you know that you know nothing about your own life and the people in it. It's about betrayal at its most profound.*[32]

Those of us who have experienced it know twists don't only exist in fiction. In the memoir *The Bigamist,* Mary Turner Thomson suddenly receives a phone call that her husband and father of her two younger children is also the husband of the woman who called her. They had been married for fourteen years and had five children together. Another memoir written by a woman who could not use her real name because of a confidentiality clause in her divorce decree describes how, after her fairy tale courtship, her husband turned on her after marriage. She eventually discovers he has acquired hundreds of thousands of dollars of debt in her name and is involved in an international underground prostitution ring. Journalist Abby Ellin got engaged to a man calling himself The Commander whose military heroism had supposedly won him a Purple Heart and a Medal of Honor. She later learned that in reality, the stories he told of politicians he'd met and missions he'd taken part in were only that: stories. In addition, he was simultaneously engaged to someone else. She ended up using her experience to write a book about people who live double lives.[33]

These real-life nightmares aren't limited to books. Deborah Newell's experience with "Dirty John" inspired a newspaper serial, a podcast, and an eight-episode miniseries on Bravo. Deborah fell for a man named John Meehan, who claimed to be a doctor who had been hurt in Iraq. In reality, he was a homeless parolee who had a past littered with dozens of restraining orders filed against him by women he had stalked and abused. When she eventually left him, he set her car on fire and attempted to kill her daughter. She told *NBC News* that by the time she left, her primary emotion was confusion.

"I believe I looked at it as 'What was real and what was not real?' I thought, 'How could this man fake it to this degree?" You know, did he love me or . . . was this all a game?"[34]

Within the past few years, because of stories like Newall's, pathological love relationships have started to creep into mainstream awareness. As the stories enter our entertainment and news and, by extension, our social consciousness, the tactics abusers in these relationships use have become more recognizable. *Love Island*, which airs in the United Kingdom, featured a contestant whose gaslighting behavior prompted a warning from domestic abuse charity Women's Aid about emotional abuse.[35] The 2019 season of the United States version of *The Bachelorette* held an average of seven million viewers captive each week watching bachelorette Hannah Brown struggle with her relationship with one of the contestants. Using the show as an example, publications from *Cosmopolitan* to *Men's Health* published online articles about the warning signs of emotional abuse and gaslighting.[36]

Other reports have also quietly made their way into the news of entertainers and politicians whose lives have been touched by the pathology of a low-conscience individual. In 2018, Natalie Lewis-Hoyle, the daughter of the deputy speaker of the House of Commons of the United Kingdom, ended her life. Natalie suffered through a toxic relationship for two and a half years and spent long periods on the phone with her boyfriend leading up to her death. Her mother described Natalie as a "feisty character" and full of life but one who had deteriorated significantly. In the aftermath of her daughter's death, she started a website to raise awareness about gaslighting. "When somebody is in psychological torment, you don't get the bruises and the fat lips and the black eyes," she said.[37]

In 2019, actress and model Pamela Anderson expressed her shock on social media that the soccer star she had been dating for two years, Adil Rami, had been "living a double life.

> *It's hard to accept. The last (more than) 2 years of my life have been a big lie. I was scammed, led to believe we were in « big love »? [sic] I'm devastated to find out in the last few days. That he was living a double life. He used to joke about other players who had girlfriends down the street in apartments close to their wives. He called those men monsters.*

She further explained that Rami was physically abusive, dangerously jealous, and had isolated her from her friends and family and monitored her behavior on video cameras, despite his multiple secret affairs. Notably, Pamela had learned he was still carrying on a relationship with his ex-wife, and after speaking with her, both women were shocked to learn of the seriousness of the other's relationship. Pamela wondered how Rami had been able to "control two women's hearts and minds." She described how, when she had tried to leave, Rami had begged her to marry him and told her he would die without her.[38]

Pamela may have never used the words "narcissistic abuse," but I wonder, by now, if she's stumbled across an article about it and had that moment where she's had an epiphany about what she went through?

You Are Not Alone

As painful as it was, the moment your relationship with your partner changed—or the moment you realized it—was inevitable.

This is one of the hardest things to accept.

Before many of us had ever learned the words "narcissistic abuse," something happened that led to a fundamental shift in the way we viewed our partners and the relationship we were in. Nothing was ever the same after that.

Pathological Love Stories

"I Knew Something Wasn't Right When . . ."

"We were 'working' on our marriage for a year after I left, and then I discovered he was having sex with multiple strippers while I waited for him to come and visit me on weekends. All the while, he would profess his love for me and how much he wanted to make things work and get back living together."

"A month after marrying me, he went on holiday with a Japanese lady whom he had introduced me to prior to our marriage. She is now pregnant with his baby, and he has also married her, too, illegally in the USA."

"I accidentally discovered my wife was leading a second-track life while maintaining a 'normal' family life with me and our children. I launched a covert investigation. When I had enough information to confront her, I demanded that it stop. That's when things got crazy—blatant denial of verifiable material fact, gaslighting, childish enragement, even violence. She refused to stop but continued to try to hide her behavior."

"We were in a committed long-term relationship one day. The next, he said he needed time. Found out he gave my commitment ring to [someone else] and moved in with her in less than a month."

"I was a victim of sexual assault by a stranger. [He] made the experience about him, tried to make me feel sorry for what I was putting HIM through. Instead of being there for me, he

disappeared because he couldn't handle the thought of that happening to me, and HE had to go to counseling."

"He just abandoned me one day after twenty-three years . . . no reason, no explanation. One day, it was 'I love you more than anything in the world' while he desperately hugged me. The next, it was 'I'm never coming back,' said coldly over the phone."

"He was avoiding me for the past six weeks, not letting me see him, and I went to his house without being invited, and there was a woman in the yard with him doing yardwork. He told me to leave his property, or he would call the police to have me removed. He called me 'bitch' many times and tried to hide the woman from me. He texted six days later, unloading on me and saying he was never in a relationship with me."

"After trying for a baby, he became very violent and scary once I discovered I was pregnant. I was forced to terminate my pregnancy, which broke my heart in pieces."

"He walked out and ghosted me. I later found out he had a girl pregnant, and then two months later, he got his niece of nineteen pregnant."

"He did not come home from work one night and would not answer my texts or phone calls. Came home much later than he got out and had no explanation of where he was. When I confronted him on it, he told me he 'hated me,' to 'get the fuck out,' and that he 'had no friends because of me.' . . . Attempted counseling (at his request). He was dating another woman while we were going to counseling."

"He is married, and he told me in the beginning, his wife and him had an open relationship. That was a lie! So, after dating

him for 2.5 years, found out he had been cheating on me with other women at work (our relationship was open to all at work), went through two rounds of antibiotics to cure myself of the STD he gave me."

"When I was bedbound with a lack of support, he told me to give up and die. He later was physically abusive."

"Besides writing to my university to cancel my master's degree scholarship so that I could spend most times with her at home over the weekends, she didn't love me enough to fight for our relationship. [He notes elsewhere that she left the relationship to be with someone else.] She went to file a threatening violence case with the police, saying she feared for how I will react to the situation, and so she feared for her life and of her 'friend,' yet I was 410 km away from her and [the new person]. Then, she later came back to me, begging for forgiveness for what she did."

"Flirting with another woman in front of me. 'Accidentally' showing pictures of other women. Treating me like a piece of nothing. Saying I lay down with someone else (he did)."

"He lied about his age. He said he had a sister, introduced me to an Erica, then said his sister's name was Nicole. So many lies. He never picked up his phone before 6 p.m."

"We had been divorced for five years but still 'friends' when I was diagnosed with colon cancer, and he said he wanted to 'help' me, and I started living with him again. . . . I was still very weak after surgery to remove about half my colon, and I had to use a walker because I could barely stand up. I made the mistake of disagreeing with him about something, and he flew into a rage, threatening to kick me out of the apartment and 'put me out on the street with the other homeless beggars where

I belonged,' because if I couldn't appreciate that he was 'killing himself' to provide a place for me, I didn't deserve to be there at all."

"The day he came home raging and kicked me while I was bent over. . . . Then, his mom called, and when he answered, in this eerie moment, I watched the mask he put on, and I'm telling you, it was insane how different he looked. His entire body and face morphed in front of me."

"I found out he had destroyed my credit. The lies kept coming out. Told me we were having financial difficulties, and then he came home with a brand-new motorcycle. My father had passed away and my twenty-five-year-old niece, two months apart. I was not allowed to grieve. I had to run our business no matter what. He started yelling and screaming in my face no matter what I did or did not do."

"When I was pregnant and on bed rest for six months and scared out of my mind for the baby, he would yell and rage and make me sob and hyperventilate and bleed and still feel no remorse, and that's when it finally hit me."

"I realized something was wrong when he'd ignore me for days if I did anything to upset him . . . which was trivial. Then after a week, he left flowers/creams/books at my door to say sorry."

"The breaking point was when my son was diagnosed with brain cancer and then demanded all the attention for his own 'needs.' I began to see a cycle, like the cycle of violence. Initially, it was very small things, comments, etc."

"I worked a full-time job. . . . He was home on disability. Small items came up missing—'STOLEN'—my mother's wedding

ring, jewelry, clothes, sentimental items. . . . The moment my mother went on hospice is the moment he dropped the loving act."

"The day after I purchased a house for us and was reliant on him for some of the house expenses . . . was the first time he psychologically attacked, and when I sat there, destroyed and in tears, he told me I was a mess, got into his car, and disappeared for several hours."

"I was sexually assaulted when I went for a walk in the early evening in my neighborhood, and just a few weeks later, I was in a car accident. I needed to go to a neurology appointment because I had suffered a head injury. I took three buses there, and my partner was supposed to pick me up after work and bring me home. He didn't show up, and although I called at least a dozen times, he didn't answer his phone. . . . When I got home, I saw his car. He was in his recliner, watching TV. He said he didn't forget he was supposed to pick me up. He said he didn't answer his phone because he didn't feel like driving. He said, yes, he knew I was scared, but that was my problem, not his."

"I realized there was something wrong when he hit me with the tailgate of our car (on accident). It hit me so hard I could see stars and couldn't speak for a moment. He yelled at me for not speaking straight, then yelled at me again for crying, and he said it was all my fault."

"Had been married for two years, and we were buying a house. He stopped informing me of decisions or providing me information but started to show more and more anger when I spoke in public or questioned him. I tried discussing with him my concerns. This led to passive-aggressive behaviors and eventu-

ally contempt toward me only in private. In public, he showed no aggression but was friendly."

"Exactly a year after our relationship, he vanished for a month. He came up with an excuse that didn't fit with facts that became available to me. I thought he was a compulsive liar."

"I discovered he'd been living a double life for twenty-two years."

"The first time I noticed a double standard. After enduring two months of accusations of infidelity and having to prove my loyalty [where] I was made to jump through hoops—everything from doing their laundry to providing sexual favors and paying for most of their bills—I discovered that they were cheating on me since the beginning of the relationship."

"When I found out that he took all our money and put it in his name only, then put his two children on the account to inherit the money when he died . . . if he died first, I would not have any money to live on. I had a stroke when I found out."

"I called her at midnight because I was having an anxiety attack. I just wanted to talk to her to feel better, and she was busy. So, after hanging up the call several times, she finally picked up the phone only to say, 'I'm worried if anything happens to you, I'll be blamed for your death.' She said this while I was sobbing uncontrollably, and then she hung up again and turned off her phone."

"Found a dummy account on his Facebook page. It was an escort site. He lied."

"At a very special and personal moment which I THOUGHT he was sharing with me, he was simultaneously emailing love letters to four other women."

"He was living a double life. He has/had a partner and child in a nearby city. His whole family and many of our friends knew, and it had been going on the entire time we were together."

"He brought a woman home to stay, claiming she was his manager and would leave soon. When I objected to seeing their closeness, he turned into Jekyll and Hyde. Then, his phone opened up in front of me and showed his messages to other women he was seeing and prostitutes he was dallying with. Then, an ex-wife contacted me after sixteen years of not knowing where he was, and I discovered a galore of ex-wives in the U.S. and numerous children he has abandoned."

"Our son was stillborn at three weeks, three days, and he told everyone I faked the entire pregnancy. Then, once I 'proved' I was actually pregnant by providing a death certificate, he intentionally didn't come to the burial. Then, he told everyone that I didn't invite him. Actually, I begged him to come. No normal person does that. Then, he gives me the silent treatment for three weeks, only to tell me I killed our son to hurt him. The autopsy report confirmed I was not at fault."

See Appendix A.

Across all the wide-ranging descriptions of cruelty and deceit included in this chapter, what unites them is the inexplicably profound disregard for each of the people who had the courage and strength to share it. There are as many creative and damaging ways to degrade a person as there are people in the world who feel entitled to exploit the personhood of others.

The moment we have the realization for ourselves that it's happening to us is the moment an unanswered question slithers its way into our minds. It's the moment we wonder, *What is wrong with my partner?* and can't come up with an answer.

"Why does he act like he hates me so much?"

"Why would she do something like this to hurt me?"

"Why go to all this trouble?"

"What is he trying to accomplish? This doesn't make any sense."

"Why not just let me go? He had what he wanted already."

Why. Why. Why.

In the movies, we always get our reason. Goldie Hawn in *Deceived* realized her husband, Jack, had always been after the precious museum artifacts. As horrible as the things he'd done were, at least we knew the purpose behind them. The universe made sense.

Right now, if you're still entangled with your partner, you're not in your own universe anymore. You're sitting somewhere in your partner's unfathomable dream world, where he or she can conjure up anything they want to and make you believe it's real.

Nothing will ever make sense again until you are free of your partner forever. You probably don't believe me. You're holding out hope your relationship is an exception.

But isn't there another part of you that thinks those words ring true?

5

Out of the Fairy Tale and into the Nightmare

One of the most well-known children's stories across the world is *Little Red Riding Hood.* Almost every culture has a version of this story, going back centuries, but it was the Brothers Grimm who collected the German version into their collection for children in 1812.[39] Depending on which version you read, this tale has several different endings. All versions, however, center around the interactions between two characters: Little Red Riding Hood and the Big Bad Wolf.

Little Red Riding Hood is a young girl who, while traveling through the woods to take food to her sick grandmother, meets the Big Bad Wolf. The girl has no fear of the Wolf and innocently tells him of her plans. The Wolf plots to eat both the grandmother and the child and distracts the girl by telling her to pick flowers while he hurries to the grandmother's house and, in the original version, eats her. He then disguises himself as the grandmother. When Little Red Riding Hood arrives, she is not at first aware she has instead encountered the Wolf, although her intuition tells her something is not right. After questioning him, eventually, the Wolf throws off the disguise, and depending on which version you read, he either eats her, or she is rescued by a woodsman outside who hears her scream.

It was only upon reflecting on this story as an adult that I've realized how terrifying this story really is—even the versions where all children and grandmothers live. *Little Red Riding Hood* is the story of a predator who targets an unsuspecting and innocent little girl. Yet, instead of just attacking her at the first opportunity when he so clearly could have done it with no apparent difficulty, he gains her trust, then devises a plot to deceive her by disguising himself as someone she loves so he can take her by surprise and kill her.

The implied moral of the story of *Little Red Riding Hood* for children everywhere is clear: "Don't talk to strangers."

Yet have you ever considered *why* the story unfolds as it does? If the Wolf had eaten her in the woods, wouldn't the moral still be the same? Does the Wolf have to be so cruel?

Why does the Wolf talk to her at all? Why doesn't he just kill and eat her when he first encounters her in the forest? Sure, he learns about another potential victim through the conversation. Yet once that happens, does the Wolf really need to trick Little Red Riding Hood before attacking her when he could presumably just kill and eat her the same way he did Grandma? Why go to all the trouble to execute an elaborate plot to deceive her when it all seems so unnecessary?

Whereas the Big Bad Wolf is wearing a literal mask, predatory people construct false selves. They pretend to have commonalities with their victims, fake emotions, carry on secret lives, and lie excessively to construct a past, present, or future that isn't real. Psychiatrist Hervey Cleckley called this "the mask of sanity" when describing the psychopathic personality. It's not that the psychopath doesn't understand the ethical rules by which most people live—he or she just doesn't abide by them.

Psychopaths are not held back by their consciences from engaging in behavior that they know hurts other people. They're not interested in conforming socially unless it benefits them. Often, the benefit is the appearance of normality. To conform, they wear a mask in which it appears to others that they follow the same social rules as everyone else. The really dangerous part is that they don't appear nervous that they're not following the same moral code. There are no cracks in the mask to give them away, and it makes them untouchable.[40] We feel safe enough to let them seamlessly into our comfort zones and make ourselves vulnerable before the masks come off.

The lies I uncovered about Amir's other relationships were not the first. When I later pieced together what seemed like small lies at the time, I realized he was not only telling stories—but he was shifting his entire identity depending on who was around. When we met, Amir gave me a false name, and I didn't learn his real one until over a month later after we had already been on several dates. He contradicted himself about his job history, relationship history, family dynamics, finances, and often, even his whereabouts throughout our relationship. Nine months into our relationship, when I was planning his birthday party with some of his friends, it also became clear I didn't know his true age. His friends shared an elaborate story Amir had told them years before about why his driver's license didn't have his real age on it. Privately, Amir insisted the age on his license was accurate, and he had lied to his friends out of embarrassment and provided me with a different elaborate story. Which elaborate story was true? I kept seeing and hearing evidence that both were true—which is obviously not possible.

The important point, however, was that he had created two divergent realities for two sets of people. It felt trivial to keep pursuing it—I really didn't care either way how old he was. Yet it nagged at me that I couldn't ever corroborate which was one was true. I never knew the truth. By the time I uncovered the secret engagement and ongoing relationship with his ex-girlfriend, I had learned of so many lies and half-truths it felt like peeling back layers of an onion.

A key feature of pathological love relationships is the abuser's false construction of reality to manipulate people in social and romantic relationships.[41] It may sound Shakespearean and dramatic, and it's true that Shakespeare plays have a lot of characters who would probably fit the bill. In *Hamlet*, Claudius, Hamlet's uncle, kills Hamlet's father to take over the throne, then marries Hamlet's mother, Gertrude. It was clearly a strategic move, but he may also be sincere with his outpourings of love toward Gertrude—or is he? It's hard to tell. Yet he has no qualms about plotting to have Hamlet killed as well when he feels threatened by him.

In *Macbeth*, there's also Lady Macbeth, who plots a murder for the power of the crown as well. She convinces her husband it's something they want, then manipulates him into murdering King Duncan by questioning her husband's manhood.

Finally, there's Iago, a character in *Othello* who most exhibits traits that resemble those of a malignant narcissist, in my opinion. When the play opens, Iago harbors secret hostility toward his so-called best friend, Othello. He feels slighted Othello didn't choose him to be a lieutenant. He also believes Othello may have slept with his wife (but doesn't appear to have any evidence). His animosity toward Othello feels either disproportionate or unwarranted. To get vengeance on Othello, while still pretending to be his friend, he lies to make him believe his wife, Desdemona, has slept with someone else and eventually manipulates Othello into killing her. He is gleeful about the destruction he causes.

Fictional characters like these always remain at the heart of the legends we pass down and the stories remade again and again. They give those stories depth while giving the heroes something to overcome (or not).

Interacting with someone like this in real life, however, is not entertainment.

The Savior, The Bully, and The Magician

In her early research, Sandra L. Brown, M.A. identified five stages of pathological love relationships:[42]

- **Pre-Relationship**: This predatory stage is characterized by the psychopath's "luring and trolling" to see who takes the bait, seeking out and taking advantage of opportunity wherever it opens up, and specifically targeting individuals with high-value traits or qualities.
- **Early Relationship**: This seduction stage is characterized by the psychopath's intense, dramatic behavior, which they express through a persona modeled after and conjured specifically for the personality of the intended target.
- **Mid-Relationship**: The turning point in the relationship comes when the constructed persona begins to fall apart, and the survivor sees another side of the psychopath for the first time, then continues to shift between both views of the psychopath until the relationship ends.
- **End-Relationship**: The survivor has struggled with understanding the psychopath's two sides by trying to communicate with the psychopath, and the psychopath

has no use for a partner who can no longer be manipulated using the same methods as before. Therefore, the psychopath departs in a way you would expect a conscienceless person to leave: "devaluing, discarding, or disappearing."

- **Post-Relationship**: Psychopaths return to draw the survivor back into the cycle, often when the survivor is vulnerable or caught off-guard. However, the psychopath may have multiple people caught up in all these stages at any given time and are constantly cycling people in and out.

This model has been condensed into three stages and institutionalized in the narcissistic abuse literature. The early, middle, and end stages characterize what's commonly called the narcissistic cycle of abuse and labeled ubiquitously as "idealization, devaluation, and discard."[43] Focusing on these three stages is useful for explaining the contradictory and irrational behavior of the pathological partner within the relationship itself.

In the idealization stage at the beginning of the relationship, the low-conscience individual puts his or her partner on a pedestal and showers them with excessive praise and attention, causing "soulmate syndrome" and extreme emotional bonding. Author Shahida Arabi puts it best: "The idealization phase can only be described as pure, unadulterated ecstasy—both for the victim and the predator. Love-bombing—the excessive praise and flattery the predator showers on the prey—might as well be crack cocaine."[44]

At some point, the partner of the low-conscience individual will fall off the pedestal, usually due to no fault of their own. The low-conscience individual may begin to see his or her partner as flawed or even grow bored. Then, the devaluation phase begins, characterized by verbal abuse, withholding, humiliation, smearing, and various forms of betrayal on the part of the low-conscience individual. Often, pathological partners have had others on the "back burner" all along—"friends," exes, a phone full of mystery numbers—and now they may trot one or more of those people out and wave them in your face.

Finally, when the low-conscience individual no longer sees any value in the partner, they may discard the partner and the relationship for one or more of the bit players. This often happens if the survivor acts or reacts in a way the pathological partner perceives as critical or demanding.

You may have noticed immediately that something seems missing from this model. The cycle begins again after the discard stage when the pathological partners initiate contact. If that contact is successful, then the idealization stage will begin again. The action pathological partners take in between the discard and the idealization stage is called "hoovering." What makes the contact, or hoovering, successful for the low-conscience individual is when the survivor continues to accept their version of events or reality. The pathological partner does not come back because he or she is contrite or apologetic. If the survivor accepts the low-conscience individual's reality, they will start the cycle again by idealizing the survivor.

By introducing this action, hoovering, into the model, it becomes clearer *how* the cycle persists.

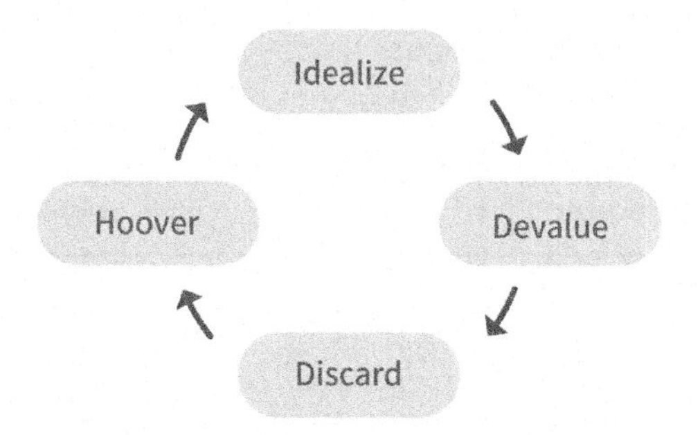

Figure 5.1:
The Narcissistic Cycle of Abuse

What I find so interesting about this model is that, in isolation, the stages are all so different from one another. It's easy to call out the devaluation stage as abusive. It most resembles our traditional model for overt abusive behavior. When people describe narcissistic abuse tactics, they usually describe these devaluation behaviors. Yet, to an outsider, the discard stage may just look like a bad breakup. The hoovering and idealization stages may look romantic.

These manipulative actions disguised as romantic gestures are why pathological love relationships are confusing, even to outsiders.

What is rarely pointed out is that it's the entire cycle that is abusive.

Manipulating someone to cycle repeatedly through four stages of such opposing environments is psychologically disorienting.

To keep with the theme of characters and fairy tales, let's talk about the roles pathological partners play at different times in the relationship: The Savior, The Bully, and The Magician. These are the masks. By alternating between these three roles, you never see your partner as he or she truly is. These three roles keep us from being unable to reconcile the incompatible images of our partner we keep seeing throughout the relationship.

The Savior sets the stage. He is the character your partner becomes when he needs you to trust and forgive him for egregious behavior. Your partner created this persona for you when you first met, and he wanted you to open up and make yourself vulnerable to him. This persona is special and likely exists only for you, based on your needs, desires, likes, and dislikes. But your partner cannot keep up this mask all the time. When he is upset with you, he punishes you. The Savior disappears, and The Bully takes his place. The Bully is brutal. When The Bully appears, we are stunned and confused about what happened to The Savior. Sometimes, we may even try to leave if it seems like The Savior is gone forever.

Then suddenly, The Magician materializes. The Magician makes The Bully disappear. He tells us The Bully isn't really a bully. The Bully didn't mean to hurt us; The Bully is just misunderstood. We should forget about The Bully and only focus on The Savior. If we'd do that, The Bully would *never* come back.

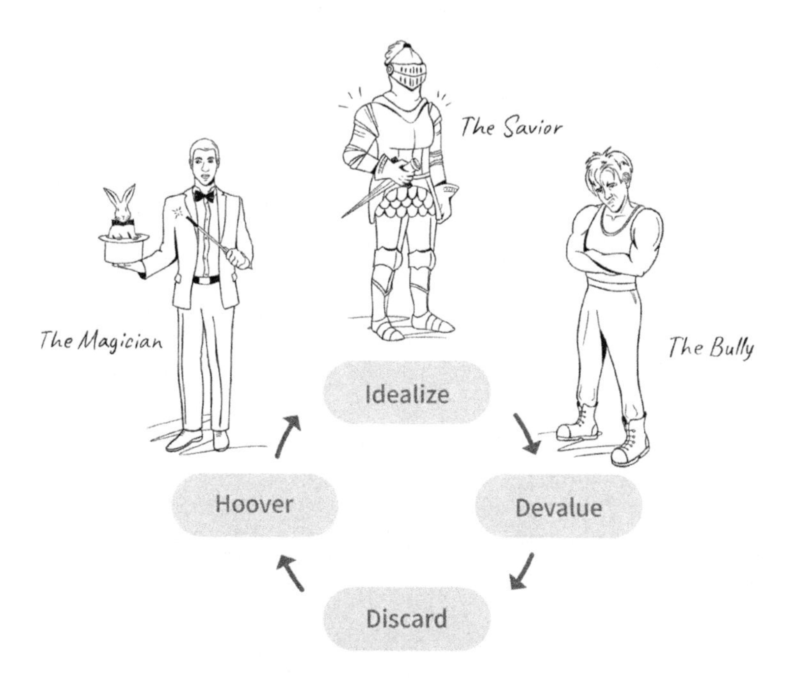

Figure 5.2:
The Roles Played by Pathological Partners

What is so nightmarish and abusive about pathological love relationships?

Making yourself vulnerable to someone else is like giving someone you trust with your life a key to your home. If you watch that person physically morph into someone you didn't know, run through your house smashing your prized possessions and laughing maniacally, then morph back into your friend and pretend it didn't happen, you'd probably want the key back.

But it would be too late.

6

But . . . Can My Partner Change?

I wish you were not reading this right now.

The fact that you are means you have learned something painful about your partner. The knowledge you now have about your partner, whatever it was and however you learned it, has put you on a path that has changed your life forever. You can never again turn back and unknow what you know.

Late in my interactions with Amir, the question of whether he could change or not haunted me. I'd seen him act loving, and I'd seen him act cruelly. If he could act loving sometimes, could he ever stop acting cruelly?

This internal argument we have with ourselves can be a complicated and confusing issue to sort out. Conflicting information exists on whether change is possible. Just as we can stay confused about whether our partner is pathological in the first place or how to categorize our partners, we can also remain trapped in a state of confusion trying to figure out whether our partners can change. We may read an article saying they can't, then read another article saying they can, and that gives us hope. Our partners return to us promising to change, and we can't get off the hamster wheel.

Let's talk about why disagreement exists about why pathological people might be able to change so when you read that type of information, you'll know why it's out there. When people describe "change," they're often talking about people who have narcissistic traits but may not have NPD. As described in Chapter 2, narcissism isn't categorical. Mental health professionals who treat those who fall on the unhealthy end of the narcissism spectrum have found that some people with narcissistic traits who seek treatment have successfully controlled and regulated some of their behaviors. They can make changes because they are self-aware and motivated, and they can self-reflect. They spend years or decades in intensive therapy because they want to. They change their behavior over time when they slowly adopt a different way of viewing other people's actions and themselves.[45]

However, these actions require self-awareness, self-reflection, and the ability to contemplate the consequences of their actions on their relationships—and to care about those consequences. The more conscience-impaired someone is, the less within reach these abilities are. Sandra L. Brown, M.A., points out that the *DSM-V* considers personality disorders to be pervasive—that is, affecting all areas of functioning.[46] These areas include the way a person views themselves. NPD and ASPD are examples of ego-syntonic disorders, which means that even though the behaviors associated with the disorders are problematic for the rest of society, most people who have them don't think there's anything wrong with them. They are unlikely to be self-aware enough to recognize that their actions have a detrimental impact on others or to consider their actions to be an issue. If people with these disorders recognize they may be "different" from other people, they often feel how they approach the world makes them superior, and other people are weak and bogged down by their empathy. If someone doesn't think they have a problem, they're unlikely to believe they need to change.

When conscience-impaired individuals are confronted with the criteria for personality disorders, one of two things often happens. If they are satisfied that their behavior is acceptable but view the disorders as negative, they will reject the idea that their behavior fits the criteria. Suppose they identify with the criteria and view the disorders themselves in a positive or neutral way. In that case, they may accept that they have the disorder but fail to view having it as problematic. They may even secretly wear it as a badge of honor. For example, they may like the idea of being a psychopath or being narcissistic, believing it makes them superior to others—even if they won't admit to it out loud.

Either way, whether they accept a diagnosis or not, what pathological partners have difficulty understanding is why their *behavior* is inappropriate. To view it as problematic, narcissists would have to be able and willing to reflect on and analyze their interactions with others and see that their interpretation of others' behavior causes the problem and not how others treat them. For antisocial-disordered individuals and psychopaths, they would have to care about what most other people consider appropriate and acceptable behavior.

Part of what makes this a losing battle is the biology of these disorders. The brains of psychopaths are different from the brains of other individuals. The amygdalae are smaller, and the fibers connecting the amygdala with the pre-frontal cortex are less pronounced.[47] These areas of the brain control emotions and social functioning, so psychopaths may be hard-wired to get something out of our suffering. Begging and pleading with them to stop hurting us not only isn't going to work, but it's also probably going to get them off.

The pleasure-seeking areas of the brain seem to gain a reward when they are in the company of someone who feels pain or when chaos reigns.

Psychopaths and individuals with ASPD usually only begin therapy because of a life-changing event that causes them to lose control. They are put into a court-ordered class or therapy, or they lost something or someone in their life and want it back. Once they get it back, they often leave therapy, and they soon revert to their previous behaviors. If they change, it's usually in a way we wouldn't want. Some of them learn from therapeutic intervention, anger management courses, and treatment for batterers how to be even more manipulative and fool therapists, lawyers, and the criminal justice system.[48]

If all of this sounds very pessimistic—it is. If you are holding out hope that your partner is one of those people who only has narcissistic traits and can actually change, there are some important questions you should ask yourself:

Being in Control When a Pathological Partner Says "I'll Change"

1. What will change **look like**? Be specific. What *actions* will you see that you don't see now? Words don't count.
2. How will you know change has ***not*** occurred? What are the red flags?
3. How will you know change has **actually** occurred? That is, how will you know their intentions are aligned with their actions?
4. What will be the consequences if he or she reverts to old behaviors or has not actually changed? What will you do?

Independent of how you respond to these questions as they pertain to your relationship, one of the key red flags to recognizing your partner has not changed is your continued confusion. If your partner has promised to change and is still doing the same things he or she did that have caused so much harm, even when you've explained how much damage they've caused to you and the relationship, your partner almost certainly will not and cannot change. The *DSM-V* states:

> *The pattern in personality disorders is maladaptive and relatively inflexible which leads to disabilities in their social, occupational, or other important pursuits, as the individuals are unable to modify their thinking or behavior, even in the face of evidence that their approach is not working.*[49]

That is an excruciating truth to face, and you may not be ready to face it right now. Just know this information is here for you to re-read at any time to help you understand why when you're ready.

I understand on so many levels why it's hard to accept this idea. Why would we want to accept that someone who has the capacity to be so loving with us is unable to stop being cruel? It almost defies reason. If we have seen that side of them, if it exists, then surely, they must be able to reduce or eliminate the cruel side of them. We wonder why it should be the other way around. There will be so much more in later chapters in the book to explain why we think this and why it's not the other way around. For now, however, I just want you to acknowledge you feel that way.

However, I also recognize that it can go even deeper than that. One of my core values is that anyone can change. Maybe you're like me, and you have this core value too. Or maybe you don't like the idea of giving up on people, or you feel uncomfortable from a spiritual or philosophical standpoint making judgments about the capacity of other people to change.

There is still room to hold in our hearts a core value such as this one while accepting the idea that our partners almost certainly are not going to have the capacity to change. Since my relationship with my ex-boyfriend ended, I have added a caveat to that core belief: Yes, anyone can change; however, they must personally want it, and they must work for it.

In other words, just because everyone can change in theory doesn't mean everyone will. It's not up to me to decide who will change and who won't, no matter how much I might want it to happen. Not making a judgment about someone's capacity to change means putting all the responsibility on them, even if the odds are stacked against them because they are conscience-impaired. It means not sharing the burden of waiting around for change if their behavior doesn't show they're making progress, regardless of whether they have the best of intentions or they're lying about what they promised. The outcome is the same either way.

Instead of trying to guess or know what's in someone's head based on what they say—whether they have gained insight or whether their intentions are true and their attempts are real—I can base what happens on their actions. Abusers don't get a free pass.

I learned how to strengthen and navigate my core belief so someone predatory can't come in to exploit it.

What I know is that if you're reading this book, you're currently suffering from manipulation, exploitation, deception, and maybe other forms of abuse. You're under no obligation to stay on deck while they figure things out. I encourage you to go beyond asking yourself whether your partner can change and ask how the relationship is changing *you* in ways you find disturbing.

Given where the momentum currently lies, what do you think has a better chance of happening: that your partner will suddenly change or that you will continue to change in a way that makes you continue to feel worse?

QUESTION TWO:

Is My Partner "Good" or "Bad?"

[The worst part of the relationship was] knowing he was lying and cheating, but he always denied it even when facts were presented. Made me feel crazy, lost, alone. Told me I was crazy when all I wanted was the truth and to get our relationship back to the way it was at first . . . until it wasn't. I just couldn't wrap my head around it when I was so in love with him and had truly believed everything. I went from feeling so loved to feeling completely worthless and not knowing why.

—*Megan,* survey respondent

When you first had the realization that something was wrong with your partner, you had bright flashes of clarity in which you knew you had to leave the relationship. Then came the anxious moments in which you doubted that thought, that everything you'd realized about your partner had somehow only been a big mistake. Shell-shocked, you waited for an explanation that never came.

Over time, too long caught between those two extremes muddied your thoughts. You fell into a struggle with yourself as your partner blinked in and out of your life and stepped into and out of the golden circle he drew around himself when you first met. You no longer remember the last time your mind settled on a thought about your partner and stayed there.

And the degradation . . . the things your partner did seemingly crawled straight out of your imagination, gristly and wet, as if your partner knew exactly how to reach into your heart of darkness and pull out your deepest fears. They are things you will only begin to accept once your partner is gone from your life, and you can then turn each piece of the relationship over in retrospect and without his influence.

There is nothing your partner won't do, no line they won't cross in trying to hurt you. Part of the horror is that the answers you receive when you ask, "Why?" pose an existential threat to your sanity: "Because I felt like it." In the next moment, your partner soothes your fears, kisses your tears, and whispers about the promised land.

Your worst nightmare becomes the dream from which you cannot wake up. You become obsessed with your new realization: *I don't know who my partner is.*

Which one is he? The good one or the bad one?

It is panic-inducing. It is mind-numbing. It is crazy-making.

My Story

Amir was silent on the plane ride home from Jamaica, stony and contemptuous when he wasn't asleep. My body cried out for sleep as well, but I was too edgy. His silence continued as he drove us back to our apartment. This anger was different than the anger he'd expressed before we'd left. Before, he had wanted to punish me for seeing through his lies. Now, it was as if I had ruined his life, and he had cast me out of his mind as someone worthy of his attention, and he couldn't wait to be rid of me. I had no doubts he would keep his agreement to move out.

This is what I had wanted. Through all the torment of the past week, I had told myself that if I could just survive, maybe he would leave me in peace when we returned, and it would all be over. Now, here we were, and it was happening. There was an unreal quality to it.

I sat on the couch in the living room as he slowly packed up his clothes, seeing things but not really seeing them. I was in my body but not really. Everything happened at lightning speed, and I watched it from mid-air. I couldn't process that two weeks ago, none of this had happened. The man I'd lived with two weeks ago didn't really exist, I kept telling myself. Yet I couldn't get the words to stick because there he stood through the doorway to the bedroom where I could see him folding things up and putting them in a gym bag. He looked up at me occasionally as he did it, and something about his attitude seemed to have changed.

My mind kept turning in circles. When he was calm, when he treated me kindly, he seemed the same as he always had. If that man didn't exist, then who was that person who had been doing all those loving things for eighteen months? He was the best boyfriend I'd ever had. If that wasn't real, then what was it? Both sides of him can't be real because he can't possibly feel that much love and hate for me. It wouldn't be rational or sane. One of them is a false emotion.

One of them is a false emotion, but both of them feel so real.

Amir gave me a long look through the doorway as he zipped up the bag. He kept his eyes on me as he walked into the living room to say goodbye.

"I love you," he said. "Can I get a hug?"

I couldn't speak, and I could not and did not resist him. Instead, I melted into him and let him be my comforter and my protector, this time comforting me and protecting me from what he'd done.

"Thank you for everything," he said, pulling back. His eyes filled with tears.

I could only nod.

He walked out, and a few minutes later, I received a text. "I wish you happiness. I'm sorry for everything."

A rush of memories overwhelmed me. Flashes, mental snapshots, of our perfect summer together the previous year came crashing unwanted into my mind, where the debate raged about which was the false emotion: his love or his hate.

That summer, it had been as if each time we saw each other, it was the first time, and each time we touched, it felt as if it would be the last. We'd figured out how to stop time, stretching out the seconds we spent together into something that stopped being measurable and agonizing over the seconds we wrenched ourselves apart.

He would drive over to my apartment, where our ritual stayed the same. I would meet him at his car out in front of the building when he arrived and ride down to the third-floor guest area of the parking garage. He would turn to me after shutting off the engine. It was a look he gave me—as if he'd never seen me before, or he'd somehow forgotten what I looked like. It wasn't that he'd tell me how beautiful he thought I was; it was that I could tell he believed it.

He'd pull a dozen roses from behind his seat and present them to me. I would cry out in happiness, closing my eyes, inhaling the scent deeply into my body as if I could hold it inside me as a proxy of his love. While I was preoccupied, he'd pulled out a dozen more roses in a different color, and I would hug them all to my chest.

Then, our eyes would lock, and our lips would crash together. We were an escalating wildfire. We would clamber into the backseat, clutching, grasping, tugging at clothing until skin was on skin. His hand would be on my face, my fingers tangled in his hair, and through it all, we would exhale whispers again and again: I love you.

Upstairs in my apartment, we melted into a universe that belonged only to us. I would flit around my bedroom, lighting the array of candles strewn across all the surfaces. He would open his phone to find a new song he wanted to play for me, a Hindi song.

"'My heart keeps asking me every moment . . . why I am so devoted to you'—No, that's not it!" He looked up at the ceiling, lost in thought, then wagged his finger when the correct translation came to him in English.

"'Why I am so in love with you,'" he said, nodding.

He would kneel in front of me and continue translating the words, looking at me unblinking as the haunting melody played in the background. "'Why is it my biggest desire to be with you? Why is it only your name on my lips?'" I would listen with a pounding heart, captivated.

When the song would end, he would grab my hands. "I had a dream, and we were getting married. You had your wedding dress on, and we were somewhere really beautiful. It had a lot of trees and flowers, and right when we were about to kiss, my alarm went off. Oh my God, you looked so beautiful in your wedding dress. So, so beautiful. When I saw you in that dress, I couldn't believe I was marrying someone that beautiful."

My skin would tingle.

"I don't have enough money for us to get married," he would say. "But when I open a 7-Eleven, we can do it."

I wouldn't speak, afraid to break the spell. But sometimes, after he'd express jealousy about my male friends on my social media accounts or demand to review my friends' list and expel the ones he disagreed with, I'd question him about the double standard.

"You want to go get married right now? You think I don't love you? We can go to the courthouse right now," he'd say.

And then, I wouldn't speak at first because something wasn't right. Yet it had made my heart pound faster and my head feel light when he had said it. So, I had to wade through all the "he wants me, he loves me" chatter and the tingling I couldn't control to see what my brain wanted to say to me about his words. Then to actually pour ashes all over that fire he'd just lit inside me was self-control I didn't realize I had.

"It's too soon. We don't know each other well enough," I'd finally reply slowly. "Besides, that's not a reason to get married."

But there were weekly proposals. They'd been coming since four weeks after we'd known one another. The first one came over a long, sleep-deprived President's Day weekend in Las Vegas about six weeks after our first date. He'd said we should go to a Las Vegas chapel and get married, and he would move in with me. He hadn't even come over to my apartment yet. No, I'd said, flattered by his proposal but chalking it up to naïveté.

At first, it was one night a week, and then the entire weekend, then three nights, and then five. We would spend that time isolated together, barely eating, falling asleep only when we couldn't stay awake any longer. When I wanted to go to trivia night with my friends on an "off night," he'd decide he couldn't stay away from me and want to have a spontaneous visit. Although I knew it was supposed to be unhealthy to spend that much time together or to let that relationship take over all my others, I couldn't seem to find a reason why I should dial things back. How could someone who loved me that much be bad for me? Why shouldn't I spend as much time with him as I could if all I wanted to do was show him how much I loved him?

We might put on a movie to watch if we weren't listening to music. If so, he always chose a love story.

"I love you more than Jack loved Rose," he said as we watched the Titanic plunge into the sea, and the film's two main characters braced for the water's impact.

"That must be a lot."

"It is."

"But if you were Jack and I were Rose, I never would have let you die in the water like that," I said. "If we couldn't both find a way to stay afloat, then I would get in the water and die with you."

He didn't yet know it, but I had considered the possibility of converting to Islam. I'd spoken with one of his cousins about it and purchased a Qur'an and begun reading it. I planned to surprise him and let him know when I'd read all of it, and then I would tell him what I had been thinking, and we could have a discussion about what it would take for me to convert. Each night when we were not together, I pulled the book out of the bottom drawer of my nightstand and read it to myself, running my fingers along the deckled edge, feeling closer to him as I did it. It wasn't him loving me that made me happy; it was my love for him. He had pried open my ability to feel vulnerable at my deepest level, and for the first time, I could show someone how much I could trust and love them. When I imagined my future, I no longer had any clear goals for myself. All I could think about was how to make him happy. The transformation was nearly complete by then.

Thinking of those memories now—in the apartment where he and I had made our home together, and I'd learned of his secret lives, then afterward spent a week wondering if he would kill me—nothing made sense. Those memories must have been a lie, yet I was there. I experienced them. They couldn't have been.

A few minutes later, I received another text. "Can I please come back over? I'd like to spend more time with you and try to show you how sorry I am. I can bring over some wine, and we can watch movies."

I sat lost in thought. No. NO. Absolutely not. *My instincts screamed at me not to let him back in. But the other voice inside me was speaking too.* Where did that Amir go? The one who had spent so much time with me and who loved me so much? Why would you spend thousands of hours with someone, months, years, if you didn't love them? How could anyone fake all of that? And *why* would they? Maybe . . . there's a reason for all of this. *Then, the first voice spoke again.* No. Shut up. You know that's not true, and nothing ever will be the same again. You don't even know who you are anymore because of this.

My mind flicked to the legal things we still needed to do to end our relationship. We had some joint accounts we'd need to close. He was still officially on the lease. I also realized at that moment that I'd forgotten to get the apartment key from him before he'd left. If I said no to him, if I told him I didn't want him to come, would he hold those things over my head too? Would he come and go in the apartment anyway? Terrorize me exactly as he had on the trip?

Almost twenty minutes went by. I couldn't think clearly.

What do I do? *My mind flipped back and forth. Practically speaking, I needed him to take care of some things. A part of me was repelled by him and said,* No, don't do this, you can't handle it, you've had enough, you're dying inside. *And as much as I couldn't explain it and didn't want to acknowledge it, a part of me wanted him.*

"Well, let me know because I'm just sitting in my car, and if you don't want me to, I'm going to go inside my parent's house."

"Okay. Yes," I typed quickly before his texts turned angry.

My heart started pounding. I couldn't believe I was letting him come back into the very place I had just gone through torture to make sure he left.

He arrived with the wine and put on The Notebook. *Like* Titanic, *it was another* Romeo and Juliet *story.*

On screen, Noah stood in front of his foiled love interest, Allie. "Stop thinking about what I want, what he wants, what your parents want," he said to her. "What do you want? What do you *want?"*

I gasped and looked over at Amir. He was looking at me. I could feel my pulse behind my eyes.

"I'd like to start our relationship over again," he said.

"But . . . the engagement."

He shook his head and scoffed. "I did lie about when it happened. I just got my head caught up in the excitement of my sister's wedding, and, yes, I did ask my parents to get me engaged. But that was before I met you. When I came back after the wedding, she and I talked online for a few weeks, and we didn't have anything in common. We want completely different things, and I realized she wasn't the girl I want to be with. I told my parents, and they know that."

"But is it called off or not?"

"Yes!" he said.

"Does she know that?"

"We have barely talked to one another, but she should know. I had my parents call her house and tell them about six months ago. When she does send me messages now, I just ignore them."

"That doesn't sound like she thinks it's called off if she's still sending you messages."

"But I did all I can do. I called it off, and I told my parents to tell her family. I can't help what she does."

"Why didn't you tell me? Why did you lie?"

"Would you have dated me if you knew I was trying to get out of an engagement that I asked for?"

"Maybe you shouldn't have been dating anyone at all until the engagement was actually over."

He shrugged.

"It wasn't right," I continued. "You should have told me and let me decide for myself if I wanted to date you or not."

"I should have, but I made a mistake. Will you forgive me?"

"But what about Julia?"

"She doesn't mean anything to me. She's just someone I would talk to when we would argue."

"But why would you ask her to marry you?"

"Just having fun. She was using me for attention; I was using her."

"You think she was using you, so you asked her to marry you? What are you saying? That you were just manipulating her? Do you know how this makes you sound?"

He shrugged again.

"How do I know you're not just saying these things about marriage to me then if you can just so easily say them to her, and they don't mean anything?"

"Baby, think about it. Why would I have moved in with you if I wasn't serious? I've never lived with a woman before."

I couldn't think of an answer to that question.

"Can't you see how much I love you?" he said. "I can't live without you. Please give me another chance.

"How could that possibly work?" I said. With his words, all the things that had happened in Jamaica already slid out of view into some dark corner of my mind where I didn't have to think about them.

"If you want me to stay here with you, I will. If you want me to stay at my parent's house and come over sometimes until you trust me again, I will. If you want me to stay here but sleep on the couch, I'll do that too. But I want us to date again."

"I need to think about that. I need to process everything before I could even know whether I can agree to something like that. I just . . . I don't know." There was too much now. Too much information about him I needed to sort through to figure out what I really believed.

"Okay, I can understand that," he said, to my surprise. "But in the meantime, can you agree not to go out with other guys?"

I didn't respond. Something felt wrong about the request, and at first, I couldn't understand why. I had no desire to even talk to another man. What had happened with Amir was making me question everything about myself and the world around me. I wouldn't be introducing anyone new into my personal safety zone until I could figure out how to get myself on solid ground again.

So, why should his question matter so much? Then, I realized it was his desire to control me that bothered me.

What was the difference between the implied exclusivity that came with a relationship commitment and a promise not to date others? I didn't trust him, and that's why I didn't want to be in a relationship with him, so why should I promise him things people give one another when they're in a relationship? Instead of worrying about whether I could ever see him as trustworthy again, he was more concerned with ensuring I remained bound to him by a commitment he had already broken. If I said yes, I would lose another piece of myself. Giving him power over my life like that would be giving up my freedom from being subjected to his arbitrary rewards and punishments.

I tried to explain that I needed to be completely out of my commitment to him so I could see things clearly and heal.

Angrily, he pulled away from me and stood up. "I get it. I get what this is about. I fucked around. Now, you think it's your turn."

I blinked, stunned at his sudden turnaround in demeanor. "No. That's not it. You don't get it."

"Yeah, I see how it is. No, Kristen." He shook his head as if he couldn't believe how unreasonable I was being. "Well, I tried."

He turned away from me in disgust and, without another word, walked over to the door and stalked out, slamming it, leaving behind a searing silence far deeper than the one that had filled the air when he'd walked out tearfully three hours earlier.

7

Poisoned at First Sight

Nothing starts in the middle. The twist in our relationship when everything changes is never the beginning. If it were, it would probably be a lot easier to walk away. Survivors in pathological love relationships must manage two extremes of treatment by their pathological partners. We are revered and denigrated, worshiped and maligned, treasured and tortured. The biggest problem may not be the treatment itself but not knowing which one is "real."

Oprah Winfrey once related a story in which she had a conversation with Maya Angelou that changed her life. She came away from the conversation with a mantra: "When someone shows you who they are, believe them the first time."[50]

But what if the person they showed you at first was seemingly dependable, loving, and caring? What if that person's loving behavior is so extravagant that when their later actions contradict it, they seem so out of character you can't tell which ones represent who they really are?

To unravel why we can't seem to get past this question, "*Is my partner 'good' or 'bad?*'" we must go back to the beginning to when we first met our partners. Although each of us has a different key that unlocked the secret way into our deepest selves, our partners used a similar method of turning that key. This technique is a hodgepodge collection of romantic, over-the-top gestures, and it has a name: love-bombing.

Sun Myung Moon, the founder of the Unification Church of the United States, also known as the Moonies, gave a speech in 1978 in which he first used the term: "Unification Church members are smiling all of the time, even at four in the morning. The man who is full of love must live that way," he said. "What face could better represent love than a smiling face? This is why we talk about love bomb. Moonies have that kind of happy problem."[51]

Love-bombing itself is like using that persona you want someone to see against them. The smiling, happy faces of the members of the Unification Church lured in new recruits who were unaware what they were joining. More specifically, the members showered potential new recruits with attention and praise, giving them an all-encompassing sense of belonging and acceptance. Ex-members have described how a steady stream of invitations and what seemed like genuine interest made them feel as if they had found people who shared their values and goals. They formed attachments to the other members and soon were encouraged to join the Church, its true purpose hidden behind the targeted messaging, based on whether a member seems to be a "thinker," "feeler," "doer," or "believer."[52]

If you think back to the beginning of your relationship, you may remember developing strong feelings of belonging and acceptance too. People with narcissistic tendencies use love-bombing as a strategy to form relationships.[53] In pathological love relationships, love-bombing corresponds with the idealization stage of the narcissistic cycle of abuse described in Chapter 5. Psychiatrist Dale Archer describes love-bombing as an attempt to influence another person using dramatic spectacles of positive attention. He says, "We're not just talking about romantic gestures, flowers and trips."[54] Love-bombing is so over-the-top and intense that it overwhelms the person's ordinary psychological defenses and speeds up their emotional attachment to the relationship.

When your partner is love-bombing you, they are fully present with you and completely focused on you. This is why it may appear that you were truly seen, perhaps for the first time in your life.

Your partner may have made extravagant or emotional gestures, such as:

- Asking you to get married within days or weeks of knowing you
- Claiming you should get tattoos to commemorate your love
- Publicly declaring their love in a dramatic way
- Using their body language to emphasize the intensity of their love; for example, staring into your eyes for long periods or spontaneously falling to their knees and hugging you
- Telling you they have never felt the way you made them feel, and they have never loved anyone the way they love you—that the two of you are destined to be together

They will "mirror," "mimic," and "parrot" back what you do to establish something called "twin-ship," which plants the idea that you have found a soulmate who has had similar experiences and understands you.[55]

A tactic both cult leaders and pathological partners use to make others more compliant is the "trance-state."[56] Trance-states have the misfortune of dwelling in a stereotype of a traveling stage show where audience members are called onstage to perform silly acts after being hypnotized. In a real trance-state, we become hyper-focused mentally to the point where we become almost oblivious to the outside world. No one needs to perform any mystical procedure on us first. Certain things about our atmosphere can lull us into that state, or we may get there on our own if we're intentionally hyper-focusing. Daydreaming, fantasizing, and ruminating over an event are all examples of mental activity that can pre-occupy us to such an extent that we go through the motions of performing routine actions but have no memory of doing them. If you've ever zoned out while doing something else on autopilot, such as walking or driving somewhere, you've been in a "trance-state."[57]

Cults often have ritualized activities overtly designed to put their members in a trance, such as meditating or chanting. Our partners may not explicitly set out to hypnotize us—at least not as a ritualistic part of our relationships. However, you may have participated in or been coerced or subjected to one or more of the following:

- long periods staring into one another's eyes
- commonly repeated phrases that felt almost like mantras: "*You're the love of my life.*" "*No one else will love you like I do.*"
- activity that feels ritualistic, such as listening to the same songs or watching the same films again and again
- re-enactments of dates or positive events that occurred during the love-bombing period

- sleep or food deprivation
- substance abuse

These actions can all help produce conditions for inducing a trance-like state, especially when combined with the emotional and mental exhaustion of the relationship.

What's the big deal about trance-states? They make us highly suggestible.[58] Sandra L. Brown, M.A., notes that eye-gazing is a tactic pathological partners use to create an intimate connection and establish control. When pathological partners use a series of gestures while their partner is already in the trance-state, including touching the partner's face while speaking, it ratchets up the intensity and implants "set commands:" "I know that you will always give to me this way and that we will be together forever. I know that you would never hurt me or leave me or lie to me, or cheat."[59] The use of intoxicants or lack of basic needs, such as food and sleep, can put the mind in an even more suggestible state.

We filter our memories and judgments through the ideas we formed in this altered state. "This [trance-state] makes it challenging for the individual to make competent assessments about what they are being asked to do, whether to stay or leave," wrote Bonnie Zieman in her book for therapists, *Cracking the Cult Code,* "and if they determine they want to leave, to actually do so."[60]

There's Nothing Loving about Love-Bombing

During this time, our brains release several chemicals associated with rewarding behavior. We develop a very real addiction that is no less pleasurable and habit-forming than cocaine—it releases the same chemical in the hypothalamus, dopamine. This is the stage and type of love that motivates people to write songs about not being able to eat or sleep—and drives us to listen to them on repeat. We may replay memories with our partners repeatedly, re-read old texts, or look at pictures of our partners, hoping to prolong the enjoyable feelings. Our brains eventually release oxytocin and vasopressin, the "cuddle hormones," as our trust in our partners grow. It's not as if we recognize consciously that this is chemically-induced behavior—but our bodies are helping us along in responding to our partners as we develop this bond.

It's not just an active decision we're making. In fact, the bond forms at least partially because we can't help being slaves to our biology, especially when we have no knowledge or awareness of what just happened to us.[61]

The one-two punch of having someone overwhelm us with their outpourings of romantic gestures coupled with the validation of someone who seems to have so much in common with us and the chemicals that flood our brain is intoxicating. Without even realizing it's happening, we quickly and naturally drop our guards and let our partners into our lives, giving them access to our secret thoughts, insecurities, and fantasies—all of which they use against us later. They listen carefully to us to find the parts of what we tell them that have emotional resonance for us. They use this in many ways:

- Learning what we like so they can morph themselves into our "perfect partner" in a way that feels natural. Meeting someone who seems to be a naturally giving person in a way that is so meticulous and with such attention to detail of what it is we love creates in us the desire to trust and give back to them. Who would take the time to know this much about us and do all these things if they didn't really care, we ask ourselves?
- Inventing a story about having had a similar experience about the emotional touchpoints we describe. Emotional touchpoints may be positive or negative: an experience of adversity, a hobby or interest, somewhere

we have traveled or lived, something we have studied, or other things. These experiences make us feel heard and understood by them and closer to them by default. It also makes us feel as if we are deepening our level of intimacy with them; however, the sharing is one-sided. What we have described about our lives was real, and they are creating a fake persona for us to fall in love with.

- Sniffing out our insecurities and filing them away. During the early period of the relationship, they build us up. Later, they will use these insecurities to control and degrade us.

Before we know it, we're swept up in a passionate union with them that feels deeper and more intense than any relationship we've ever experienced before. "Relationship" isn't even a strong enough word to capture the extent of what we're in with them because it's a bond whose boundaries surpass the components of a typical relationship. You have barely gotten to know one another yet, and the pathological partner is declaring eternal love. What makes it feel so real is that our pathological partners overwhelm us with behaviors that flood the biological and emotional "processing centers of the brain" and generate these feelings in us that more natural processes would if a normal relationship unfolded over time. This tricks our brains into making us feel as if the relationship is built on a more solid foundation than it really is.

Up Is Down and Down Is Up

In most relationships, we settle into a comfortable routine. Occasionally, you may have a disagreement, and the other person may even say or do something they wouldn't normally say or do. However, what happens is still within the bounds of normally accepted behavior. Nothing so dramatic has taken place that you're shell-shocked by it, wondering who the person is with whom you've been building the foundation on which your life currently rests. Furthermore, the person makes a verbal repair to you with an apology, and you believe the person cares that they have hurt you. You sense remorse. The world has not been upended. There's nothing else to explain. Everything keeps moving forward.

A pathological love relationship gives us a different sequence of events.

When we first entered our relationships with our pathological partners, we bonded closely with our partners because they held us captive with melodramatic declarations that they couldn't live without us. They called us "home," and we believed they meant it. The bond we formed to them carved its way right into the middle of our lives until we couldn't live without them either. Their theatrical displays of their love, while abnormal, certainly aren't viewed as abusive by us or by anyone. If your friends or family members met your partner during this time, they were probably just as charmed by them as you were.

When the bottom dropped out, it wasn't just that they stopped the extravagant displays of love and settled into more neutral behavior—it was that their behavior was the mirror opposite. It was punishing. What we learned showed us there was something contemptuous in them directed at us. Sometimes, their behavior made it appears as if we didn't exist to them.

The irrationality of it turns everything inside out and freezes us in place. We're not quite sure where to step because everything feels like a landmine.

Then, as we're frozen, understandably struggling to process the enormous gaps between the types of behavior they've started to show us, they're quick to step in and nudge us in the direction that benefits them. They use a form of psychological manipulation called gaslighting.

According to Preston Ni, author of *How to Successfully Handle Gaslighters & Stop Bullying*, gaslighting is "a form of persistent manipulation and brainwashing that causes the victim to doubt her or himself, and to ultimately lose their own sense of perception, identity, and self-worth."[62]

The gaslighter intentionally tries to convince the person they gaslight that they have a distorted view. Gaslighters may deny facts, provide conflicting information, or tell outright lies repeatedly, even in direct contradiction to evidence to convince the victim to adopt a different reality because it benefits the gaslighter somehow.

The term gaslighting comes from a 1944 play turned film, *Gaslight*. In the plot, a man purposely tries to drive his wife insane by making the gaslights flicker. He then tells her she imagines it when she points it out. Gaslighting examples in real life could be overt like this "gaslight" trick; for example, a very manipulative abuser may purposely hide items belonging to the victim and tell the victim that he or she misplaced them.

More common examples of gaslighting occur, however, when abusers try to convince their victims something didn't actually happen. The gaslighter may also try to convince others they are the true victims in a situation when they have caused harm or been abusive or to minimize or invalidate the victim's thoughts or feelings.

Have you ever had conversations with your partner that devolve into nonsense? You feel as if you could just explain why something hurts you, they will stop doing it. It seems so obvious you wonder why you have to explain it—it's the kind of thing everyone should know would hurt someone—yet you've explained it a dozen times, and it doesn't stop. Your conversations are circular, and your partner always seems to project what he or she has done back onto you or bring up something unrelated you did in the past, claims to be the true victim, or accuses you of not letting go of the past.[63] Shannon Thomas, a trauma therapist who treats narcissistic abuse survivors, puts it this way:

> *When a survivor tries to talk to a psychological abuser about their negative behaviors, a favorite maneuver of toxic people is to simply not reply. . . . When a survivor asks why they didn't reply, the toxic person will spin the situation and say something like, "I am not going to argue with you." Can you see what just happened? The survivor was blamed for causing drama, or an argument, and the toxic person never addressed their behaviors.*[64]

One example of gaslighting that has gone viral on the Internet, called "A Narcissist's Prayer," provides an accurate demonstration of how gaslighting statements work together, not in isolation. They build a mental trap around a victim until there's only one path left to take: "it's not me, it's you."

A Narcissist's Prayer

That didn't happen.
And if it did, it wasn't that bad.
And if it was, that's not a big deal.
And if it was, it's not my fault.
And if it was, I didn't mean it.
And if I did,
You deserved it.

Each of these statements individually are not uncommon ways our partners may use to try to gaslight us. When our partners try to gaslight us, we have a choice. We can reject the reality they offer and choose instead to believe their contemptuous actions were intentional. That's an extremely painful choice. It's also a very difficult one, and the odds are against us. First, we have the conflicting evidence against it of their love-bombing, which is what we used to form our first opinion of them. Second, let's be honest—the dopamine chemical addiction makes that choice of rejecting what they say a near-impossibility until we prepare ourselves. And then, third, we have our partners—offering up their reason for why we shouldn't accept the evidence that that cold or hateful side of them is the real one.

There's a price to be paid for accepting what they say when they gaslight us. When we accept their reality, they give us a message about something they want us to believe about ourselves. If something didn't happen the way we perceived it, then the problem lies with us. Depending on the ultimate conclusion about reality our pathological partner wants us to draw, he or she may imply or eventually move to secondary gaslighting statements about our thoughts, emotions, or behaviors to help us come to that conclusion. In the table below, look what happens when we take apart *A Narcissist's Prayer* and examine it one line at a time—plus a few more gaslighting statements.

Table 7.1:
Gaslighting Statements about Partners That Support General Gaslighting

Gaslighting Statements That Distort Reality	*Gaslighting Statements about Partners*
That didn't happen.	"You're crazy." "You can't trust your own judgment."
It wasn't that bad.	"You're blowing things out of proportion." "You never remember anything good I do for you—only the bad things."
It wasn't my fault.	"You always think the worst of me." "You don't trust me. Everyone says you're too controlling and always looking for a reason to be suspicious."
It's not a big deal.	"You always want to start an argument." "You've done a lot worse than I have. Do you remember that time you . . . ?"
I didn't mean it.	"There's no need for you to talk about your feelings because it's over now. I can't change it." "You always have to bring up the past. I made a mistake, and you won't let it go."

You deserved it.	"I'm hurt because you [don't trust me/aren't there for me/don't believe me], and that's why I did [x]." "You're so angry/jealous/emotional/needy/crazy/untrusting/abusive/bipolar/obsessed, and I can't take it anymore."
You didn't say that/You meant something else.	"You're lying." "You're not trustworthy."
I didn't say that/ That's not what I meant.	"You misinterpret things." "You're so sensitive."
Your emotional reaction is out of proportion to what I did.	"You're too emotional. This is why I do things you don't like." "Why do you cause so much drama?"

Pathological partners gaslight for different reasons. They may maliciously include intentional denials, lies, and accusations in conversation, which are meant to deflect from the truth. These can quickly devolve into messages implanted into our minds. However, Robert Hare, one of the first researchers to study psychopaths, determined that at least some of the time, the lies they tell occur because of what's happening in their brains. They make contradictory statements at least partially because there is an "inefficient 'line of authority'—each hemisphere tries to run the show, resulting in speech that is unmonitored and poorly integrated."[65]

Additionally, they seem to lack the ability to process and understand abstract concepts such as love, loyalty, and cheating. Areas of the brain that are normally engaged when reading emotionally charged words register the same way as neutral words in psychopaths. When survivors use abstract or emotionally laden words, conscious-impaired individuals may interpret something different and use the concepts differently themselves. If a survivor uses the concept to explain why something is inappropriate, the pathological partner may respond in a way that looks like intentional gaslighting. When pathological partners say they love their partners, they mean they love how their partners make them feel. When they say their partners don't love them anymore, they mean their partners won't stop asking them questions about their irrational behavior. When pathological partners accuse their partners of disloyalty, they mean their partners weren't compliant with their wishes.[66]

Our emotional investment in our partners makes resisting it almost impossible and means giving over control of our perception of ourselves. Once you've accepted those messages, the messages further spiral down into justifications for their abuse.

Pathological Love Stories

When They Called Us Crazy

"He made constant comments and insinuations that I was crazy. He would say one thing and do another every single day. He would tell me he was going to a sporting event for one of the kids, and he would not be there. Or go get his haircut at an establishment that had a 'closed' sign on the door. He told me once he was going all day to a basketball tournament in a completely different city all day long. He was constantly looking at other women he passed, regularly watching porn, and having flings with women but told me basically that nothing I saw, heard, or felt was happening. The most painful part is having him convince his mom and his whole family I was crazy.

And having him make me feel like I was not worth his love or respect by constantly messing with other women. I questioned everything about myself."

"When he started hiding my things—like keys, cigarettes, reading glasses—and then they would reappear a few days later in places that I never would have put them, I knew he was doing it but didn't understand it. I couldn't figure out why he would do something like that . . . but never thought he would cheat."

"I found an email he had written to his ex-wife, basically begging for her back, and I literally thought we were perfect. . . . His response was that he was just trying to manipulate her because she can't be real. She was going on a trip to get remarried, and he was asking her if she wanted him, did she want to run away with their kids, quoted romantic movies, etc.—and that was his answer. It was so disturbing to me. I already thought she was a narcissist, and I started piecing together what was really going on. It only got worse. So much worse."

"I discovered everything I suspected was true, and I was called 'crazy' and 'jealous' for twelve years. I was discarded like a sack of garbage when he was caught 'cheating.' Everything was turned upside down and inside out, and instead of him begging for my forgiveness and return, it was me who was destroyed and left questioning every decision. I will never be the same."

"[The most painful part of the relationship was] constant affairs he was having yet denied. He made me feel like I was going crazy. The distance, then the love-bombing. The mind control. The false dreams and hopes."

"He makes me question my sanity, my memory, calling me delusional, crazy, on drugs."

"He hid my things and then called me crazy because I couldn't find them, tried turning my family against me behind my back, cut me off of all access to our money, secretly videotaped my meltdown the day I found out he was cheating, and then threatened me with showing it."

"I doubted my own mind of what I believed to be true because of what she had asked for and, then when it no longer suited her, went back on it. . . . There was cognitive dissonance and double standards . . . I thought I was an angry person and needed help."

"I feel like I am going insane when I know I am not, but then I start to believe I might be."

"I have many stories of things that actually occurred that if I told people, they would wonder why I stayed as long as I did. I couldn't make this stuff up if I tried. We would go out to the movies, for example, and while we were standing in line, someone would come up . . . and say things like, 'Man, that was a good party the other day, wasn't it?' And he would not really respond in a way someone who had actually not been there would. He would say, 'He got me confused with another person. He must have thought I was someone else.' When I confronted him on it, saying he called him by name, he would reverse it on me and say I was paranoid or crazy and that I had trust issues from a previous relationship that I was taking out on him. Same thing with the girl who was calling and texting him in the middle of the night. It was never his fault—he can't control when this girl calls. Even though I talked to her, and she said she did not know he was married."

"The lived reality vs. my vision and beliefs about what a loving relationship should look like. The circular arguments . . .

> *always my fault? How? Why would you want to hurt me if you really love me? Self-doubt—always second-guessing he's right. 'I made him this way.' The self-blame and responsibility for destroying such a wonderful person. So, if I made him this way, then I alone am responsible for 'fixing it.'"*
>
> *"He would yell at me, telling me something that I had said or done, and in my head, I was thinking to myself,* Did I say, do that? Was that what I was thinking? Did I come at him like that?"

When you have a pathological partner, gaslighting is a multi-pronged attack on a shared narrative for how the relationship unfolds. Conversations become the flashpoint for keeping the peace, and you learn to walk a line that language divides. You can either adopt a pathological worldview in which you are to blame for causing problems by talking, yet your partner is never held accountable for wrongdoing. Or you can continue to speak up and be further shamed, threatened, and diminished. You leave conversations feeling drained and may accept a response that resolved nothing just to end them.

Just as our brains brought us closer to our partners when we first met them, our brains can work against us once we get on this verbal roller coaster with them. Psychologist B.F. Skinner performed experiments with rats and pigeons by putting them in boxes with levers that, when pushed by little rat hands or beaks, released food pellets. He learned that even though the animals received an award for it, eventually, they got bored of pushing the levers. When he changed the experiment so the food pellets released randomly, the animals would not stop pushing the levers.[67]

This phenomenon is known today as intermittent reinforcement. Casinos use it to keep us in front of slot machines as long as possible. Slot machines are programmed to pay out different amounts and at random intervals—and it works. Usually, when we play them, we lose. Occasionally, however, we do win, and that's what keeps us sitting there pumping our money into the machines. Just think about it—there would be no point in playing if each time we put a dollar in, all that happened was a certain percentage of it paid back out. Not only would it not be any fun, but we would also lose money over the long term.

The same concept happens in our relationship when our partners treat us first with love, then with contempt. They sometimes lavish us with praise, attention, gifts, apologies, and approval, but they withdraw it on their own timetable—it's not tied to our own behavior. They also punish and degrade us often without warning. The anticipation of not knowing from moment to moment when we will next receive their love or when they will suddenly attack chemically reinforces the bond we have with our partners.

This reinforcement may seem counterintuitive. Why would contradictory behavior reinforce a bond, rather than weaken it?

When our relationship was in its early days and our partners love-bombed us, our brains released all those love chemicals like oxytocin and dopamine. Later when our partners inexplicably withdraw that affection or inflict more cruelty, the valve for those chemicals is shut off very suddenly. We feel the loss painfully as if we were suffering withdrawal. When they return and we start the narcissistic cycle of abuse with them again, our hypothalamus produces and releases oxytocin into our brains as they repeat their idealization of us. Each time this cycle repeats, we wait for crumbs of their affection so a hit of dopamine will take that pain away.[68] Gaslighting can feel like salve to a wound during a repeated idealization period when they offer it up: "That didn't happen." "It wasn't my fault." "I didn't mean it."

When you're in a pathological love relationship, you become obsessed with trying to figure out who they really are. You never really learn the answer. You just keep choking on the answers they want you to swallow.

8

Our Brains, Our Enemies

In the 1950s, social psychologist Leon Festinger studied a group of people who were convinced an apocalypse was looming, and UFOs were going to visit from planet Clarion and take the group members away in their spaceships before destroying Earth. The group members sold all their possessions and waited on a mountaintop on the designated day of the apocalypse for the alien visitors to arrive and save them.

The next day when the UFOs didn't come, instead of giving up their beliefs, some of the group members were even more firm believers than they were before. They believed the aliens had been so pleased with their faith that Earth had been spared. In other words, the group members changed what they originally believed rather than accept the fact that the original belief was wrong. In their view, nothing about what they believed changed because the real-world event proved their beliefs were true. Objectively, what they had done was incorporate this real-world event into their beliefs in a way that wouldn't contradict them.

Festinger and his colleagues came up with the term "cognitive dissonance" to describe what happened to the group members when they had to confront the new reality. This term "cognitive dissonance" really means that both ideas—aliens are coming to destroy Earth and the aliens didn't come—cannot "go together" in the minds of the group members. One of them has to be false. When thoughts and/or behavior clash like this, it causes psychological discomfort and anxiety.[69] Though it might seem that the most rational thing to do is to look at all the evidence and keep the idea that has the most evidence behind it or change what doesn't work, that's rarely what happens.

As we go about our daily lives, we are all regularly confronted with ideas and choices that result in cognitive dissonance. None of us can hold competing beliefs in our minds simultaneously. Sometimes, we have competing values and priorities, or we are presented with conflicting information. Most of the time, we resolve our cognitive dissonance quietly without even recognizing what just happened.

In a hypothetical example, let's say I think of myself as a climate change activist, but I recently read about how driving is one of the most environmentally destructive acts an individual can perform. In this example, I'm disturbed by this new knowledge because I own a car, and climate change is such an important issue to me.

I'll have to resolve the cognitive dissonance by reconciling my car ownership with my view of myself as someone who cares about the environment. Let's slow down these thoughts in my mind to look at how I might do that.

I could sell or donate my car, deciding it just isn't compatible with my beliefs to own one. However, that would require me to do more than just make the decision and get rid of it. If I've been driving my entire adult life, that's a major change in how I go about almost everything I do. There are billions of people in the world who live without cars. It's not that it can't be done, but if I've never done it before, it will take some effort and forethought. I'd need to map out some routes, learn how long it takes to get around, and figure out the best ways to avoid dangerous situations. I would have to sit down and develop a plan for how I will get to work, get my groceries, and make it to the doctor if I get sick. If I have children, I'll have to figure out how to get them to school. I'd have to develop new habits. In other words, this would be a major change.

Figure 8.1:
Resolving Cognitive Dissonance

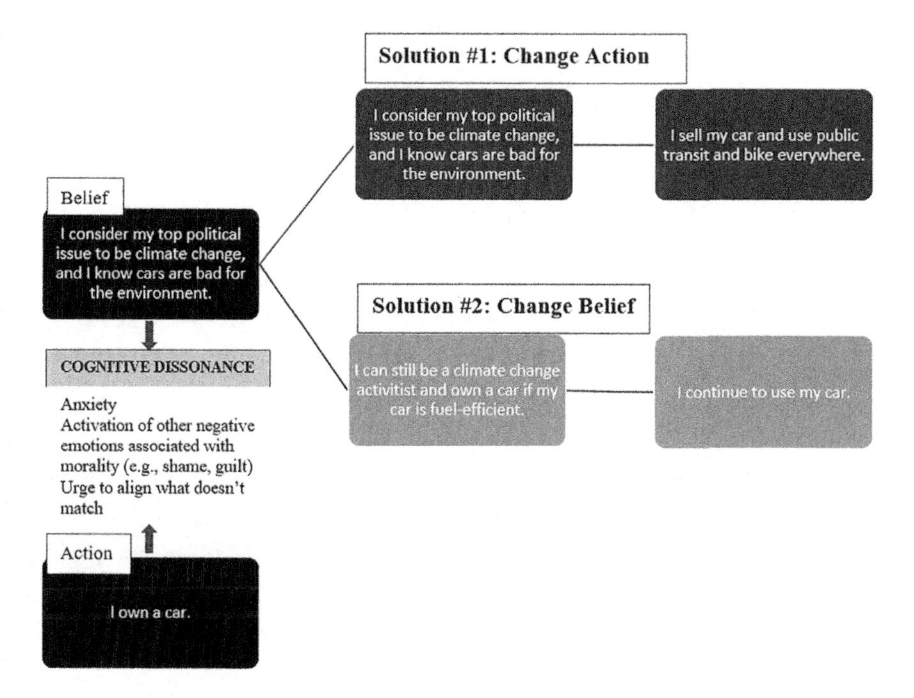

Unless something happens that forces us to change or decide consciously to commit to change, we almost never choose to resolve our cognitive dissonance by changing our actions because making major changes is difficult, time-consuming, and detracts from our feelings of security. Instead, we frequently just modify our thinking slightly, absorbing the new information into our existing beliefs somehow. If every time we were faced with a mismatch in our beliefs and our actions, we made a major life change, our lives would lack stability.

Instead, most of the time, we make a compromise with ourselves about what we believe. In this example, I resolve the cognitive dissonance by reminding myself how my car is a hybrid, fuel-efficient car, so it's about as good as it gets environmentally if you're going to own a car. Another thing I might do is make a list of all the things I do that are good for the environment, such as recycling, that offset my driving behavior. Or I could dismiss the research that shows driving is bad for the environment as alarmist and unrealistic.

The point of this example is not to make a judgment about how to resolve cognitive dissonance but to show that it's impossible to avoid experiencing it. By doing any of these things, I would have made the idea of owning a car more compatible in my mind with being a climate-change activist and eliminated my cognitive dissonance. Maria Konnikova, author of *The Confidence Game*, writes of reducing cognitive dissonance:

> *We can revise our interpretation of the present reality: there actually isn't any inconsistency; we were just looking at it wrong. We achieve this through selectively looking for new, confirming information or selectively disconfirming information. The study . . . was flawed. The sample was biased. It doesn't apply to me. We can revise our prior expectation: I thought this would happen all along, so it's actually not discordant. . . . I was prepared all along and made the decision anyhow: I think my experience will defy the odds.*[70]

As much as we might like to distinguish ourselves from the UFO cult members in Festinger's study, as much as we'd like to believe that when evidence is staring us in the face that we don't reject it outright, none of us are immune from the irrationality of cognitive dissonance. Additional research has backed this up: if we say or do something that contradicts our opinion, we will usually bring our opinion in line with what we said or did rather than avoid saying or doing what contradicts our opinion.[71]

Well, most of us will anyway. Individuals who don't feel any cognitive dissonance when they contradict themselves don't seem to do either one.

Who do you suppose doesn't feel cognitive dissonance when they say or do something that contradicts their opinion?

How to Change Your Mind

Festinger was very clear that the three important features of cognitive dissonance are psychological discomfort, a motivation to act to resolve it, and relief once it is resolved.[72] However, he didn't explain why dissonance causes us discomfort. We know it has something to do with the need for consistency. Consistency brings stability and predictability. But what exactly needs to be consistent and under what conditions?

In 2009, researchers gave functional magnetic resonance imaging (fMRIs) to a group of people and told them to argue that they enjoyed the fMRIs. They also gave fMRIs to a control group of people who weren't asked to do anything. They wanted to see what happened to the brains of the individuals who had to give statements that contradicted their true feelings (no one enjoys getting an MRI!). They found that three areas of the brain were activated among the group of people asked to describe enjoying the procedure: the anterior cingulate cortex, which helps with error detection and cognitive conflict; the anterior insulate, which helps with perceiving pain and negative emotions; and the posterior cingulate cortex, which helps with self-processing. This is a complex area of the brain that serves functions in memory processing and self-reflection. Their conclusion was that we are motivated to eliminate our negative emotions caused by the conflict we feel internally by producing an attitude that will justify our action or our belief.[73]

There have also been hundreds of studies on cognitive dissonance that have provided us with information about what the conditions are under which it occurs. For example, when we have the excuse to blame someone or something else external to us for an action that would otherwise contradict our beliefs, we don't feel cognitive dissonance. In other words, when we don't have a choice, the pressure is off.[74]

A study on cognitive dissonance that also measured psychopathic traits in the subjects also gives us clues about the conditions under which cognitive dissonance appears. In it, college students were asked to use an abacus to do some counting by sliding a ball across one wire at a time, then reporting the outcomes. It was intentionally designed to be as boring as possible. Then, what the experimenters wanted them to do was lie about how exciting it was to the next person who arrived to complete the task. With the benefit of knowing how choice impacts cognitive dissonance, the researchers varied the level of choice among the participants to compare how psychopathic traits impacted cognitive dissonance. Some of the participants were directly instructed to lie, and some were only strongly encouraged to do it.

When individuals had more choice, individuals who were lower in psychopathic traits rated the task as more fun than those who were higher in psychopathic traits. Individuals with fewer psychopathic traits resolved the cognitive dissonance of telling someone it was fun by telling themselves it was fun. Students higher in psychopathic traits still rated it boring, which points to the idea that they didn't feel any dissonance about their belief and the lie they told about it being fun.[75]

This corresponds with what the MRIs showed, but it gives us a little more information in that it provides support for a theory of cognitive dissonance called the "New Look" theory, which says:

- We experience cognitive dissonance when believe we are harming ourselves or others.
- Our cognitive dissonance is triggered by negative emotions such as guilt, shame, regret, and sadness.
- The cognitive dissonance comes to an end when we change our belief about why we are harming others.[76]

One of the strongest arguments for cognitive dissonance is that we are protecting our concept of ourselves. If we think of ourselves as "good" and moral, then harming ourselves or someone else or doing something that violates our values of what a good person should do would cause cognitive dissonance. Somehow, we would need to neutralize our actions.[77] This makes sense when compared with the research on psychopaths and cognitive dissonance. If someone has no moral dilemma about hurting others or their positive self-concept doesn't rest on whether their actions are harmful, they won't experience cognitive dissonance.

Research by Sandra L. Brown, M.A., found that cognitive dissonance impacts survivors of pathological love relationships on three levels: the pathological partner, the relationship, and the self, and she also found that these levels follow a sequence. The cognitive dissonance about the pathological partner hits first in the early stages of the relationship. In the mid-stages of the relationship, we begin to have cognitive dissonance about the relationship. Finally, we begin to have cognitive dissonance about ourselves. Interestingly, these layers of cognitive dissonance follow a similar sequence to the five major questions I found in my own research on survivors and their experiences. These are the five questions that form the organizational structure of this book.

Table 8.1:
Major Relationship Questions as Products of Cognitive Dissonance Layers

Layer of Cognitive Dissonance	Major Questions
Cognitive dissonance regarding the partner	*What's wrong with my partner? Is my partner "good" or "bad?"*
Cognitive dissonance regarding the relationship	*Why can't I just leave?*
Cognitive dissonance regarding the self	*Where did I go? How do I get out of here?*

Brown's research has highlighted cognitive dissonance as "so universal it is the hallmark symptom in all pathological love relationships." It results from the psychological manipulation of our partners, which is something that may or may not be present in other types of abuse. "If a survivor does not have cognitive dissonance, they were probably not in a pathological love relationship," Brown says.[78]

Cognitive dissonance *is* the "inevitable harm" of the pathological love relationship.

9

But . . . Does My Partner Mean to Hurt Me?

A question you may ask yourself again and again is whether your partner knows what he or she is doing.

Shannon Thomas, author of *Healing from Hidden Abuse*, puts the answer like this:

> *Psychological abusers know when and where to turn off their manipulative games. They know precisely how to push all the right emotional buttons to get the victim's frustrated response that the abuser craves. They know how to triangulate people and make themselves appear to be the victim. You tell me, does that sound like someone too 'dumb' to know what they do? They know.*[79]

If we are being honest with ourselves, we knew that already, didn't we?

We asked them why dozens of times. We tried to confirm our suspicions or ask why things didn't add up. We tried standing up for ourselves. We begged them to stop hurting us. How could they not have known?

They know.

So why isn't Thomas's answer to that question satisfying?

Because we are asking the wrong question.

What we are really asking is something much more sinister than "did they know?" What we really want to know is, *"Knowing that they had to know, how is it possible they could have done these things?"*

There is a chess-game-like element to this question that implies the pathological people sit down and plot to hurt people in their lives. Their behavior sometimes seems so intentional and systematic, especially as we read the stories of other survivors and realize how similar they have behaved. It's difficult to believe they didn't plan it on purpose.

How could they *not* have targeted us, poured on all the flattery and attention, then slowly torn us down to gain control over us? That sounds like a deliberate strategy. And it seems so deliberate when they say cruel things to us, then smile when they watch us crumple in pain, or they sit there, bored or annoyed, as we burst into tears and beg them to stop.

Accepting the answer to this question—*how could they?*—requires understanding how low-conscience people view the world.

As described in Chapter 2, narcissism is not categorical. Some narcissists are on the more extreme end of the spectrum, and some also have overlapping traits with ASPD. The degree of narcissism and the type of traits they have can govern the extent to which they are aware of their behavior on their partners. Some may be more calculating about what they do than others. It may not be possible to tell from the outside how much your partner is calculating anything.

Pathological partners, whether they are consciously calculating or not, enter relationships with others based on whatever resources they want to extract from the person. They may then do things that *intentionally* hurt you or that *incidentally* hurt you. Let's look at three examples:

1. A low-conscience individual hides a camera in the room where he sexually humiliates his partner for no other reason than because he enjoys it.
2. A pathological partner in a relationship becomes angry and offended because dinner was not on the table when he arrived home from work. He says verbally abusive things and storms into the kitchen, swiping pans of food from the stove into the floor and ordering his partner to clean up the mess. He blames her for his outburst; it's her fault she didn't have everything ready when he got home. His actions are spontaneous and not well thought-out, but they are intentional.
3. A low-conscience individual has several secret relationships simultaneously, in which he lives in different homes with different women, and none of them know about one another. His actions harm or have the potential to harm multiple people. His goal is not to harm anyone outright. His goal is to benefit himself, and he doesn't consider how what he does hurts anyone else, yet he knows enough to keep the relationships hidden.

The pathological partners in these three examples each behave in harmful ways for very different reasons, and the scenarios can help us think through intent to harm and premeditation.

Table 9.1:
Intent vs. Premeditation

	Example 1	Example 2	Example 3
Intent to Harm	Yes	Yes	No
Premeditation	Yes	No	Yes

Only in the first example did the pathological partner plan ahead to deliberately hurt his partner. In the second example, the pathological partner intended to punish his partner, but he didn't premeditate his actions ahead of time. Finally, in the last example, the pathological partner methodically calculates his relationship interactions carefully so none of the women will ever know about one another, yet he isn't intentionally trying to hurt anyone as he does it. In fact, as far as he is concerned, what they don't know *won't* hurt them.

When we view these three examples together, it becomes clearer what it is that bothers us so much about pathological people when they hurt others. What they all have in common is not intent or pre-planning but callousness. In each of the examples, the pathological individual knows exactly which acts they engage in are socially unacceptable and harmful—*they just don't care.*

M.E. Thomas, a diagnosed sociopath, states that when confronted with a decision that has to be made quickly or without knowing all the information, most people use "emotional shortcuts," such as automatically choosing not to do certain things that would hurt others because of how it would make them feel. She claims emotional shortcuts are not available to sociopaths, so they use other ones:

> *Many sociopaths use the shortcut of 'anything goes' or 'I am only in it for me. . . .' Some sociopaths are capable of reigning in their*

> *impulses enough to decide that jail time is not to their advantage so they avoid major violations of the law. Other sociopaths have settled on a more 'principled' approach to life. . . . The one thing that sociopath 'codes' tend to have in common, though, is that they don't fully map with prevailing social norms, those unspoken rules, and customs that govern behavior in a group.*[80]

It's not that they don't understand what others consider moral. That may only factor into their decision-making when considering the chances and consequences of getting caught. Often, they don't weigh the pros and cons at all. They may believe everyone is trying to exploit others in the same ways they are, so they take advantage where they can to avoid being one of the victims. They also seem to lack the ability to comprehend the long-term consequences of their actions.[81]

This is a hard pill to swallow. When someone does something we don't understand, we are driven to find out why. Sociologists Marvin Scott and Stanford Lyman asked the question, "How is society possible?" and proposed that one of its fundamental components are verbal accounts we give to one another that explain our problematic behavior when we violate expectations.[82] These explanations reestablish equilibrium in relationships, which provides a stable foundation to society as a whole.

When pathological partners hurt us and can't give an account that adequately explains how they could have done it, the imbalance is not corrected, and social order is not restored. However, it's likely it never existed in the first place.

Waiting for them to provide us with an account that can explain how they could have hurt us assumes they adhere to a shared standard of cultural norms and they need a reason to break them. People who walk through the world wearing a mask of sanity and living according to their own rules are telling the truth when they say they did something because they felt like it.

That explanation seems like a non-answer to the rest of us. From someone with low empathy and who lacks a conscience, however, it's probably the most honest answer you'll ever get.

QUESTION THREE:

Why Can't I Just Leave?

I have tried escaping this relationship on multiple occasions. Sometimes I put myself back in it because it seems easier than the pain of dealing with the reality that I have wasted more than six years of my life, but the past few times, he has lured me back into it. He uses every approach—anger, guilt, shame, love, promises, and "accidentally" running into me literally everywhere I go. Until eventually, it feels easier to say yes than continue to deal with the confusion. Granted, that just leads to self-loathing and more confusion.

—*Simone,* survey respondent

The people around us help construct our version of lived reality. Those closest to us have the strongest influence. We share experiences with them, then develop a narrative that creates order out of those experiences.

But what happens when someone you trust has intentionally constructed a reality around those experiences for you with holes in it?

Some parts of the dreamworld you have been sharing with your partner were blatantly false. You know that now, and as those fragments were ripped out, it rattled you to the core. Yet just enough is still true, or at least seems true, to keep the base intact.

You can't quite be sure.

Each shared moment between you and your partner, each word your partner says, each action he or she takes, has its own duality. Because you cannot know for sure, they are all both true and false. Your partner reassures you the holes in the world the two of you inhabit together are all patched up, yet you know sometimes they're not.

What you don't yet know is that when the truth was eroded, parts of you were eroded too. When those lies were uncovered and pasted over, the holes still left behind left voids in you too. You can't know this because the parts of you that would know were the very parts that were stripped out. You're in a dream within the dreamworld.

Now, there is only the suffering your partner inflicts, first by her presence and then by her absence. You are now suspended by the hopelessness of your dual motivations, paralyzed by powerlessness: "I don't want to stay in this relationship, but I can't leave."

My Story

I got a text one evening as I was packing things up. In two days, I planned to move out of the suburban apartment Amir and I had shared and back into the heart of Washington, D.C., which I considered my home.

I opened my phone, and my heart drummed in my ears when I saw Amir's name. "If you need help with taking your bed apart or anything, let me know. I think I owe you that much."

"Okay. Thanks," I texted back.

"Anytime." He sent a picture with a quote on it. The quote said: "It all comes down to the last person you think of at night. They have your heart."

I looked at the picture for a moment, feeling a tug in my chest. As part of the process of moving out, I'd gone down to the lobby of our building earlier to get the last of our mail. Our names were listed together on the mailbox, and the grief I'd been stifling threatened to spill over. That could not happen. I wasn't sure I could stop it from taking over everything. I was surviving, and that's all I had to do.

After Amir had walked out of my apartment that first day back from Jamaica, I had been shambling ghost-like through the life I had formerly inhabited, eyes staring and seeing shapes that resembled real-world objects, though the world did not feel real. I did not occupy my body, except when I was forced to out of absolute duty or mortal danger. As I walked on autopilot to the Metro on my way to work one morning, a blast of car horns jarred me out of my waking sleep-state and caused me to hop backward onto the sidewalk. I'd almost crossed the street without looking to see whether I had a "walk" sign or not.

He was gone, yet I still felt his presence everywhere. I had gotten so used to feeling his control over me, checking to see where I was, monitoring me on GPS, reviewing my actions on my social media apps, that I was sure his control was still present. Had he parked somewhere in the parking lot of the apartment building? Did he watch me leave to go to work? I felt his eyes on me, watching me to make sure I arrived home at the regular time and wasn't going out anywhere. I would see a man walking toward me, Amir's face grafted over the man's face, then I'd real-

ize it wasn't him. Arriving home one evening, I absent-mindedly pressed the button in the elevator for the floor I worked on instead of the floor I lived on. When I turned the corner in the hallway and saw the welcome mat was missing in front of my door, my heart leapt into my throat as I thought he had come by the apartment or was perhaps even waiting inside. I reached the door, then confusion washed over me when I saw the apartment number was "4" instead of "2." For a split second, only a millisecond, I thought he must have done this to me. He had switched out the numbers to show who was in charge and make me feel like it wasn't my apartment anymore to make me feel crazy. It was only a tendril of an idea that didn't grab hold because the truth of what I'd done, that I'd made a mistake, washed over me. I felt faint with relief as I hurried back down to my floor.

Untangling. I needed to untangle us. What was it I needed to do? The bank account seemed very important. Amir and I had opened a joint bank account for the sole purpose of paying joint bills, such as rent and utilities. We deposited our portions of each into it, then paid the bills as they came due. My fear was that he would start writing checks or using the debit card indiscriminately against the account, even though there was no money in it because we weren't using it anymore. I'd have more to lose, and he'd already made the apartment threats.

"I want to close the account," I said into the phone.

I heard clicking on the other end as the bank clerk typed in the account number. "There are two of you on the account?"

"Yes, but I can't get in touch with Amir. I don't know where he is." Obviously, I knew how to reach him. But if I thought he might use the account against me, I certainly could not count on him to help me close it.

"I'm sorry, but since both of you are on the account, I'm going to need permission from both of you to close it."

"Okay, well can you just take my name off of it then?"

The man hesitated. "I'm sorry. Since it's currently a joint account, I'll need to get approval from both of you to remove you and change it to an individual account."

"Wait . . . so you're saying I can't even take my name off of it?"

"I'm sorry."

"But I don't want to be on that account anymore. I don't know where he is, so how am I supposed to get his permission?"

"I'm sorry," he said again.

"What is this? Saudi Arabia?" I said and hung up.

Something else struck me the week he walked out. What if there had been others? I found myself in a doctor's office.

"I want to get tested," I told the nurse once I got into the examining room.

"For?" she said, looking up from the computer she was typing on.

I cleared my throat. "STDs."

"Have you been exposed?"

Once again, how could I explain? I simply said: "My boyfriend cheated on me, so I don't know."

"Did he tell you whether he used a condom?"

The sheer magnitude of what I didn't know was an ocean that threatened to drown me, but I stared at her, my face mask-like. "All I know is he cheated on me. We aren't in contact anymore."

She gave me a cup, and I wrote my name on it in blurry blue Sharpie in the bathroom. Afterward, she ushered me down the hall where a man drew three vials of blood. The nurse pointed me to the exit, and I squinted as I walked out into the sunlight.

About a week later, I received a text from him asking if we could have dinner that night "one more time before I leave for Pakistan." My heart stopped when I saw his name on my phone before kicking again at my ribcage, faster than before. I felt my fingers go cold as I struggled with what to type back to him. Beyond the bank account, I needed to break the lease early. Now that I had his attention, would he agree to sign something saying we wanted to move out? Maybe he would even pay some of the fees for breaking the lease, which was going to cost thousands of dollars. Yeah right, *I thought.*

I agreed to see him, and that night, he showed up at my apartment. As we walked over to the Mexican restaurant next door and waited for the light to change so we could cross the street, he suddenly dug into his pocket and pulled out a handful of what looked like colorful mesh.

"Here," he said. He stuffed it into my hand.

I opened my hand and looked at several small bags. Opening the first one, I found a ribbon necklace with a black glass heart on the end and matching earrings, another pouch holding a red and silver beaded bracelet, and, finally, one with a silver ankle bracelet on which dangled a silver charm.

"That one's my favorite," he said, holding it up so I could see it. "It means love . . . infinity . . ." The figure-eight infinity symbol twinkled in the sunlight.

"Anyway, I know you don't want to be with me, but please, I hope you'll keep these forever." He looked away, back at the street. The light had already changed once while I'd opened the pouches. I felt a strange tightening in my chest, and I struggled not to cry.

At the restaurant, I unfolded the letter I needed him to sign, giving our sixty-day notice to break our lease and move out of the apartment, as per the lease we had signed. I had listed the amount it would cost in the letter, and as he signed the paperwork, I asked him if he would be willing to pay his half. I cringed inside waiting for him to respond, but he was in a conciliatory mood, and he agreed that he would do it.

"But . . . is there anything . . . we can do?" he added.

I asked him what he meant, and he said he wanted to stay together even if we didn't live together. Going to Pakistan was something he only planned to do if I said no, he said. I didn't know what to say. There were two months to go until I moved out. I was well-aware that he wasn't agreeing to pay his share of the fees to move out because it was decent and honorable. He wasn't doing it because he regretted anything or because it was fair since we were both on the lease. I recognized it as conditional agreement that he would withdraw if I wasn't complying with his expectations.

What would that mean? I tried to guess. I'd need to act as if the things he'd done and the way he'd treated me were no big deal. He'd probably want to come and go in my life whenever he felt like it. I'd be expected to drop everything and respond to him. He would demand I not "date" anyone else. No problem there since the thought of dating under the circumstances made me nauseous. Could I just hang on and treat this as a business arrangement?

Two months didn't sound like a very long time. I told myself it would be a type of revenge in a way, that I would let him think he had some type of control over me, but he wouldn't know my motivations for interacting with him.

Back at my apartment, I was still so raw because of all that had happened, and I started crying. His face hardened. "If you're going to cry, I'm just going to go home."

I sniffed. "I can't help it. Do you expect me not to cry?"

"I can't change it. You have to start a new relationship with me if you want this to work." He held his arms out. "Come here."

I moved close to him, and he wiped my tears away as each one fell from my eyes, as if he couldn't bear to see it on my face.

"Let's watch a movie," he said. He had put on a movie where two college friends started a social media company together. Later, one of them double-crossed the other.

"If you did that to me, I'd kill you and then be on a plane to Pakistan before they even knew it was me," he said.

I couldn't recognize it at the time, but what I was doing, the silence and the "role" I was trying to play, were not "revenge," and I wasn't "letting" him think he had control. He had actual control over me, and what I told myself was only a rationalization to manage my fear and make myself feel just psychologically strong enough to get through that time and get out from under that control. The motivations I had for interacting with him were not a game I was playing—they were choices I made in a no-win situation to survive.

By the time I moved out, I could no longer tell the difference between reality and his lies. His very presence reminded me of his betrayal, and I could show no emotion about anything he'd done. He became increasingly more controlling, yet he mixed in his cruelty with flowers, surprise gifts, and more marriage proposals. A pattern had developed in which he would appear suddenly for a few days claiming how much he loved me, harass me about his paranoia that there were other men in my life, and violate my privacy by going through my phone. I would cry, and he would rage at my tears and drop hints about other women in his life, storming out and disappearing. I became frozen, every action punished, all the strength I had left focusing on that date I would move out.

Before the text message about my bed, he had disappeared again. We hadn't talked in a couple of weeks. This seemed like a strange and shallow way of trying to show me he cared about me after everything that had happened. I struggled with my response.

"I want to make a joke out of this and say, 'So, which one of us is it?'"

"Fuck you," he said. "Thanks. It was you, but it won't be from now on."

His words stung, but after everything, I should have expected them. "It never was. Don't contact me again."

"Okay, slut. The more I talk to you, the more I hate you anyway."

I wished I could figure out how to block text messages on my phone. I'd never needed to block a number before and didn't know how. Every time I tried, it seemed unnecessarily complicated. Between the move, the shock and trauma of everything that had happened, and walking on eggshells never knowing when he would contact me or just show up, I persisted in a state where everything felt overwhelming, terrifying, and exhausting. My inability to figure out how to block numbers left me at his mercy.

And then, I was free—or so I thought.

The day I moved out, he sent me another text letting me know he had gone into the apartment after I had left. The apartment was completely empty then, as he'd known it would be. He had already moved out his own stuff, so I wasn't sure why he would have gone back to an empty apartment. "It smelled like your perfume," he said. Only years later did it even occur to me that he probably never went back, that he probably used the idea that he did and the line about my perfume as an excuse to send me another message.

Surprisingly, he had paid his share of the fees for breaking the lease, but a lot of harm had been done in the months between our return from Jamaica and my move to a new apartment. He was emboldened, and my cognitive dissonance was further entrenched. Sometimes it was as if the bad things he'd done didn't exist, and sometimes it was as if the good things he'd done didn't exist. Now, the nightmare during which he controlled my life physically was finally over, yet it wasn't over. Following the perfume comment, twenty more texts arrived from him over the course of only a few minutes.

"I want you in my life. I have learned from my mistakes."

"I will treat you like a queen."

"Don't give up now."

"Please."

"Just give me thirty days."

"One last chance."

"I'll be loyal and trustworthy."

"I love you so much, and I know you hate me, but I can turn that hate to love."

"I'll treat you like a princess, baby."

"I'll do everything right and make you fall in love with me again."

"I won't treat you like I did."

"I'll do anything I have to do to make you happy."

"I can change. You will see in a month, baby."

"I can't live without you. You're the best thing that ever happened to me."

"Let me show you how much I love you."

"I just want you to sit back and let me do my magic."

"Thirty days."

"Please."

"I love you."

I didn't say yes, but I didn't say no. Instead, I would ask him why he would want to bother after everything he'd done, and he would respond with one of same answers he'd already texted me: "I can't live without you. You're the best thing that ever happened to me." The conversation continued over the course of days. When he invited me to his birthday party the following week, I agreed to that because it seemed harmless. That wasn't a commitment. It turned out, however, that I was walking into a trap—I just didn't know it. His friends bombarded me with reassurance that he really loved me. They said they had never seen him act this way with any other woman, and I was surprised to hear he'd told them he'd lied about the engagement and about Julia. If his friends say these things, then what Amir says must mean something, *I thought.*

Saying no to his persistent request to give him thirty days never felt like a real option, so I never really said yes. Instead, we just never really stopped talking or making plans together after that. My body was clamoring deep below surface level that I was in danger, but the part of my mind that could feel that alarm seemed submerged, as if I was sleepwalking, and the warning was a dream.

Amir promised this time, it would be different. He deleted all the social media apps from his phone except for Instagram and Facebook and gave me his passwords. It should have made me feel safe, yet I always felt on high alert. He brought me flowers, gifts, and chocolates, and it made me happy he wanted to show me his dedication to what he'd said, but it did not get rid of the rot underneath. When he'd sense my anxiety, I'd tell him that I felt something wasn't right, that I couldn't trust him.

"Are you sure the engagement is called off now?" I asked him. I told him I couldn't open my heart and give everything to him and

trust him again if there was this thing in the background. It didn't matter if that wasn't the life he wanted if he was still engaged, and if he was, then I couldn't let down my guard and be with him.

He reassured me there was no engagement. He repeated that it was over many times, that he told his dad to call his fiancé's house and call it off.

Yet there was such a feeling of dread—it was as if a sickness was spreading beneath the surface of our relationship, and I had an unshakeable feeling something bad was going to happen. I couldn't concentrate at work; I couldn't focus on anything going on around me. Cotton strands wrapped themselves around my thoughts, and I was slow to react, overwhelmed and haunted by my nightmares. At other times, when he was with me, the dread and anxiety just faded away as if they had never been real, and soothed by his presence, I convinced myself that what was in front of me was the truth, and everything else was my imagination.

When we were apart, however, my brain immediately started looking for signs that there were other lives he was still living. In the shadows, there were shapes I couldn't make out. I asked Julia if Amir had contacted her again, and she said she hadn't spoken with him in a long time. When I confessed that we were dating again, her response came quickly, and she told me I had Stockholm Syndrome.

One night, I was feeling particularly anxious after he became unreachable, and he had his friend send me a text to tell me his phone was installing an update that was taking over an hour. I couldn't take it anymore and logged into his Facebook account. What was I doing? On some level, I realized how absurd my behavior was. What was I even looking for? As I scanned through his messages, I searched for some kind of clue about what else was going on in his life I might not know about or even what else might be in his head that he didn't tell me. His messages seemed pretty sterile. There weren't many from before two or three months earlier, even between many of his closest friends. He had wiped them clean, and there was nothing incriminating.

But then, I saw his archived message folder was full. I didn't know whether I should click on it or not, but my curiosity got the best of me. There were hundreds of messages going back almost eight years, the length of time he'd had a Facebook account. I clicked on some of them randomly, hoping they might help me fill in some of the gaps in my mind about who this man was. There were messages to several women he appeared to have dated. The time periods seemed to overlap with one another. There were messages from women asking him for money in exchange for sex. He'd offer them fifty or a hundred dollars, and they'd arrange a time when he was to go over to their homes. There were several messages where he just invited women to parties at his house, and there would be no response. It didn't even appear he knew the women very well, if at all. Then, there were dozens of messages to women, messages that only said simply, "Hi" to make contact and start a conversation, most unanswered. Oh, he is that guy, *I thought . . . the one who's in every woman's inbox trying to see who will take the bait and continue the conversation. I saw a conversation in which he tried to convince a woman that a second woman they both knew was not his girlfriend, then other messages to the second woman in which it appeared that she was, in fact, his girlfriend. There were conversations in which he appeared to be encouraging women to cheat on their boyfriends with him. I saw messages he sent to Sandi wherein he had told her she was the love of his life and sent her a link to one of the exact same songs he had once sent to me, one he had sung to me.*

I realized some of these conversations or messages had taken place during our relationship. They weren't recent, but they had still happened. This long history gave me a better picture of who Amir was and how he acted online, and I found it hard to believe that suddenly, he had just stopped trolling the waters. Maybe he just deleted all the new messages he was sending and receiving before I even saw them now since I had his password. For all I knew, he had an entirely different Facebook account I didn't know about. Or used a different social media app for things like this now.

"I worry that you're still talking to other women," I told Amir later. "I worry I'm not enough for you. That you need attention from several women at the same time."

"Baby, you are enough. I haven't talked to any women, and I have no desire to. I love you. I have you back, and why would I mess that up? I want to marry you and start a family with you."

"I wasn't accusing you," I said. Maybe he wasn't. I had no evidence he was. Just that sickness spreading underneath. "I just can't get rid of the feeling."

"You'll trust me and believe me again one day."

"I worry you'll change your mind about me."

"I'm never changing my mind. I want you in my life, and I'm going to make my dreams come true. I can't live without you anymore."

"Thank you for being patient with me."

But the fear never went away. I was always waiting to confirm that he had a secret, other self, an idea that my body had absorbed as truth at the cellular level. We would say goodnight, and I would fall into an uneasy sleep, then wake up after a nightmare. I would open my Facebook app and happen to see he was online. Who could he be talking to at four o' clock in the morning?

I felt ridiculous, but I'd ask him about it the next day. He'd insist he hadn't been online at all, that he'd been asleep. My anxiety would only grow when he made that claim. The next time I saw him online in the middle of the night, I felt paranoid and needy, but I took a screenshot and sent it to him to show him I wasn't crazy.

"My phone must not be logging me out of the app when I close it," he responded.

I felt reassured, and I was also increasingly skeptical.

The crack inside me that threatened to rip me apart grew just the tiniest bit wider.

10

Invisible Chains

In a 2017 article, *Buzzfeed* broke the news that musician R. Kelly was holding six women seemingly against their will in properties outside of Chicago and Atlanta. A former inhabitant of one of the homes described the conditions in which the women lived. Kelly took away their cell phones, forced them to cut off almost all contact with their friends and family, and forbade them from leaving the house. They had to call him "Daddy" and ask permission to eat, sleep, bathe, or use the bathroom.

In addition, he confiscated the women's clothing, made them wear jogging suits so his male friends couldn't see their bodies, and forced them to turn and face the wall when his friends came over. He also forced the women to perform sex acts, which he filmed and showed to his friends.

Kelly has been embroiled in scandals related to child pornography and sexual assault for decades; however, these new revelations came to light when the parents of one of the women contacted the local authorities. They told police Kelly was abusing their daughter and holding her in the house against her will. Yet when the police went out to the home to check on her, the woman claimed she was fine.

Her parents told *Buzzfeed* the last time they saw their daughter, "It was as if she was brainwashed . . . she just kept saying she's in love and [Kelly] is the one who cares for her." No one has ever referred to this as narcissistic abuse. In fact, her parents stated they wanted to get her out and get her treatment for cult indoctrination.[83]

When Your Human Rights Become Their Offense

"I never told you that you couldn't hang out with your friends!"

Amir never controlled what or when I took care of my basic needs or kept me from talking to my family members, but he did exert quite a bit of control over my wardrobe, where I went, who I saw, and with whom I interacted. Yet that's the type of thing Amir would say to me in a tone that suggested I was crazy for implicating him when I'd said I was tired of not being able to see them.

He was right. He had never explicitly said to me I couldn't do things with them. He had, however, done the following:

- Intentionally made plans for the two of us at the last minute on a night I had plans with my friends, then became hostile when I didn't break my plans to be with him.
- Insulted my friends and made comments that implied they didn't like him or our relationship, and I was being disloyal if I saw them.
- Started arguments right as I was about to leave, then accused me of not caring about his feelings if I tried to walk out of the argument.

- Made sexually degrading comments and cruel remarks such as, "If you get raped, don't come crying to me."
- Requested pictures of me while I was out to prove to him I was where I said I would be.
- Insisted I turn on my GPS while I was out.
- Bombarded my phone with dozens of demeaning, accusatory, and threatening texts if I didn't respond to him while I was out.
- Stalked my social media pages afterward to see if I had added any new men.
- Made false accusations without cause that I was actually on a date instead and made me go to exhausting lengths to prove my faithfulness.
- Exploded in rage if he didn't find out until afterward and questioned me relentlessly about what had taken place.
- Threatened to cheat on me or break up with me if I went out.
- Actually cheated on me.
- Withheld his love and pretended as if I didn't even exist, gave me the silent treatment, or broke up with me.
- Accused me of doing the things to him he was doing to me—all the other things in this list.

Do any of these behaviors look familiar?

The last one is particularly tricky, because on the surface, it looks harmless, maybe even ridiculous, especially when you know you haven't done any of those things. However, it turns out that this can become one of the most powerful methods of control they have. In this example, they may label choosing to spend the evening with our friends as disloyalty and draw a false equivalency to their actual betrayals. Or they may claim going out with our friends is us walking out on them. If we don't respond to their many attempts to contact us while we're out, we are giving *them* the silent treatment. If we challenge them on any of this, we are being disrespectful and degrading their feelings on the matter.

Wait, wait, wait. What happened there?

Our normal, everyday human behavior and our right to engage in it were pitted against their attempts to stop it. Yes, exercising our rights gets framed as an attack. Once they can cast themselves as a victim, they turn their abuse into a method of defending themselves.

So you see, pathological partners don't actually need to tell us not to visit our friends—and in fact, they get to explicitly deny they have forced us into anything. They look innocent—and sometimes victimized—as they put on the different masks to get us to comply.

The types of actions in this example create an invisible forcefield around us that has a name called "coercive control." Coercive control has been criminalized in England, Scotland, Ireland, and Australia, which is promising since many of its abusive qualities are so hidden. Traditional definitions of abuse focus on individual incidents of physical injury. However, coercive control uses dominance and conditioning that have the cumulative effect over time of restricting the victim's human rights to result in entrapment.[84]

Coercive control can manifest itself through behaviors such as:[85]

- excessive monitoring
- isolation from loved ones
- privacy violations or spying

- trivial "rules" (usually one-sided)
- controlled access to basic self-care or resources
- verbal abuse, degradation, and humiliation
- threats
- forced acts that violate the law or the morals and values of the survivors
- destruction of personal property
- sexual and reproductive coercion
- covert or overt dominance over one or more areas of a survivor's life, such as finances, career, friendships, clothing choices, hobbies, or other areas

All these behaviors do not need to be present, and this is not an exhaustive list. It usually begins slowly and may be subtle, especially at the beginning of the relationship. The abuser is usually charming to outsiders, and the control could be disguised as concern or as caring behavior. It may even be disguised as a loving behavior, seemingly carried out because of the abuser's passionate nature or deep love for the victim. The incremental, fog-like way it creeps around the victim can make it difficult to recognize as threatening. Eventually, the abuser degrades or criticizes almost all the actions or choices of their partner. When this happens, it's only then that the survivor finds herself with restricted access to others and almost all her choices overtaken or made very challenging to freely act upon.[86] Outsiders may see what's happening, but either fail to see it as abusive or fail to understand why the survivor doesn't walk away from the pathological partner's excessive control. From the inside, many victims don't recognize themselves as victims of abuse.

Sam Vaknin, author of *Malignant Self-Love* and who is himself a malignant narcissist, characterizes the environment in a situation like this one using the term "ambient abuse, which he describes as:

> *The stealth, subtle, underground currents of maltreatment that sometimes go unnoticed even by the victims themselves, until it is too late. Ambient abuse penetrates and permeates everything—but is difficult to pinpoint and identify. It is ambiguous, atmospheric, diffuse. . . . It is the outcome of fear—fear of violence, fear of the unknown, fear of the unpredictable, the capricious, and the arbitrary. It is perpetrated by dropping subtle hints, by disorienting, by constant—and unnecessary—lying, by persistent doubting and demeaning, and by inspiring an air of unmitigated gloom and doom ("gaslighting"). Ambient abuse, therefore, is the fostering, propagation, and enhancement of an atmosphere of fear, intimidation, instability, unpredictability and irritation. There are no acts of traceable explicit abuse, nor any manipulative settings of control. Yet, the irksome feeling remains, a disagreeable foreboding, a premonition, a bad omen.*[87]

Ambient abuse cannot be seen. It can only be experienced.

Pathological Love Stories

How We Were Objectified and Threatened

"I didn't care much for Facebook and was on it but not an avid user. He said he didn't want to go out with anyone on Facebook, but he would try and cope with the fact I was. It became such an issue; I said I would deactivate my account. But that wasn't good enough. I had to delete it. He wasn't happy about LinkedIn even though I said it was for work. He made me change my profile picture, as it wasn't appropriate. He made comments if I wore makeup, saying I was so beautiful I didn't need it. I stopped wearing makeup. He said he loved me in casual clothes and said that if I did dress up, he would never say how beautiful I looked, as that's a look he doesn't like. I stopped dressing up. At no point did he forbid me, but somehow, I ended up doing and thinking just how he wanted me to."

"He had hacked into my phone and had access to all of my personal data, emails and old text messages and would regularly threaten to 'expose' me to people from my past—ex-boyfriends, old co-workers, friends, even though I hadn't really done anything wrong—he'd just exploited context to fit some narrative of me being 'evil' and disgusting."

"I am isolated and have no friends in my life. There are constant accusations and threats."

"He treats me with complete disrespect. He will threaten and bully me every day regarding finances, the very home that I have built. . . . The isolation because I need to rely on him for everything, which means that he plays take away if I don't behave. His constant 'if you're not nice to me, you get nothing!'"

"I knew in my gut he was being unreasonable or controlling, but he always turned it on me—I was misunderstanding him. I had such fear if my phone had a notification or if one of his friends wanted my number (he didn't like me being friends with his friends and disliked all my friends). It was the sudden issue out of the blue. Continually walking on eggshells. I remember going to a spa day, and he said that if it is a male masseuse, I should ask for a female. Not to go in the jacuzzi if anyone else was in there, as it's 'weird.' If I met friends for lunch, he would call, and if I didn't take his call, he would say, 'There is no time I wouldn't want to talk to you' and make me feel bad. I lost my mind. I couldn't trust my thoughts."

"I wasn't able to express myself because I was always treading on eggshells so as not to upset him."

"Being accused of things I didn't do, lies, cheating, etc. Abuse and rage at times that came from nowhere and for no real reason. Betrayal."

"All of it—the gaslighting, lies, betrayal, intermittent reinforcement, using their friends and family to help in the con, actively turning people I knew against me to collaboratively abuse me too. Lastly, drugging and poisoning. I had no idea at the time that this was happening. Just was so unwell and disabled by them."

"The betrayal and the lack of consideration of me as a human being. I slowly realized that he literally did not care about me as a living person. The way he lied, cheated, and used my money, apartment, and car without any shame were completely pathological. He didn't even care about my body or my health. I couldn't get him to think about or care about the fact that he was putting my health and my actual life at risk by cheating.

It became terrifying to be around him as I started to realize the way he must actually think about me, which is like I was an object."

"He tried to force me to commit suicide over and over, knowing my sister did and that I'm still devastated from losing her. My mom would have lost two daughters, and this made him happy. That still makes me sick to my stomach the most. The extent he went to cover his cheating. He photoshopped his maps, location history, added countless overlays, filters, and added animation to them, thinking I was too stupid to know."

"The abuse started to get physical toward the end. Throwing things at me, pushing, shoving, physical intimidation, blocking my way when I tried to leave. Every time we got in a disagreement or he was bored or needed attention, he would go on Facebook and smear me to his followers. He went back and forth between love-bombing me and smearing me. He posted dirty pictures of me on a dirty fetish site. I started to get physically ill from the stress."

"Never knowing which version of him I was going to get, not just day-to-day but moment-to-moment and in complete ignorance, being terrified that I could trigger a reaction."

"He talked about me to others as if I was not there. I felt like a possession, not a person. I never could have an opinion, or a thought, without him downplaying it, ridiculing it, or making me feel insignificant."

See Appendix A.

Coercive control looks a lot like the tactics pathological partners use, but there are some important differences. Are the women who live with R. Kelly being held there against their will, or are they there by choice?

We See What They Want Us to See

In 1973, four hostages were held captive in Stockholm, Sweden, during a bank robbery by a man named Jan-Erik Olsson and his fellow former jail cell mate. When the police finally arrested the two men, the hostages and the men hugged goodbye. Two of the women who had been held hostage begged the police not to hurt the bank robbers who had just held them at gunpoint for six days. None of the hostages would testify against the men; in fact, they defended their captors. After the men returned to prison, at least one of the hostages visited them in jail.

A year later when *The New Yorker* published an interview with the hostages, they described the terror of being bound by rope and having a submachine gun stuck in their ribs and of being threatened with death so the gunmen could have a getaway car. They also described moments where their captors soothed them, showed them kindness and compassion, provided them with comforts, and cared about their well-being.[88]

One of the hostages described how Olsson draped his coat over her when she shivered. "Jan was a mixture of brutality and tenderness. I had known him only a day when I felt his coat around me, but I was sure he had been that way all his life," she said in her interview. One of the other female hostages said that in her fear, she had held hands with one of the captors: "Perhaps it sounds a little like a cliché, but Clark gave me tenderness. Yes, we held hands, but there was no sex. It made me feel enormously secure. It was what I needed."

The sole male hostage recalled how he would be overwhelmed with feelings of gratitude for Olsson when Olsson described his plans and referred to him as an "emergency God." While captive, Olsson pulled him aside to let him know he wasn't going to kill him as he'd originally planned but shoot him in the leg instead. *What an incredibly kind man*, the hostage thought.

Afterward, even the hostages couldn't understand their own behavior. Thinking of their captors as kind and wanting to defend them didn't seem rational. Psychiatrists explained their reactions as a phenomenon called "identification with the aggressor," which they noted had also been seen in prisoners of war. Eventually, their actions came to be known in this circumstance by one of the treating psychiatrists as "Stockholm Syndrome" and was explained as a way for hostages to cope with the extreme stress of life-threatening situations.

The FBI has identified three environmental conditions that result in Stockholm Syndrome:[89]

(1) inability to escape

(2) a threat to life by the perpetrator

(3) the rise of positive feelings by the victims for the perpetrators when the perpetrator offers any kindness

Victims develop these positive feelings because the kindness the perpetrator offers casts him or her as a savior, sparing the victim from ongoing terror in a situation in which his or her life can be taken at any moment. Anything that offers salvation offers hope. When the victim sees the perpetrator behaving kindly, it casts the perpetrator in an almost god-like role. The victim knows the perpetrator held her life in his hands and chose kindness instead, and extreme feelings of gratitude involuntarily may overwhelm the victim. It doesn't matter that the perpetrator put her in that position because the victim has no power relative to the perpetrator in these situations.

Stockholm Syndrome looks a lot like what happens to survivors in pathological love relationships, but there are some important differences.

Their Word Is Not Their Bond

There is an important element missing from both coercive control and from Stockholm Syndrome. What the two have in common with one another is that the rights or freedoms of the survivor are overtly and forcefully taken away. Coercive control focuses on the tactics the abuser uses to do that. Stockholm Syndrome is the effect on the survivor, although it has been more commonly applied to even more restrictive situations, such as kidnapping.

Pathological love relationships are not hostage situations or kidnappings. No one keeps us in it by force. This truth can be one of the most confusing of all to understand, much less explain to others. *If I'm not being forced to stay, then why can't I leave?*

The element that's missing in coercive control and Stockholm Syndrome can help to explain why we stay: deceptive influence. Not all the tactics used by pathological partners are openly forceful. Some are deceptive, and we don't recognize them for what they are.

The deceptive influence is what creates cognitive dissonance. There are two parts of you right now: the one that wants you to read this book and the one that wishes you could put it down and forget what's in it. Those two parts of you are splitting off to manage the two different sides of your partner because they can't be rationally reconciled into one coherent person. Yes, read that again. To cope, a part of your brain has begun compartmentalizing your partner's actions to keep you sane.[90]

Let's go through what's happening here, then the rest of this book will be dedicated to bringing the two back together so you'll be the one in charge again.

Our brains can't function in two realities at once. Sandra L. Brown, M.A, found in her study of approximately 600 survivors that cognitive dissonance is the symptom they reported as the most traumatic, disruptive, and intrusive.[91] She reminds us that harmonious and consistent thoughts, emotions, and behavior are important because they lead us to:

> *Knowing who we are and what we believe. We rarely recognize how important this is to our own well-being until our consistency is interrupted and we begin to feel "all over the place" and not ourselves. We feel our best when our thinking, emotions, and behavior reflect what we believe. That's when we are living our truth, when we are on point, when we feel settled and balanced.*[92]

Brown also found that survivors struggle with inconsistencies on three different levels:[93]

- ***Thoughts*** (e.g., drawing contradictory conclusions based on evidence of both the pathological partner's love *and* cruel and unloving actions)
- ***Emotions*** (e.g., feeling both ecstasy and despair)
- ***Behavior*** (e.g., having a core value of not tolerating abuse, yet stays in the relationship)

As we saw in Chapter 8, when our perceptions are inconsistent, we will feel cognitive dissonance.[94] When our pathological partners hijack our cognitive dissonance, that's when the real crisis in the relationship begins. In a pathological love relationship, our hearts and minds are indoctrinated with a script about who our partners were early on. It was a powerful one that involved our emotions and an intense physiological response: "Love-bombing and manipulative language used in the early relationship embeds in the survivor certain perceptions of [the pathological partner] and corresponding emotional and sexual responses," says Brown.[95]

Yet once the love-bombing phase ends, our partners intentionally and repeatedly put us in a position of having to compare words and actions that do not match. We are forced to choose what we see and experience with our own eyes at one moment versus what happens in the next. They can use that script to hook us around the throat indefinitely so they can continue to do to us whatever it is they don't want us to see.

She identified three types of cognitive dissonance women in pathological love relationships encounter. They face cognitive dissonance about their pathological partners ("He's good" and "He's bad"), about the relationship ("This relationship makes me feel so happy" and "This relationship makes me feel devastated"), and about themselves ("I'm beautiful and loved" and "I'm worthless"). We can't resolve the dissonance because we can't see both sides of our partner at the same time, and we can never settle on which one to accept. We are constantly being pulled first in one direction, then the other. Brown refers to them as "relationship dichotomies," such as:[96]

- Feeling extreme bonding yet expecting probable abandonment
- Feeling highly protected yet exposed and at-risk of danger because of him
- Feeling sexually worshipped yet treated like a whore
- Feeling as if he understands her completely, yet he is totally clueless about her needs, emotions, and motivations

When we struggle with whether our partner is "good" or "bad," what we are struggling with is which version of their extreme behavior characterizes their "true self." They manipulate our natural tendencies to trust our intuition that they are dangerous by seamlessly re-creating the biological and psychological processes they activated during love-bombing phase. This redirects our attention to the memories of how they once behaved early in the relationship. The cognitive dissonance we feel as we try to reconcile their actions creates an all-consuming confusion that can quickly overtake our lives.[97]

This may feel familiar. In Chapter 5, we looked at roles our partners play in the relationship. He or she repeatedly shifts between The Savior and The Bully. Plunging you in darkness, then turning on the light. Poisoning you violently, then injecting you with the cure. Pushing you off a cliff, then swooping in like Superman. Pushing your head underwater, then pulling you to shore at the last second.

Figure 10.1:
Hero or Oppressor?

Your partner pushes your head under water, watching you struggle, then pulls you back up for two seconds so you can breathe as you gasp for air. Then, he does it again. And again. And again. And ...

You say: *"I don't understand. Why are you doing this? I thought you loved me. Do you love me? Please stop."*

Every time your partner pulls you up for air, he or she waves a wand and gives you a different response.

Figure 10.2:
The Magician: Making Cruelty Disappear

- "I'm not drowning you. What are you talking about?"
- "I'm drowning you because I love you. And stop asking me if I love you. Of course, I do. Can't you see how much?"
- "You deserve to drown. Remember that time you splashed water on me a year ago?"

- "I'm not going to talk about this. I'll walk away and leave you here if you don't stop."
- "You look so pathetic right now. I can find somebody better. Someone who's not flailing around in the water."
- "I'll stop drowning you, but you have to promise that you'll stop talking about drowning forever. We don't need to talk about it. You're just going to have to trust me on this that I'm not going to do it anymore if you promise not to talk about it."
- "I am drowning you, but so what? It won't kill you."
- "I didn't mean to drown you. I just made a mistake."
- "I'm just playing with you. Can't you lighten up? This isn't even considered drowning. You're being too sensitive."

It isn't only the cruelty of the act that disappears, but it's the act itself. Each time they take us closer to the edge of what feels like death, we're that much weaker and feel that much more grateful when they keep us alive. As we experience the highs and lows of our partner's alternating love and hate, our neurotransmitters sync up with the change in their behavior. When attachment forms as a physiological response to traumatic or intensely emotionally charged events, they are called "trauma bonds." We become extremely loyal to those with whom we form trauma bonds because our physiology tricks us into believing we have formed a deep connection. Yet it's actually the hardship we've been through with that person that makes it feel as if we have shared something only the two of us can understand.[97]

Patrick J. Carnes, author of *The Betrayal Bond*, describes how trauma bonds can form between people who experience negative situations together and that they are not always bad. When one person forms a trauma bond to another because the negative situation in that circumstance is abuse and exploitation, however, the trauma bond is an extremely important way that the abuser maintains power over the victim because the bond is so difficult to break and can be long-lasting.[98] Trauma bonds that develop with pathological partners are based on power and control.

Our partners keep us in the relationship where it benefits them but at the expense of ourselves. The benefits to our partner and the costs to us may be almost invisible. There are times we can't use any of our five senses to explain why we feel that way, and it can make us feel crazy—yet we feel it in the shadows where we know something isn't quite right.

11

A Cult by Any Other Name

The women who lived with R. Kelly claimed they were free to leave any time they wanted to. They did not meet the criteria for the traditional definition of Stockholm Syndrome. However, Sandra L. Brown, M.A., describes how pathological love relationships have their own version of Stockholm Syndrome because the pathological partner indoctrinates the survivor into his pathological worldview and traps her with his occasional kindnesses, isolation from outside perspectives, and the perceived inability to leave.[99]

The fact that the parents who were interviewed about their daughter's situation mentioned they wanted to get her treatment for cult indoctrination doesn't come as a surprise. By most definitions of cults among people who study them, it isn't so much what cults believe as what they do that identifies them.

The International Cultic Studies Association defines a cult as "an ideological organization held together by charismatic relations and demanding total commitment."[100] This definition is broad, but three things are mentioned: ideology, a charismatic leader and his or her followers, and the commitment of the members. There is no limit to how large a cult may become, and they can be as small as one family. They can be based on any type of ideology: political, racist, spiritual, business, cults of personality, or something else.[101] In the United States alone, experts claim there are up to 10,000 cults operating at this time, most operating in secret.[102]

One of the most famous examples of cult behavior took place in Jonestown, where Jim Jones urged almost 1,000 of his followers to drink poisoned Kool-Aid in the 1970s because of his delusional conspiracy theories as part of a mass murder-suicide (although many of his followers tried to protest).[103] More recently, Keith Raniere, founder of the NXIVM multi-level marketing company, used his professional development seminars as a front for the more insidious purpose of recruiting a smaller group of women. By enticing them with the promise of a secret, elite group who would receive "special knowledge" that would impart important psychological wisdom, he persuaded the women to fork over incrementally higher amounts of money, always in service to the ideology and their belief in him and his mission. He eventually forced some of them into sex acts and branded his initials into them with a hot iron.[104]

It's easy to be deceived by examples such as these into believing cult behavior is rare, easy-to-spot, and revolves around bizarre beliefs. Mostly, however, cults are operating in plain sight yet invisible to most. This is only one way they are like pathological love relationships. There are so many similarities between cults and pathological love relationships that some cult abuse researchers and activists make no meaningful distinction between them. They refer to high-control relationships as micro-cults, cults of personality, one-over-one cults, or cults of two.[105]

There are important things we can learn from the research on cults that help us understand the answer to the question we ask ourselves in this section about why we can't leave. As we saw in Chapter 10, there are some important concepts that help explain our loyalty to our partner and what keeps us from leaving—for example, Stockholm Syndrome. Stockholm Syndrome is an extremely important concept because it explains why we identify with our partner's pathological worldview and defend their destructive actions directed toward us. The rare research on pathological love relationships that describes cognitive dissonance as a significant factor often lacks all the context the research on cults provides. Almost no research on pathological love relationships describes the larger social psychological and situational factors that operate on us all.

My theory on why that has happened is that issues within romantic relationship first attract researchers and mental health professionals who use existing frames about relationships because those are the frames they have available. These frames provide us with important information, yet that information is incomplete. We often tend to forget our romantic relationships are also two-person "groups." Despite the fact that every group type has a unique dynamic, all group types are also subject to general social norms that are often invisible to us and that hold our larger society together. Pathological personalities can manipulate the conditions under which we follow or break these norms to their advantage. It's important to understand how these norms operate to become fully aware of how we got here and how we can untangle ourselves from our partner's manipulation and exploitation.

The Free Will Paradox

The plot seemed like a gimmick: would an ordinary person walk into a situation with harmless intentions and end up committing murder less than ninety minutes later?

For Derren Brown, a British illusionist who uses sociology as the basis for some of his magic tricks, this was the question he wanted to answer. Brown's performances center around demonstrating how much mind control plays a role in magic and other mystical phenomena, such as fortunetelling. To show his audience how much mind control matters, he created an elaborate social experiment, with a set—a charity event—and over seventy hired actors for his television special, *The Push*. An unsuspecting man named Chris is brought to the "charity event" under the pretense of meeting someone for whom he will perform some work, not knowing every single person he meets is playing a role, and everything they are doing is scripted.

When things veer off course for him, as the script requires, we see that the small but unexpected changes in the environment that Brown wrote into the "plot" that require Chris to act quickly under pressure have the intended effect. Chris incrementally changes his behavior to match in reaction to events, violating his own morals and values in small ways at first, but then in what he believes are increasingly more alarming ways.

It's not a magic trick. Viewers can see exactly how and why Chris makes the choices he does as Brown reveals off-camera what social psychological principles he drew from to try to manipulate Chris into taking an action.[106] For example, he had an actor encourage Chris to think he was committing a minor act of deception by putting out food at charity event that was labeled vegetarian when it wasn't. The purpose of that act was to give Chris a shared secret with that actor to create a small bond between them. This primed him for a later moment when he was easier to influence and perhaps more willing to share a much larger and even more morally questionable secret.

Things we have learned about compliance and human behavior from some of the most iconic social science experiments ever conducted were on full view in *The Push* as well. Low-conscience individuals have personality traits and disorders that lead them to attempt to gain control over and compliance from the people around them.[107] Many of these same factors also play a role in how we find ourselves in the middle of a pathological love relationship, doing things we don't understand.

Social psychologist Solomon Asch performed an experiment on the ability of a group to influence our behavior. The people who signed up to be in the study believed it was about visual perception, and the instructions were to identify a set of two matching lines out loud in front of one another from across the room. This group of lines was designed so the two who matched were obvious. However, only one of the people in the room each time the experiment was conducted was an actual study participant. The others worked with the experimenter and had been instructed to intentionally select an incorrect response that would result in a mismatch between the two lines. As they selected their choices out loud, the participants in the study had to hear them select the wrong answer. The experimenter recorded whether they went with the group or selected the correct answer.

Asch found that each time he did this experiment, 75% of the participants in the study gave at least one incorrect response. One-third of the responses overall were incorrect, most of the time matching the group's incorrect response. When Asch briefed the participants after the study and let them know what the study had been really measuring, he asked them why they had selected their responses. Most said they felt it easier to go along with the group.[108]

Brown did something similar on his show. He had three confederates stand up and sit down every time they heard a bell ringing. One by one, he had individuals who didn't know what was going on also file into the room. Most, after observing everyone else, also began to sit and stand at the sound of the bell. He then had the confederates leave. The study individuals continued to sit and stand at the sound of the bell, although, as Brown points out, no one had told them to do so.

His experiment to see whether a man will commit murder relies on the desire to fit in but also on the idea of compliance. Psychologist Stanley Milgram demonstrated that most people are willing to knowingly harm another person if someone in authority gives them the instructions and a "good reason" for doing so. In his experiment, Milgram told people they were teaching word associations to someone else, and if they couldn't get the words right, they should use a machine sitting in front of them to administer a shock to the person. The "learner," however, was really an actor in on the experiment, and the machine didn't really administer any shocks. Milgram wanted to study whether the "teacher" would really administer shocks to another person, even when that person screamed and asked them to stop. Most of the participants administered some shocks, and 65% of the participants in the study administered the shocks at the highest levels they thought were available, even to the point where the actor pretended to lapse into unconsciousness.[109]

At around that same time, another psychologist, Philip Zimbardo, recruited several male students for the Stanford Prison Experiment, an experiment about the power of social roles to dictate behavior. He assigned half the students to be guards and half to be prisoners and instructed the guards to treat the prisoners with an authoritarian attitude. The guards did not question him, and their actions grew so cruel and humiliating that the "prisoners" began to break down psychologically. Zimbardo had to shut down the experiment after six days.[110]

So, did Chris "commit the murder" in Brown's experiment? During the hour and a half, he helps someone else hide what he thinks is a dead body, impersonates the dead man, lies to several people about the man's whereabouts, and assaults the body. He did not, however, push a man to his death and commit murder when presented with that horrifying option. Brown notes he was an exception. He ran the experiment multiple times, and of the other three cases where he showed the result on camera, each played out their designated role through to the outcome, bowing to the social pressure to "murder" the actor.

When the show aired, there was shock, outrage, and disbelief. Across social media, people posted their thoughts. Some were quick to denounce the individuals as weak, and others called for them to be arrested as "murderers." Still others were skeptical the show was real.[111]

If they had ever heard of these social psychology experiments, they might not have been skeptical. A series of sinister real-life compliance incidents played out in the United States from 1992 to 2004 when a man called up fast-food restaurants and grocery stores claiming to be a local police officer. In over seventy calls to businesses in thirty states, the caller convinced managers to detain female employees or customers on the basis that they were wanted for crimes. Then, using a "foot-in-the-door" approach like what Derrin Brown used in his script when he had Chris label food inaccurately as vegetarian, the caller asked the managers to comply with small acts, then eventually to strip search and sexually assault female employees or customers.[112]

Pathological partners use many of the identified compliance strategies such as the "foot-in-the-door" approach.[113] One of the most effective tactics they use is what Edward E. Jones describes as "ingratiation." They spend so much time during the love-bombing phase aligning their opinions with ours, flattering us, and presenting themselves in a way they know we will like that they know we will be less likely to see them as villains later when they behave like them.[114]

Free will is what we choose at any moment to do given the situation we're in and the choices available to us. Dr. Janja

A. Lalich describes how, to outsiders, the choices individuals in cults and other high-control situations appear irrational, however, they are perfectly rational in the context in which they were made by the individuals who were led one step at a time into making them, a concept she calls "bounded choice."[115]

What it's always important to recognize is that those choices are shaped by the information available to us, and the situation can be manipulated to give others power over us if we're not paying attention. This is often not recognized in the books and articles about pathological love relationships, but it's crucial to understand.

Under the Influence

Cult research often incorporates some aspect of compliance research from social psychology into why and how people are indoctrinated into cults. For some, the terminology may start to sound like science fiction. It can be difficult enough to accept that outside forces are acting on our behavior without introducing terms like "mind control." This may be less true for us as survivors, however, as once you're aware you're doing things you can't explain and you can't make your own actions match your desires, explanations that were once difficult to believe become much more convincing.

Cult abuse research uses a variety of terms to frame the abuse that takes place. While we have the term "coercive control," cult abuse research uses thought reform, mind control, coercive persuasion, cult programming, and undue influence, among others, to refer to the psychological tactics the leader and other members of a cult use to gain compliance over someone else.[116] Sandra L. Brown, M.A., found in her study of survivors that trauma bonding is not the cause of our attachment to our pathological partners but is a symptom of cognitive dissonance.[117] Pathological partners exploit the bonds by becoming both terrorist and rescuer—maneuvering back and forth between both roles with ease and erasing all trace of how they make us dependent. The body of research on cults can help us understand why. It has focused on how the impact on member recruits and the real harm is *identity change.*[118] The research on pathological love relationships mentions identity erosion and manufactured emotions but has not explicitly described the processes that produce them. Understanding identity disturbance in pathological love relationships fills in the gaps between how cognitive dissonance leads to Stockholm Syndrome.

When we put all this information together, it's easier to understand the bigger picture of what's holding you in the relationship right now.

Figure 11.1: The Relationship Between Cognitive Dissonance and Trauma Bonding

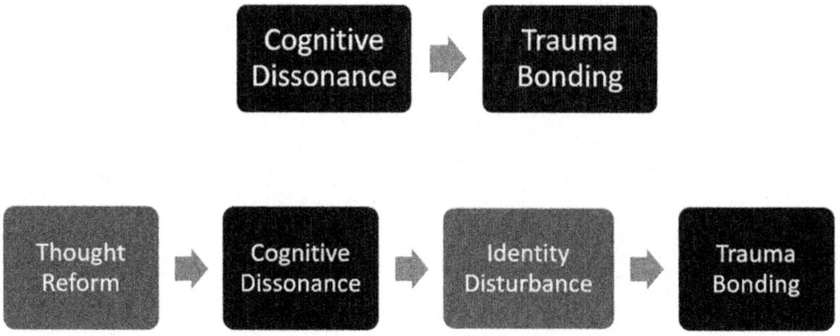

Cognitive Dissonance → Trauma Bonding

Thought Reform → Cognitive Dissonance → Identity Disturbance → Trauma Bonding

As described in Chapter 10, coercive control is characterized by dominance by a pathological partner over their partner's choices and activities, isolation, verbal insults, threats, controlled access to resources, and other overt negative actions. Coercive control is a groundbreaking and important step forward in acknowledging and prosecuting domestic abuse, and these actions are definitely present in a pathological love relationship. Coercive control describes the tactics pathological partners use when they play the role of "The Bully." As an explanation of why a survivor stays in a pathological love relationship or what the harm is, it's not quite adequate, however, as it doesn't cover all the manipulative techniques that pathological partners use. What about the roles of "The Savior" and "The Magician?"

It is the role-switching that results in the cognitive dissonance and special harm of a pathological love relationship. Models that explain mind control, or brainwashing, can help us fill in the blanks and explain the larger picture of how we are psychologically manipulated more completely.

The term "brainwashing" goes back to 1950, when Edward Hunter used it to explain how the Chinese government could coerce its citizens to adopt communism. It literally derives from a Chinese word meaning "wash brain."[119] A few years after the term first appeared, psychiatrist Robert Jay Lifton used it again after he interviewed Americans who had been prisoners of war during the Korean War. They had undergone a personality change during confinement, and some had even made false confessions or defected to the other side. Lifton identified eight elements that had contributed to this personality change:[120]

1. **Milieu Control**

   Domination and restriction of the environment, making communication with outside influences that don't align with the group's ideology difficult or impossible.

2. **Mystical Manipulation**

   Interpretation of ordinary events, experiences, or the group leader as special or superior to justify extraordinary actions and behavior.

3. **The Demand for Purity**

   An unattainable demand to abide by an ever-shifting set of rules. Members work harder to gain approval and redemption from the leader that is never given.

4. **The Cult of Confession**

   The expectation that there is no privacy, and there are no secrets. Weaknesses and vulnerabilities can be and are exposed at any time.

5. **Sacred Science**

   The requirement that all ideology of the group is superior to outside information and is absolute. Questioning it is not allowed.

6. **Loading of the Language**

   Using language to control perceptions of reality.

7. **Doctrine Over Person**

   The expectation that the ideology of the group is so important that outsiders who oppose it should be avoided or rejected. Group members who undermine the ideology will be expelled.

8. **Dispensing of Existence**

   Anyone in the group is dispensable. Those who fall out of line will be shut out and treated as if they do not exist.

Lifton noted that these eight elements all contribute to an atmosphere that fosters brainwashing, which he termed "thought reform." He claimed all eight must be present for thought reform to take place. According to Margaret T. Singer, another a brainwashing expert who also studied prisoners of war:

> *The goal [of thought reform] is to produce specific attitudinal and behavioral changes. The changes occur incrementally without its being patently visible to those undergoing the process that their attitudes and behavior are being changed a step at a time according to the plan of those directing the program.*[121]

One of the many major contributions of Singer was that she was able to show the conditions for thought reform don't have to be as exacting as Lifton described because not all circumstances under which it takes place are coercive. "Contrary to popular misconceptions . . . a thought reform program does not require physical confinement and does not produce robots," she writes.[122]

Singer points out that cults and authoritarian groups differ because the rules of the latter, though coercive, are always visible.

> *Because cults profess to help members but in actuality, exploit them, cults develop a double agenda in which they employ a dual set of norms in operation at the same time, with the surface norms subservient to the deeper, hidden designs and purposes of an organization or group. Surface norms stress the idealism and the righteousness of the cause. Below the surface, however, are a set of underlying norms that efficiently run the organization.*[123]

A "dual set of norms" is exactly how pathological love relationships operate, with our expectations that we are in a normal relationship on the surface and the reality of our exploitation underneath. For this reason, though we might see some of the eight elements of Lifton's model in our own relationship, it's probably not the best fit for explaining the psychological manipulation we've endured. A better one would consider the deception behind the dual set of norms.

World-renowned expert on cults, Dr. Steven Hassan, focuses on the harm of what he terms "destructive cults," in that the cults violate the rights of the members, have a hierarchical structure members are not allowed to question, and a rigid ideology and rules for members to follow. Hassan's emphasis on the deceptive aspect of the recruitment into the cult provides a useful model for explaining why it's so difficult for cult members and people in other similar situations to let go of the identity and beliefs they develop afterward. The person embeds themselves at their most intimate level and develops positive relationships that are intertwined with negative experiences. There is conflict and confusion about how to move forward and leave one aspect behind without leaving the entire self. Even Hassan makes the connection between his ideas around cults and deception to abusive relationships. He states:

> *The tactics that cults use to recruit and indoctrinate people are similar to the tactics that abusive individuals use to make someone "fall in love" or become dependent and obedient. Controlling and abusive individuals usually try to isolate their victims from their families and friends. They may encourage physical, emotional, or financial dependence.*[124]

Hassan has put forward a model for mind control, called the **BITE** Model of Authoritarian Control, which he uses to explain how destructive cults recruit and control people—which are conditions under which individuals have been deceived. When they are deceived, force is rarely used. In conditions where people have been deceived, different tactics are needed to make them compliant. The model has four components:[125]

- **B**ehavioral control: control over the group member's physical actions and interactions, such as,

- Access to basic resources
- Clothing choices
- Who the person can interact with and how
- Where the group member lives
- Rewards and punishments imposed for following "rules" and restrictions
- Physical isolation and controlling access to transportation
- Physical abuse and rape

- Information control: control over access to information to and between group members and about the cult and the outside world, such as,
  - Intentional deception and withholding information
  - Controlled access to other people or material that might disclose negative information or competing views
  - Pitting people against one another
  - Information categorized as "black and white"
- Thought control, or domination over the ability of group members to engage in critical analysis that might challenge the control of the cult leader, such as,
  - Questioning the doctrine is not allowed, and ideology must be internalized
  - Use of language, repeated phrases, and key words that shut down critical thinking
  - Hypnosis techniques
  - Gaslighting, denial, rationalizing

- Emotional control, or suppression of some emotions and amplification of others depending on usefulness to cult leader, such as,
    - o Instilling guilt, shame, and fear
    - o Suppressing anger and doubt
    - o Making the person feel responsible for "punishments"
    - o Making the person fear what will happen if they leave

Hassan claims that destructive cults use these tactics as methods of control to break down the identity of the recruits. What makes Hassan's model so applicable to pathological love relationships is that it was specifically designed around the concept of cognitive dissonance and the idea that dissonance results when our behaviors, thoughts, and emotions are not in alignment with one another. Hassan himself explicitly makes the connection between high-control relationships and cults through his model:

> *Controlling, unhealthy, abusive relationships share the characteristics of destructive cults. . . . Abusive people use tactics listed in the BITE Model to control and exploit others. Isolation from family and friends, secrecy, and estrangement are tell-tale signs.*[126]

One of the most crucial factors of all where pathological love relationships are concerned is deception. A deceptive element is not present in Lifton's model—but it is not needed. Prisoners of war and those living in totalitarian societies do not need to be deceived, and they don't need to be showered with attention as part of their compliance programming. When someone is unaware that they are in a situation where a person or group has a desire to change their thoughts, emotions, and behaviors, their view of reality can become warped as they struggle to figure out what to trust.

Hassan uses the legal concept of "undue influence" to describe the type of psychological manipulation, or mind control, that cult leaders use as opposed to the term "brainwashing." In law, undue influence has usually referred to exploitation of someone's ability to act on their own behalf due to factors such as age or cognitive ability to gain access to an inheritance. More recently, the idea is gaining steam that this concept can be used in abusive situations to demonstrate psychologically manipulation and mind control. Alan Scheflin, a professor emeritus of law, developed a seven-point model, the Social Influence Model (SIM), that courts could use to analyze whether undue influence has occurred:[127]

1. **Influencer**

   Who is the influencer, and what is their relationship to the influencee? Hassan notes that "often the influencer/ predator or predatory organization has narcissistic characteristics like pathological lying and lack of empathy," and "psychological testing could be done on the influencer to determine their healthiness."[128]

2. **Influencer's Motives**

   What is the gain to the influencer? For example, financial, sexual, behavioral (i.e., Does the influencee carry out the influencer's will?), ideological (i.e., Has the influencee adopted the influencer's beliefs or thoughts?), and others.

3. **Influencer's Methods**

   What tactics did the influencer use to manipulate the influencee specifically, such as those previously discussed in this book?

4. **Circumstances**

   Was the influencee in an isolating physical environment? How did the influencer control the influencee's access to outside information and other people? Note that these questions overlap with many of the methods of coercive control.

5. **Influencee's Receptivity/Vulnerability**

   Were there situational circumstances that made the influencee vulnerable to undue influence (e.g., moving to a new city, divorce, recent trauma, etc.)? Does the influencee have personality traits that make him or her more vulnerable?

6. **Consequences**

   Was there psychological trauma? Has the influencee lost money? Has the influencee done things that put themselves at risk as a result of undue influence?

Regarding undue influence, Scheflin writes:

Psychology and sociology have now produced data-based and theory-tested explanations of how influence works, or does not work, depending on the variables, that fit within the SIM. The days when brainwashing can be called mere rhetoric or an outmoded piece of political propaganda may be coming to an end . . . people who would have had little reason to talk with each other previously—the brainwashing specialists, the terrorism fighters, the child protectors—suddenly find they have much common ground.[129]

We can now add one-over-one cults, or as we call them, pathological love relationships, to that growing list.

Table 11.1:
Awareness of Coercion in Mind Control Experiences

Examples	Totalitarian societies Prisoners of war False confessions	Cults Sex trafficking Romance scams Pathological love relationships
	High Awareness of Coercion ⟵	⟶ Low Awareness of Coercion
Perception of the Abuser by the Victim	Enemy (hostile)	Friend (trusting)
Method of Gaining Control of Victim	Force	Deception
Core Coercive Element	Giving the victim no choice or making the victim believe he or she has no choice	Offering the victim something he or she desperately wants and keeping it just out of reach
Types of Coercion	Physical brutality and psychological conditioning	Incremental shifts in behavior to condition the victim to desire the will of the abuser (may occasionally include physical brutality but not required)

No one who is aware their pathological partner was attempting to gain control over their lives—and that that was the goal from the beginning—would stay. In a pathological love relationship, however, the informed consent of survivors is compromised because the true nature of the relationship is kept hidden. Survivors of pathological relationships are not aware there is any coercion taking place.

Hassan makes the excellent point that we are always under influence of other forces, including other people, and that this is not always negative. For example, we know that some forms of evidence-based therapy can rewire the brain.[130] When we enter therapy, we know our mental health provider is intentionally going to use techniques he or she has learned to help change how our brains operate so we can live a healthier and happier life.

Relationship partners may try to influence each other as well. If your partner wants to influence you to stay home on a particular evening, he or she may make a case about why it's a good idea and cajole you lovingly. This is not necessarily destructive. If your partner won't take "no" for an answer without flying into a rage or ignoring you and giving you a silent treatment, hints around with threats to cheat if you don't agree, or gaslights you about how you already agreed to it, this is manipulative and damaging to your right to be an equal partner in the relationship.

Margaret Singer, thought reform expert, writes:

> *In society there are numerous elaborate attempts to influence attitudes and modify behavior. However, thought reform programs can be distinguished from other social influence efforts because of their totalistic scope and their sequenced phases aimed at destabilizing participants' sense of self, sense of reality, and values. Thought reform programs rely on organized peer pressure, the development of bonds between the leader or trainer and the followers, the control of communication, and the use of a variety of influence techniques. The aim of all this is to promote conformity, compliance, and the adoption of specific attitudes and behaviors desired by the group.*[131]

Transparency, consent, and respect of personhood make the difference between relationships and group interactions that are healthy and those that are not.[132]

12

A Voice Is Born

Pathological partners lure.

They lure with promises, flattery, lies, and sweet words.

The mask they wear shifts with each new person in their sights, adjusting to our likes and dislikes, filling in crevices to become whatever seems to be missing, and fulfilling our long-lost dreams. What remains the same, however, is that the true nature of the pathological partner remains hidden behind their mask.

With that mask, employed skillfully at the outset, the pathological partner sets the stage to lure and trap by putting it back on again and again.

Imagine your partner with a piece of chalk. With the obsessive love they poured onto you at the beginning of the relationship, they draw a fat, white circle of protection around themselves. Their words and deeds during that time further cast a glittering, golden spotlight of goodness over them, and you formed a bond with the person standing in that spotlight that is difficult to break.

Later, each time they step out of that circle and your brain and body scream at you that you have been violated, they only have to stand under the golden goodness inside that circle so you catch them in its glow to get you to override our instincts.

"No, I'm not trying to hurt you," they tell you. *"I love you."*

Like a blade cutting into winter frost, they etch that phrase into us until it becomes permanently engraved.

When cracks inevitably start to show and lies start to unravel, when one of those worlds start to crumble and then fall apart totally, reality stops being real.

There are biological, psychological, and sociological reasons why from the day we learned or realized something was wrong with our partners, the odds were against us for walking away from them. Everything they have done since that time has only strengthened our bond with them. Yet that bond doesn't make our positive view of them absolute. Our partners haven't embedded a trigger in our subconscious minds as if we were Manchurian candidates in Richard Condon's novel, programming us to act on command when we see the Queen of Diamonds. That's not how mind control works.

It's also why you picked up this book. It's why you can't make up your mind if your partner loves you or hates you. It's why you want to leave, even though you can't.

Sandra L. Brown, M.A., found that cognitive dissonance and intrusive thoughts are the symptoms that are the most disruptive to the ability to function of the survivors she studied. She writes:

> *As soon as she tries to get herself on the "he's bad for me" page, up pops a positive intrusive thought of a time she perceives him as 'good.' When she tries to realign herself to get on the "he's good for me page," up pops an emotional pressure to find out he was cheating. She never stays consistently on one page about*

how she views him so she never really finishes a thought and never really connects to a firm decision about how to handle the relationship. Instead, she's pulled back and forth with the 'ping-ponging' without ever resolving even one conflicting thought. Nothing changes because she never completes a thought without being pulled to the dichotomous opposite belief she was just having.[133]

If cognitive dissonance exists to help us form a stable self-concept and to maintain a consistent view of the rest of the world, when someone stands in the way, what happens to the parts of the brain that use our perceptions to maintain stability and consistency? What happens when someone lives with chronic cognitive dissonance for months and years that they can resolve only temporarily, if at all?

Brown points out that most studies on cognitive dissonance explain what happens in one instance. She writes:

Today, cognitive dissonance is the most widely studied social theory, but it has the least written about psychological treatment for this pervasive phenomenon that affects almost anyone with a conscience. The handful of theorists who threw their hat in the ring had little to contribute toward the idea of cognitive dissonance resolution *or even* reduction.[134]

Although we know a lot about the conditions under which someone feels the anxiety of dissonance and why and how they resolve it, we know very little about the impact of chronic, unresolved cognitive dissonance on the brain and the mental health impact of the anxiety caused by the long-term inconsistency.

We do know that two things seem to occur: (1) executive functioning in the brain declines significantly; and (2) identity begins to break down to accommodate the two ways of viewing the pathological partner, the relationship, and the self.

How to Lose Your Mind

Normally, we manage our cognitive dissonance by using mental shortcuts so we can make a quick decision to act that won't require a major overhaul of our lives or interfere with our habits or routines. The downside is that these mental shortcuts we use to resolve cognitive dissonance have built-in biases that are easy for manipulative people like our pathological partners to exploit.[135]

Table 12.1:
Examples of How Pathological Partners Exploit Cognitive Dissonance Biases

Factor Impacting Cognitive Dissonance	Mental Shortcuts (Biases)	How Pathological Partners Exploit the Bias
New information that contradicts what we already believe	We often reject information that contradicts what we already believe because the investment in older beliefs is much higher. This is true even if the new information is true.	Love-bombing

Repetition of information	We are more likely to adopt the repetition as true information that is repeated but false, even when • it contradicts basic facts • we already know the correct information, or • we are given the correct information	Gaslighting statements; parroted information during love-bombing
Our attitude toward the source of the information	We are more likely to believe information given to us by people or sources we like and to disregard information given to us by people or sources we don't like, regardless of whether either source has true or false information.	Love-bombing; smearing others who may have information that casts them in a negative light to pre-emptively lower the credibility of others

In all three of the examples in Table 12.1, love-bombing is an important tool pathological partners use to create dissonance. Without it, there is no cognitive dissonance. Because of it, we will temporarily resolve the dissonance in their favor, absorbing the evidence of their cruel or inexplicable behavior into our view of them to make sense of it. At least until the next time they do something cruel. In each act, we are looking for the reasons why our pathological partners love us to justify why we're still there. To resolve the cognitive dissonance, we might use what Brown refers to as "rebalancing attempts."[136]

- **Rejecting the facts**: We might pay attention only to information that supports what we already believe.

- **Denying reality**: We may try to convince ourselves that no conflict really exists by focusing on only part of the information or changing our beliefs.
- **Changing our behavior**: We may do things that go against our own values or principles to avoid having dissonant thoughts.
- **Seeking validation**: We may explain the irrational behaviors, thoughts, and beliefs to others, seeking answers from someone who can quiet the constant anxiety that has taken over our lives.

These methods provide us some relief, but it never lasts.

Our brains work on overdrive, draining our levels of cortisol and adrenaline and causing our anxiety levels to spike. Months or years of unresolved cognitive dissonance result in issues with cognitive decline in memory, thinking skills, judgment, and reasoning.[137] These are executive functioning skills. They are the skills affected when someone has attention-deficit hyperactivity disorder (ADHD), schizophrenia, obsessive-compulsive disorder (OCD), bipolar disorder, depression, dementia, and a traumatic brain injury.[138]

Relationships with pathological partners often lead to post-traumatic stress disorder (PTSD). If we struggle with PTSD, too, we are being hit with both trauma and dissonance in some of the same areas of the brain: the pre-frontal cortex, in particular. Brown writes, "Survivors often complain about not being able to think a coherent thought, to remember to feed the children, or about having complete white outs of brain fog."[139]

At the worst of my own executive functioning crisis, I could not remember the steps I needed to take to get to my therapist's office. The steps were to open my phone, order a car using a rideshare app, choose my therapist's address among those already saved in the app, and go downstairs and get in the car when it arrived. Yet as soon as I opened my phone and clicked on the app, my mind would go blank. I forgot what I was trying to do. I suspect something about opening the rideshare app may have been derailing me to dissociate. The shame and fear that I was losing my mind and I would never get myself back was horrifying.

We lose the ability to process what's happening in the relationship in rational ways, to make judgments or decisions for ourselves, or to filter information in ways that will allow us to take care of ourselves. When you can't form a stable sense of reality with what's in front of you, you're at the mercy of what's missing. Our partners are all too happy to fill in the gaps for us.

At some point, all our attention, energy, and mental strength is exhausted just trying to survive, and even then, it isn't enough.

On what miracle superpowers should we draw to reality-test when our partners flip the switch on us again?

Splitting the Difference

As previously mentioned, cognitive dissonance has been reported as the most disruptive symptom among survivors of pathological love relationships. This is partially because it causes such severe executive functioning difficulties that survivors find it difficult to manage day-to-day life. However, there is a second reason why it's so debilitating: it results in a loss of "self."

"I Felt Like I Was Losing Myself . . ."

"There was the feeling that I didn't know who I was anymore. The thinking that I was in fact the abuser. Not being able to speak, because regardless of what I said, it would get turned back on me (I'm a victim, I'm complaining, I'm the one with the problem because of how I react, I'm not being kind to her, I'm not treating her with respect, etc.)."

"I was put into a little box and shut off, treated like dirt by her when she didn't want me, and the pity she would give me when she would let me have even a little affection from her. I felt isolated and yet addicted to just a word from her."

"I was constantly questioning myself, and I have had relationships end before, but no one ever said the things about me that he did. I felt very confused about myself."

"Never knowing how you truly feel because of their control! How they can act like they want you and love you and need you so much in one moment, then the next treat you as though you barely exist!"

"The confusion, the inconsistency, the mindblowingly nasty verbal abuse, and the questions it raised in me about who I knew myself to be, and the possibility that I was this whole other vile person."

"The worst part of the relationship was the decomposition of the self, the fact that you lose track of who you are/were and what you can/could do, losing agency, being unimportant, invalidated, and unheard."

"The feeling of constantly not being good enough, even when I did the things that he liked or said he liked. I also didn't like what I felt like was losing myself and being myself, which I really loved. I had always had confidence and didn't care what other people thought."

"The most painful part of the relationship was when I blamed myself for the abuse and completely lost who I was. . . . I hated who I had become, a zombie. Craving only love I earned from being good."

"I completely lost myself. I have been in a mental coma. Only a few months after our son was born, he got his (now ex) wife pregnant, and I am ashamed to say I took him back."

"I felt as though nothing I did was ever correct, and I didn't even recognize myself in the mirror. I had always been such a strong and independent woman. I was nothing in his eyes."

"The worst part of the relationship was feeling that my life was becoming smaller and smaller. I was disappearing bit by bit. My life was being drained of colour. I was doing everything I could to make the relationship work and not being able to understand why it wouldn't. Becoming emotionally numb and slowly shutting myself off from everything and everyone around me. Ceasing to exist."

"[The worst part of the relationship] was losing me and not realizing how different I was when I was with him."

See Appendix A.

As we saw in Chapter 11, cult research considers identity disturbance to be the primary harm of thought reform and cult indoctrination. Dr. Janja Lalich, former cult member, sociologist, and author of *Bounded Choice*, explains identity disturbance as a process of "reorganization of the person's inner identity or sense of self." She further describes the process as a combination of "emotional appeals, rituals, instruction, self-examination, confession, and rejection, all in a context that deftly combines stress and harmony. Most often guilt, shame, and anxiety are integral to this process." This reference to stress and harmony sounds like the idealization-devaluation stages experienced in pathological love relationships.[140] Although she does not use the term "identity disturbance," Brown did find a very similar phenomenon among survivors of pathological love relationships that she called "disorientation" that leaves survivors "unrecognizable to themselves: "Injuries to her self-perception are the greatest source of the reduction in her resiliency and overall decline due to no longer being able to recognize herself or her internal resources."[141]

There are many names for this disruption to the self: identity disturbance: dual identity, doubling, pseudo-personality, and dissociation.[142] Whatever we call it, it appears that there is some severe trauma that occurs to the "self." But what is the "self?" Ginnie Jenkinson, who wrote about the pseudo-personality, said:

> *I conceptualize the self as changing moment by moment in response to contact with the self, others, and the environment. . . . The personality function of self is the knowable, relatively predictable, verbalized aspect of the self that can be called up in answer to the questions, "Who are you?" or "What are you like?" or "How do you do things?"*[143]

Identity disturbance is about undergoing a personality change over the course of the relationship. We say, do, and think things in violation of the values with which we entered the relationship, and we are unable to explain why even to ourselves. We act as if controlled by something outside ourselves, as if we have a second identity.

The concept of "dual identities" explains that this is possible because we develop two ways of thinking, feeling, and acting to survive that correspond with the two versions of our partners. In other words, the situation with our pathological partners has created in us a second voice that identifies with and defends our partner, suppresses our authentic voice, and avoids reading or hearing any information like what you're reading right now. At other times, our authentic voice reads everything we can get our hands on, trying to break free.

As Hassan points out, the *DSM-V* includes a category for identity change due to thought reform, **Dissociative Disorders: Not Otherwise Specified 300.15 (F44.89):**

> *Identity disturbance due to prolonged and intense coercive persuasion: individuals who have been subjected to intense coercive persuasion (e.g., brainwashing, thought reform, indoctrination while captive, torture, long-term political imprisonment, recruitment by sects/cults or by terror organizations) may present with prolonged changes in, or conscious questioning of, their identity.*[144]

**Figure 12.1:
The Dual Identity in Pathological Love Relationships**

Considering identity disturbance to be a type of dissociation puts it in a similar, but still different, diagnostic category to dissociative identity disorder (DID), or what used to be called multiple personality disorder. Hassan even explicitly claims a dual identity can result in DID.[145] However, other researchers seem to have concluded that identity disturbance or dissociation alone is not the same as DID for many reasons. DID tends to develop in childhood and to be the result of extreme childhood trauma and may result in many identities, which may have no knowledge of one another. Treatment is also very difficult. Identity disturbance that results from thought reform, in contrast, does not usually have these qualities.[146]

Yet not all dissociation is the same. There are two types of dissociation: detachment and compartmentalization. Detachment is feeling disconnected to what is happening around you, as if it has an unreal quality to it or is happening to someone else. Compartmentalization is having knowledge or information that is influencing your behavior when you aren't aware of this knowledge or aren't able to control how it influences your actions.[147]

Compartmentalization is the type of dissociation survivors appear to experience in pathological love relationships. Researcher Richard James Brown explains that in normal environments, we "have a high degree of internal consistency," but in traumatic environments, when some of our goals clash with one another and negative emotions boil to the surface, we compartmentalize our goals and emotions and keep them attached to the autobiographical memories associated with them.[148] Autobiographical memories are processed in the posterior cingulate cortex, the part of the brain that lights up last as we are resolving and eliminating the painful emotions caused by the cognitive dissonance. This might suggest that in traumatic situations when we experience chronic cognitive dissonance, our brains resort to compartmentalization to eliminate the dissonance and painful emotions it causes. Compartmentalization, however, results in a lot of problems.

Long-term compartmentalization of reality compound executive functioning issues in judgment, reasoning, memory and cognition, and cognitive decline—all of which make it even more difficult to leave.[149] Sandra L. Brown, M.A., noted that in her research, women had difficulty remembering why they wanted to leave or holding the abusive acts their pathological partners had committed in their minds.[150] If memory details of the abuse cannot be recalled because of dissociation, they may seem less serious or important—like a bad dream. Further, that survivor "self" has been conditioned to be compliant with the will of the pathological partner. We act outside of who we really are inside, what we really want, and what's in our own best interest.

Duality in our actions is not unique to high-control situations. It has been noted and studied in other contexts. For example, Robert Jay Lifton, who provided the eight criteria for thought reform discussed in Chapter 11, also developed a concept he called "doubling" when he studied Nazi doctors who had to violate their own ethical beliefs in Auschwitz. He didn't intend it to excuse their atrocities. He describes how the doctors came from different backgrounds and had held different degrees of support for Nazism, yet their role as "healers" had been flipped on its head. The concept of "doubling" was offered to provide a more general understanding of how individuals who generally adhere to their society's moral code shift psychologically to engage in conscienceless behavior. He explained that they compartmentalized their "evil" acts into a second "self."[151]

Figure 12.2:
Chronic Cognitive Dissonance and Compartmentalization in Pathological Love Relationships

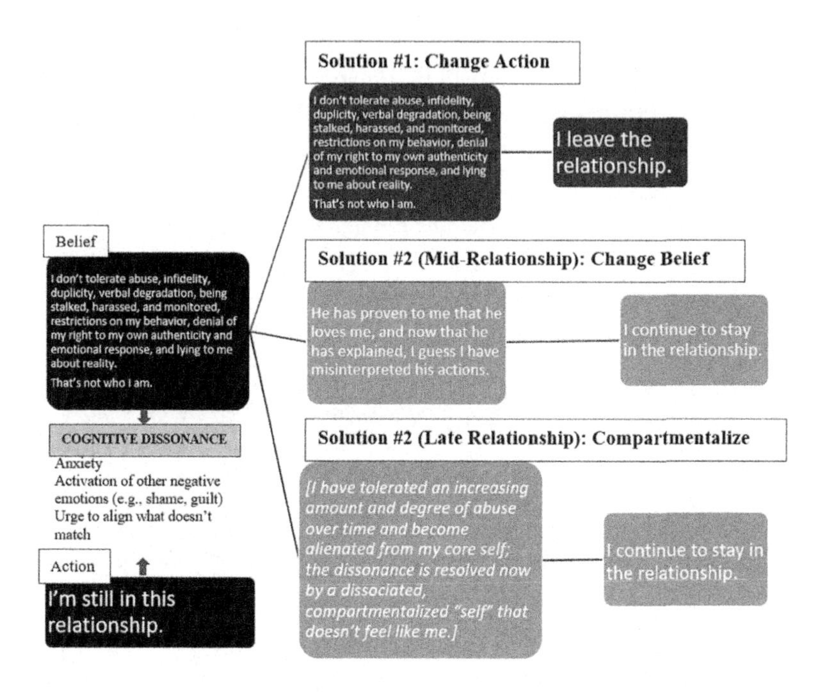

"Doubling," however is not really the same thing in this context as the Nazi doctors were not in high-control environment. The concept of a pseudo-personality, as explained by Jenkinson, provides a more complete explanation of how a high-control group dominates and subjugates the original self. In this theory, pseudo-personality "overlays" the original personality with "a way of acting, feeling, evaluating—which you have taken into your system of behavior but which you have not assimilated in such fashion as to make it a genuine part of your organism—your self." She also quotes a former cult member to explain the concept: "I feel as if my real self was like a little dot, like a seed that was buried in deep soil, and then a layer of tarmac (asphalt) laid over me."[152]

In all these concepts—dual identities, dissociation, doubling, and pseudo-personality—one thing that remains consistent is that the authentic or original identity is not erased or unaware. The new, second identity acts "on top of" or "alongside" the person's true identity.[153] This is why it feels as if we're aware of what we're doing even as we cannot stop it. Lifton writes:

> *Obviously, there must be some connecting element to integrate oneself with the other—otherwise, the overall person could not function; but the autonomy of each is impressive. . . . The two selves can exist simultaneously and confusedly for a considerable time, and it may be that the transition periods are the most intense and psychologically painful, as well as the most harmful.*[154]

This research on cult members has illuminated important information for survivors of pathological love relationships. As Hassan points out, the false identity fades when time apart is spent from the influence causing it.[155] Identity disturbance in pathological love relationship survivors is at heart of this book. It's why you can't leave yet also why you're still holding this book at the same time. Alexandra Stein, cult survivor and author of *Terror, Love, and Brainwashing*, writes:

> *This two-fold functioning...means an autonomous self remains as a part-self, and it is this part-self that may—given the right conditions--be able to resist the system. Doubling is a terrible acrobatics that the human mind performs while in totalist situation of isolation and fear—the creation of a totalist self as a means of surviving. But at the same time, the autonomous self, which experiences and senses (though perhaps doesn't compre-*

> *hend at the time) these real conditions, also exists. This gives some grounds for hope within the terror.*[156]

Breaking through the cognitive dissonance and connecting with your true identity is how you can and will leave the relationship.

13

But . . . What If the Problem Is Me?

Imagine an alternate universe where the infamous shower scene in the film *Psycho* is slightly different. (Another spoiler alert—skip this paragraph if you don't want to read the ending of the film *Psycho*). When the door opens in the background behind Marion as she enjoys the hot water spraying on her neck, we see the dark figure approach from behind her. Then when the shower curtain is ripped aside to reveal the killer, instead of a shadowy figure with a bun and a butcher knife, we see: Norman Bates standing there in a wig. Instead of waiting until the end of the film to find out it wasn't Norman's mother who killed the young woman, we would have learned who the killer was thirty minutes into the movie. It would change the entire mood of the film. We would sit through the remaining hour watching impatiently as Marion's sister and her boyfriend put all the clues together and learned the truth.

Yes, if you could go back and know then what you know now, it would be like knowing the end of a mystery before it unfolded.

Maybe you have been in a relationship like this one in the past, and you are telling yourself you should have seen this coming. Perhaps you had an abusive parent or other relative. Maybe you're telling yourself this is your pattern to overcome, that you're codependent. Maybe you have even internalized the blame your partner has tried to get you to shoulder, and you believe you deserve this or that this is your destiny.

This is no one's destiny. It's also not your fault. The most comprehensive research we have available suggests that codependent traits are not a precursor to pathological love relationships and that most survivors of pathological love relationships are not survivors of child abuse.[157] The reason why it matters is that even if you *are* struggling with one or more of these issues, pathological partners use deceptive and manipulative techniques that work on everyone, and failing to recognize that leaves you open to a lot of self-judgment—not to mention, potential revictimization. Let's recap:

Your partner made up a version of themselves that didn't exist, manipulated you into a relationship, and hid their true intentions. Remember the primary distinguishing feature of a pathological love relationship is that the abusers manipulate their partners into the relationships by creating a false persona, or "mask," based on the needs and desires of the targeted person.[158]

At the beginning of the relationship, the abuser intentionally lies about his or her past, mirrors their partner's likes and dislikes, and makes grandiose promises to fast-track the relationship. The pathological partner also puts their partner on a pedestal, intentionally "love-bombing" him or her with excessive praise and flattery. All this customized attention and affection is deliberately designed to elicit trust, vulnerability, and intense emotional bonding.

Your partner has continued to psychologically manipulate you, using tactics that:

- intentionally tear down your self-worth
- erode your boundaries
- condition you to behave in ways that go against your own best interests
- elicit feelings of paranoia and anxiety
- induce cognitive decline
- force you to lose your internal compass for knowing when to trust yourself
- alienate you from yourself

Social psychological research has demonstrated we are especially prone to comply under the right circumstances. Zimbardo, the psychologist in charge of the Stanford Prison Experiment, wrote:

> *Conformity, compliance, persuasion, dissonance, reactance, guilt and fear arousal, modeling and identification are some of the staple social ingredients well studied in psychological experiments and field studies. In some combinations, they create a powerful crucible of extreme mental and behavioral manipulation when synthesized with several other real-world factors, such as charismatic, authoritarian leaders, dominant ideologies, social isolation, physical debilitation, induced phobias, and extreme threats or promised rewards that are typically deceptively orchestrated, over an extended period in settings where they are applied intensively.*[159]

We can be convinced to override our personal morals, values, and instincts when:

- others around us are doing something that makes us question whether our instincts or beliefs are accurate;
- someone in authority pits a core value of following orders against another of our core values;
- there are other social pressures or time constraints on our actions that distract us from our values;
- we take a series of small actions and each one seems insignificant;
- and in other situations.

The manipulative techniques and principles our partners used are the same ones at work in prisoners of war and hostage situations, sex trafficking, and totalitarian societies. You are suffering some of the same symptoms as individuals who experience these events, yet very little treatment for these symptoms exists for people who exit a relationship with a pathological partner because this is a new area of domestic abuse research in clinical practice.

Maybe you're wondering if there was something about you that drew your partner to you. A range of characteristics and qualities seem to attract pathological partners to survivors. Examples of reasons why pathological partners find their partners desirable can include status, sex, money, affection, support, a home, a cover of normalcy, adoration, or other qualities or items, tangible or intangible. They often feel having a person in their lives with those qualities can elevate them or make them feel powerful. Beyond what pathological partners are looking for, however, what is it that their partners have in common?

Sandra L. Brown, M.A., worked with Purdue University to learn more about victims of pathological love relationships. In their study of 600 survivors, they found that 75% of the women had high levels of agreeableness and conscientiousness. Those personality traits are associated with being trusting, tolerant, willing to help without expectation or desire for anything in return, being upfront, thoughtful, and goal-oriented, giving others the benefit of the doubt, and being resourceful and self-confident. High levels of agreeableness and conscientiousness are also associated with having a high level of empathy.[160] It's probably unsurprising that low-conscience individuals would target highly empathetic people, right?

However, these traits may now seem problematic to you in the face of exploitation—or perhaps other people have told you they are. Your partner's pathology may also be causing you, in that dual-self state, to do things that look like the pathological versions of some of those traits—being perfectionistic about and obsessed with pleasing your partner, trying to keep the relationship together at all costs, or ignoring or denying evidence of horrendous behavior right in front of you, for example. Brown states people confuse the development of these traits with long-term codependency generated prior to the relationship because there is a lack of understanding of pathology.[161] However, doing these things may cause you to become self-blaming or mistake those *original, beautiful* qualities of yours as codependent traits.

In addition, once we broaden our scope and look across all types of deceptive, predatory, and coercive behavior, *situational vulnerability* is the only common factor. In other words, there are situations in our lives when we are more vulnerable. These tend to be situations where we are going through some type of life change or transition that causes us to be distracted or isolated from our usual support system or to feel lonely or otherwise emotionally low. Sandra L. Brown, M.A., writes:

> *Predators shop in the vulnerability aisle. While these Cluster B/psychopaths have shown a definitive preference for successful women, what makes those successful women accessible at that time is their current situation (or for him, opportunity) that has created vulnerability.*[162]

Examples of these life changes include divorce, breakups, a move from one location to another, a job change, financial crises, health crises, losing loved ones, and starting or leaving school. Any type of major shift in our lives that causes our identities, values, roles, or routines to be in flux provides an opening for someone predatory to step in and fill some of those voids while we're not quite at the top of our game. We may also become more open to change and new ideas during times of life transition. Across research from cults to sex trafficking to romance scams to pathological love relationships, this holds true.[163] In fact, it's true for general scams and cons, from the three-card Monte on the busy sidewalk to the threatening IRS phone calls. There is nothing shameful about being in a situation that makes us vulnerable to exploitation when everyone experiences life change. As Maria Konnikova, author of *The Confidence Game,* writes, "Everyone will fall victim to a confidence artist of one stripe or another. Everyone will fall for it."[164]

We are never responsible for someone else's abusive treatment. Your partner is responsible for his or her actions. You didn't know your partner was going to treat you this way when you met them—he or she love-bombed you into oblivion. You've been deceived and never consented to be in a relationship like this one. On top of it, your partner is using mind control techniques to keep you from recognizing and acknowledging the deception.

Instead of beating yourself up and wondering if you're the problem—maybe try something different. I'd like for you to try to see the bigger picture. Imagine stacking all these things on top of one another. Each individual factor is a block. You stand next to it, and it towers over you. It's not even a fair fight. Now. Remember, you didn't even know that stack of blocks was there.

Your rights have been violated.

Please ask yourself: how are you to blame? How could this possibly be because of *you*?

QUESTION FOUR:

Where Did I Go?

I went "no-contact" three weeks ago. I even changed states. When I tell him I'm done, he acts as if he doesn't understand. So before "no-contact," he would use his "Jedi mind control" to get me back, not caring whether I wanted to or not. It wasn't a choice anymore. He started to use ultimatums and violence. I would go with him to keep the peace.

—*Tara*, survey respondent

Our partners have spun a web around us of dread and hopelessness, policing our thoughts, behaviors, and emotions. The web's most important function above all the others is to disguise itself as a nest so we can't see it as the trap it is.

As the relationship continues on a downward spiral, we begin to wonder who this alien self is who now acts without our consent.

We are further compressed, and our authentic selves cry out in desperation for relief. This question may come with a realization that if we don't leave, something bad will happen. It is the second realization to emerge in a flash of clarity. The first was when we had a sudden insight that something was wrong with our partners.

This time, we suddenly know something is wrong with *us*. The relationship is making us sick. We can feel the gap between our thoughts and our actions clearly and fully, perhaps for the first time. The ways in which we resolve our cognitive dissonance in the relationship are normally invisible to us, but in these moments, the pain we suppress overwhelms our senses, and we know. We can see the horrible end for the first time. The happy ending is not coming. A part of us still longs for it, but the other part of us has become consumed with survival.

There is nothing left but fear and dread now. We feel our lives slipping away from us, a slow agonizing death. We feel it in our bodies, which have been grinding down: a tightness across the chest, dizziness, startle reflex, flopping heart, tearfulness that doesn't go away, general unease that lets you know you're sick inside. There is nothing else left. All other life activity has been crowded out—work, school, hobbies, other people, daily routines, current events. Then, there are those creeping thoughts that belie the worst possible scenarios underneath it all. *What is the worst possible ending to the relationship you have considered?*

It's all laid bare for you when you see the truth, stripped down, and a puzzle piece clicks into place.

Get out.

Your authentic voice speaks to you. It's a flame in the darkness that shines light on the pathway out if we dare walk down it.

You must walk down the path.

My Story

It was supposed to be over. Amir had gotten married.

After almost three years of being told there was no engagement, because it had been broken off, one day, he finally told me the truth over a text. In three months, the wedding would take place. He couldn't stop it, he said. His mom was already at the destination making final preparations. Still, he claimed it was against his will.

He had spent the past few months becoming increasingly tyrannical, just as he had when we lived together. He stalked me at bars when I went out with my friends, taking pictures of me talking to my male friends and sending them to me, calling me a whore. If I was out with a friend and didn't respond to a text from him immediately, he would make an obscene comment about what he assumed I was doing, call me degrading names, and cut off contact until he was ready to talk to me again, and I'd have to spend time trying to "prove" that nothing was going on—an impossible task. He found hairs on the towels in my apartment and claimed it was evidence men had been in my apartment, forgetting I not only had a roommate but that she had a boyfriend. If things were arranged on my dresser differently than they were the last time he was in my apartment, it made him suspicious about why my room looked different. He claimed one of my belts was a man's belt, and a man must have left it behind in my bedroom. I became paranoid each time my phone buzzed with a text or app notification about how he would react, knowing he would make an accusation about who was sending it, and a night could suddenly turn into one of rage and terror.

By the time I found out he was about to get married, my health was in decline. I was jumpy, unable to sleep. My heart would squeeze in my chest for no reason, and I would get dizzy and have trouble breathing. When I read the words that the wedding was really going to take place, I stumbled into my bathroom and threw up. Then, I screamed, and I cried.

"You're not being supportive," he said.

"Of what?"

"You know I don't want to get married, and all you've done is make this about you," he said.

Underneath the anxiety and grief, I felt something else: the tiniest hint of relief. There was a voice inside me that wanted to say something else about it other than how terrible it was, but I couldn't hear it yet. The threat was no longer an unknown, however. Instead of turning all around in circles looking for the unknown peril, my brain seemed to hyper-focus, narrowing in on that one date on the calendar.

The week before he was to leave, he took me to play pool at a bar down the street from my house. As we stood together at one end of the table about to start a game, he suddenly grabbed my shoulders.

"Let's get married. Then when I get there, I'll have to tell everyone I can't do it because I'm already married."

"What—no."

"Okay, then I'll tell my dad now, and he'll know it will be too late."

"I'm not doing that," I said. "I'm not getting married like that under these circumstances."

I just couldn't believe it was actually going to happen. I couldn't believe he could actually go through with it. How could you claim someone was the love of your life, then marry someone else within days?

And then, it was time for him to go. As he stood in front of me, saying good-bye, I waited to see if he would say it again: "Let's get married so I don't have to go." Maybe I'd do something crazy and say "yes" this time. I couldn't hold all the bad things he'd done in my head.

"There will be a sequel to our story," he whispered. "It's not over." It was as if he thought we were in one of the movies we'd watched together—our own version of Titanic, *or* The Notebook, *or some other ill-fated love story. He had recently given me a bracelet that had "Beauty" engraved on it, then shown me one he could wear that said, "Beast."*

I shook my head sadly.

"No? No sequel?" he said, and I could tell from his voice he didn't believe me. After all, he was standing there after everything that had already happened.

I stared at him. Every time I'm around you, I'm a little closer to fading away, and every time you go away, I hate you that much more, *I wanted to say.* You hurt me so much I crawled away somewhere inside myself to die slowly, but some other part of me was still in love with that fake person you made me so dependent on for companionship and comfort. Every time you thought I was about to stop loving you, you'd put that face back on and pour yourself all over me. You'd swoop right back in to pull me out of that darkness just so I would see you as the light. You were the only person who said good morning every day, who asked me how my day was and how I was feeling, and the only person who said good night. You were the keeper of the knowledge of me. And you used it to set me on fire.

I wanted to say something poetic like that, but I didn't think he deserved to hear it. Instead, I said, "You getting married is the best thing that ever could have happened to me."

It didn't matter. He was still smiling smugly as he left.

I thought I knew how it ended.

Yet even as I tried to move into a new stage of my life, in the weeks afterward, he continued to text me. He sent me a picture of himself on his wedding day wearing a different bracelet, one I had once given to him, swearing it was proof I was the one he loved. I didn't want to hear from him, yet I couldn't stop talking to him. One day, he was kind and loving, the next suspicious and hurling insults, claiming I didn't love him and was moving on. The endlessness of it continued a duality in my head I had tried to leave behind but had ground me down into a shadow. I was drifting through the world, but no one could see I was being kept behind clear soundproof, shatter-proof glass, slowly suffocating to death.

Then when he arrived back to the United States after his wedding, his messages became even more relentless.

"I found all of our pictures. I thought I lost them." The E-mail I received one night contained a link to a shared drive on the Internet with hundreds of pictures we had taken over the years.

I closed my eyes, breathed deeply, then began typing a response.

"This relationship was bad for me, Amir. I don't want to rehash everything. I believe you loved me, loved something in me, but you also hurt me very much."

His response was immediate. "To be honest, it wasn't all bad. I didn't hurt you all the time. We had good times too. I was wrong, and I'm sorry. One day, you will know everything, and you will know my love was real."

"You tell that to all of us. All the women you string along. You have no loyalty to any one of us."

"Okay, you believe that, Kristen. You're really going to sit there and tell me what I feel about you? You can't because you don't know what I feel. Let me just tell you one thing. Don't ever compare yourself to anyone."

"I've seen it for myself. But you can't hurt me anymore."

"Don't say I can't hurt you. It was never my intention to hurt you. I just got myself in a hole I couldn't get out of. I know sorry isn't enough, but I never wanted to do you wrong. You were my

everything. I will always love you, and no one can take your place. Can I call you? I would like to see you."

"We are never going to see each other again." Every cell in my body seemed to stand at attention, on edge at the idea of letting his chaotic presence disturb the small amount of peace I'd manage to cobble together around me in the last few weeks.

"Okay, as you wish. We can meet in public but never mind."

"For what?"

"I just want to talk."

"About what?"

"Everything."

"That isn't a compelling answer," I responded. Yeah, talk, *I thought. When had he ever wanted to talk about anything throughout our entire relationship? What did "everything" mean? It left me to fill in the blanks and said nothing.*

"I want to explain," he said.

I considered his proposal to meet. It was a horrible idea, yet I was burning with curiosity. I desperately wanted to know—no, I needed *to know—how he reconciled all the things he did and why he did them in the first place. His promises to explain things to me were the most valuable things he could have dangled in front of me, and the "meeting in public" offer tempted me.*

"I'll meet you somewhere in public after work," I told him.

The next day, however, our plan to meet in front of the Washington Monument was thwarted when the temperature dropped that September afternoon into the thirties, and rain started to fall. Against my better judgment, I told him to meet me at my apartment instead.

I'd confirmed that he was willing to answer my questions, and I was surprised when he followed me upstairs with the same enthusiasm to answer them he'd previously expressed. Yet I'd been here before with him—the trap to get me alone. It seemed different this time as we sat face-to-face, him only looking at me expectantly, not speaking. I could feel his confusion and impatience.

My stomach flip-flopped. How many minutes could he sit here with his own actions the focus of conversation before his hostility escalated? What would I do if I asked him to clear up an inconsistency and he flew into his usual rage and verbally or physically assaulted me?

"I . . . sometimes get sidetracked when we are talking because we go off on tangents," I said. "And I lose track of what I wanted to ask or what I was confused about. I wrote down some of what I wanted to say, so let me see how I wanted to start."

I didn't say why I got sidetracked. I didn't explain that I was scared of him. Instead, I unfolded the piece of paper I'd tucked in my pocket and read the first few sentences. Once I recognized I was staying focused and not dissociating, my confidence increased, and I put it down and looked into his eyes and tried to talk from my heart.

"When you were gone and we weren't really talking, Amir . . . my life made sense again. I know that when the two of us are talking, things feel complete for you, but all the anxiety falls on me because I can't make any sense out of the world."

He looked away from me and sat in silence.

I continued, "I see what you do, and I hear what you say, but the two of those things don't make sense together. I need to know what you're thinking and feeling when you do the things you do so I can understand why they happen. I've asked you this before, and you never come up with a satisfactory response. It's affecting me. It's affecting my health. It's making me sick. I can't keep doing this."

He was still looking away from me stern-faced. I could tell he wanted to speak, but he said nothing. I took a breath to stop myself from rushing, but it didn't help much. He's going to explode. He's going to get up. He's going to attack.

"All I want is for you to tell me the truth about what you feel and think and how you reconcile all these very different things going on in your life. I think I deserve to understand that. Even if you think it's not something I'd want to hear. Even if you think

it would hurt me. It would ease my heart so much. I need to fill in these gaps."

"I don't understand it either," he said, finally breaking his silence.

"But something has to be going through your mind. What are you thinking when you do these things?"

He shrugged. "All I know is I talk to you, and I want to be around you because I feel happy. I can be myself."

"But then, where does that feeling go when you're not here? What do you feel when you're not around me?"

"I mean, I do feel bad, but . . ."

"Bad about what exactly? How can you compartmentalize me, then go home and pretend like I'm not here?"

"I don't. Why did I contact you again after I got married? Why can't I stay away from you? Why do I send you messages all the time? I think about you all the time."

I chose my next words carefully. My heart still pounded in fear. "Yes, but I'm not a part of your life. And I don't understand why you've been so cruel from the very beginning if you love me so much. And what about all the lies? None of this makes any sense, Amir."

"I was just young."

"Amir, some of these things you just did a month ago. I mean, they're still happening. Do you not see that these two lives you lead are what I'm asking you about? It's not just about me. Do you think it's okay to treat everyone this way? Do you care about anyone you hurt? Do you think you're hurting your wife, too, just by talking to me? I want to know why you do things that hurt everyone."

"She's not the kind of woman who cries about things like this. I've told you this so many times that I'm here because I love you."

"But . . . then why did you marry someone else?"

"My family. I did it to make my father happy. Nobody cares about him and my family."

I wanted to cry out in frustration. Any moment now, *I thought.* Any moment, his eyes will turn hard. He will say how much he hates me, and I deserve all this, telling me I'm right: it was a lie, the whole relationship was a lie all along, and he never loved me. Then, this entire conversation is undone, and I'm back at the beginning again with the dualities I can't unravel.

"Amir—then why do you keep contacting me? Why are you sitting in this room with me? If you made such a big sacrifice for your family, why would you risk hurting your father or throwing it away? All these things you're saying don't come together. Do you understand what I am asking? What is going through your mind?"

"You. You are what is going through my mind."

Something tried to bubble to the surface. There was no detail to explain how things had unfolded, no inner monologue. It was as if he had rehearsed answers for certain lines of questioning. If I pressed a button, I'd get a certain response. If I pressed it again, I'd be sent to a different question's response. Eventually, I was just routed back to the beginning.

He asked me for a kiss, and at first, I turned my face away. The second time he tried, I didn't try to resist.

Yet something was different. I didn't feel anything. Wait, no, there was something. Buried under the nothingness, there was something almost like repulsion, disgust. I not only couldn't return the kiss, I felt an energy force inside me willing my arms to thrust forward and push him away.

But my arms were frozen, and the kiss didn't end until he pulled away and smiled, satisfied that one more time, one more piece of me could be siphoned away.

A part of me felt empty, sad. I'd once given him everything I had, and now there was nothing. I was dead inside.

I pulled away from him, disgusted by the look on his face. "You know, there will be men out there who will actually want me for me. You have tried to make me feel like no one will ever want me.

You're hollow inside. That's why you use people." I felt the words coming out of my mouth, but I didn't know where they had come from.

"What do I use you for?" I thought it was a strange thing to say. The verb he'd chosen was wrong for a hypothetical question.

"Everything. Anything," I said everything I could think of that came to my mind. "Attention. Love. Sex. Flattery. Acceptance. Having someone do things for you."

I moved away from him and sat down on the floor and started to cry uncontrollably. I expected him to get up and storm out, and a part of me wished he would. Instead, he reached out for me, but I didn't let him comfort me. I only sat frozen, my mind whirling.

The thought hit me that I would never get away from him. Until one or both of us was dead, I would never escape this relationship. It would go on exactly like this, and I would keep getting smaller until nothing remained of me.

I kept hearing the voices of other people who told me about his behavior once I'd caught on and asked, people who didn't even know each other but who said almost the same thing. People who warned me about him. The ex-girlfriends who wondered what I was doing with him. My eyes popped open.

"You're not that special," I said, calmly, without malice. "What's special about you? Tell me." I didn't expect an answer.

Something about his action of getting married proved everything everyone said, and I could see the truth I had never seen before. He was just a man and not the great love I'd held him out to be. Sure, I loved him, but what I also treasured was the special bond I thought we shared. Share. By definition, a bond is something you share. It means both people are in it. Yet he didn't think there was anything special between us worth holding onto, or else he would have held onto it. If that was true, then there never was a bond. It was all just words he had told me so I would think there was a bond he could exchange for a commitment I made because of lovesickness and confusion. Meanwhile, his actions were what spoke the truth. In fact, he'd never valued it. There were his words and my commitment, but that does not make a bond. Without his commitment, too, there is nothing.

The realization didn't make me sad. It gave me strength.

I didn't know how, but I knew I was going to do it: get out and get away.

The alternative was that I was going to die crushed under the unbearable weight of that man's presence in my life at his own whims.

14

Why Your Relationship Can Never Work Out No Matter What You Do

Our partner's behavior can remain inexplicable to us, even as we start filling in the blanks.

Sometimes it seems as if our partners intentionally try to hurt us, and other times, we may fail to see the sinister motives in what our partners do. Sometimes it seems as if they go out of their way to hurt us in ways that end up causing hardship to themselves. It can be difficult to find the reasons for what our partners are trying to achieve because each action may seem unconnected to the last. Nothing they do can be trusted to show their true intentions, and nothing they say can be trusted to indicate their true desires. We're constantly trying to put the answers together to form one cohesive picture of their behavior.

Therefore, we bounce around from question to question even when we think we already answered one of them. We have been answering questions throughout the book that explain their behaviors, yet still it probably seems mysterious. As soon as you think you understand one action, they do something to negate your understanding that made so much sense a moment before. This is why just understanding their individual behaviors in isolation is not enough, otherwise thinking about the relationship is like a puzzle you can never solve.

To put this problem in a larger context, let's re-phrase all the questions we've answered so far in this book into "why" questions.

- ***"Is my partner really pathological?"*** and ***"What's wrong with my partner?"***
    - o Why does my partner do [x]? (Questionable Actions)
- ***"Can my partner change?"***
    - o Why does my partner say he or she will change but then doesn't? (Lack of Change)
- ***"Is my partner 'good' or 'bad?'"***
    - o How is it possible that my partner can do both the most loving, thoughtful things for me I have ever experienced and the most devastating things I've ever experienced? (Contradictory Actions)
- ***"Does my partner mean to hurt me?"***
    - o Why does my partner not take me into consideration when doing such hurtful things? (Lack of Consideration for Others)

- ***"Why can't I just leave?" and "What if the problem is me?"***
    - o Why am I so bound to this relationship? Why am I so confused? Why do I always feel like I did something wrong, and at the same time, my partner hasn't taken responsibility for his or her actions? (Personal Inexplicable Behavior)

Figure 14.1:
Summary of Questions about Pathological Partners

We wonder why our partners can engage in such questionable, contradictory actions in which they don't seem to consider us before they do them. Then when they find out they're hurting us, they can't or don't seem to stop doing them. We wonder why our partners say they love us but don't act like it. Perhaps most of all, we wonder why it feels like they've wrapped chains around our throats that keep us from walking out of the relationship.

Chapter 1 described several scenarios in which you might currently be in your relationship and how you may not be sure why you picked up this book. It contained a checklist of items that can describe pathological love relationships and noted that confusion is a warning sign that you're in a pathological love relationship.

These factors in Figure 14.1 are not really inconsistent *with one another*. There is an overarching commonality they share that can help us understand what's really going on and get out of the mind maze we're in. There are two reasons we can't see it. First, some of the individual actions in those factors include contradictions so distracting we can't focus on the big picture. Second, out partner uses words that negate those actions, and those words and actions don't match. Ultimately, this creates cognitive dissonance that keeps us from seeing the truth of who our partner really is. We can't see the common thread because we're constantly bouncing between the "love" question or the "did they do this on purpose" question or the "why did they do this to me" question. We can't even get to the question of "how is all this possible?"

So, what is the common denominator for each of these questions?

**Figure 14.2:
Underlying Factor in the Questions
about Pathological Partners**

The impaired conscience of a pathological individual is the underlying factor that connects each of the puzzling elements of our relationship. People with impaired empathy make decisions that are difficult to understand, but they often cover up their decisions with what they say or with occasional actions that seem kind. They manipulate others into getting the things they want from them and often don't see a need to change. They don't see a problem with their behavior.[165] One reason it can take so long to process this is because it's difficult for people who are not conscience-impaired to grasp the mind of someone who is. Boiling down something so complex to "that's how they see the world" or "their brains work that way" doesn't feel like a satisfying answer. When you can't fathom not taking others into account or repeatedly and knowingly exploiting and causing them harm, there will never be a way to see the world from their point of view other than to simply understand it intellectually and accept it.

So, put the book down and just let this sit for a little while if you need to.

Anytime you have a question about something your partner did, see if you can answer it with "because he or she has an impaired conscience." How does it feel?

When we begin to accept what having an impaired conscience means, it doesn't mean we like it. It just means we can start to see their actions in a different way. They're not personal. We can also start to fill in some of the gaps for why they behave as they do.

As explained in Chapter 5, pathological love relationships follow a pattern called the narcissistic cycle of abuse that has four stages: idealize, devalue, discard, and hoover. It explains well what pathological partners do; however, it doesn't provide any information about why or how. Trauma therapist Christine Hammond provides a useful model that helps describe the motivations of low-conscience individuals in these situations.[166]

Figure 14.3
Hammond's Model of Narcissistic Abuse

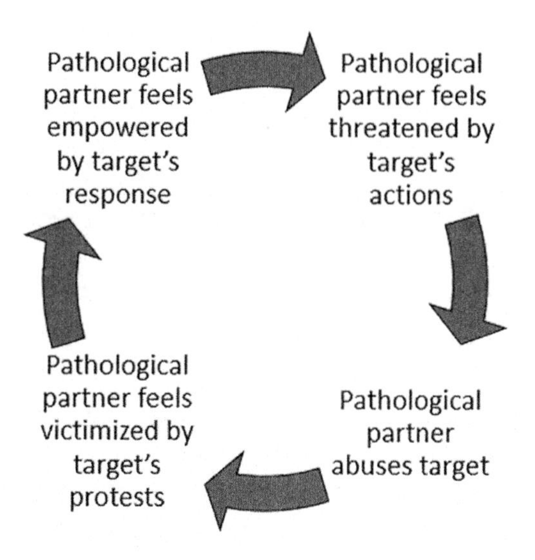

- ***Step 1: The pathological partner feels threatened by someone's actions.*** The event would likely not upset a non-disordered person.

- ***Step 2: The pathological partner abuses the person who upset them.*** The type of abuse can vary. The purpose of the abuse is to "even the playing field" in the eyes of the pathological partner and restore a sense of control or positive feelings about the self. The pathological partner sometimes lies about or denies the abuse, which they feel is justified, perhaps to avoid shame or restore the relationship to its former state.

- ***Step 3: The target of the abuse protests.*** The pathological partner feels victimized by the target's response and uses the actions as evidence that they are the ones being harassed and abused in the relationship. The switchback occurs when the pathological partner uses manipulative tactics to coerce the partner into adopting their pathological worldview.

- ***Step 4: The pathological partner feels empowered by the partner's response.*** The partner has accepted the pathological partner's version of events, and the pathological partner's abuse was never acknowledged.

In this model, pathological partners go from being an entitled victim who deserves to treat us in an abusive way in their own minds (e.g., verbal abuse, cheating, silent treatments, sabotage, etc.) to being an indignant victim when we rightly protest their treatment. It doesn't matter whether we whisper or scream, are timid or aggressive, question or accuse, politely assert our rights or demand they stop the crazymaking. They will see it all the same way: we are harassing them for something they had every right to do. It's a double hit for us. Sandra L. Brown, M.A., refers to this as the victim/rescuer/persecutor triangle, or the Karpman Triangle. She explains that when they play one of these roles, we are also pulled into the drama and manipulated into playing another of the roles in the triangle. For instance, when they are playing the victim, they will manipulate us into being the rescuer.[167]

Here's the really insidious magic trick.

By the time we are dragged through this cycle with them a few dozen times, we become unhinged and out of control trying to get off this merry-go-round with them. They often end up with the reaction they believe they always had. We may end up going toe-to-toe with them, saying or doing something "crazy" we would never say or do under any other circumstances. *See—no wonder I act the way I do,* your partner may say. *Look at how you're acting*. And there it is. You swallow your partner's projected shame, and while you've been hiding all your partner's abuse and defending their actions, they take this manufactured person you've become and parade it around in front of everyone to prove how they're being victimized by you. Jackson MacKenzie, author of *Psychopath Free*, writes:

> *They want you to confront them about these things because they are so seemingly minimal that you will appear crazy and jealous for bringing them up. They will calmly provide an excuse for everything and then blame you for creating drama. Covert abuse is impossible to prove because it's always strategically ambiguous.*[168]

The Expanded Cycle of Pathological Love Relationships

Now let's put everything we've talked about in the book so far together into one big model. We'll call it the Expanded Cycle of Pathological Love Relationships. What I hope to do with it is explain the entire dynamic of what's going on in your relationship. This includes your partner's actions and motivations and your reactions to your partner's behavior and motivations.

In addition, a complete explanation of the cycle shows how the dynamic changes over time. We don't act the same once we go through it a hundred times as we did the first time around. Neither does your partner. We may become more anxious, and our behavior may become more contradictory to match theirs as we struggle with our cognitive dissonance. Our behavior may also become more extreme. We may become both more contrite to win back their favor, and we may become angrier at their mistreatment. As we grow weaker and more unhinged, their behavior grows more abusive and violent, and they become further emboldened.

No matter where you are in this cycle right now, hopefully now you'll be able to see how things got here and why.

Figure 14.4: An Expanded Cycle of Pathological Love Relationships

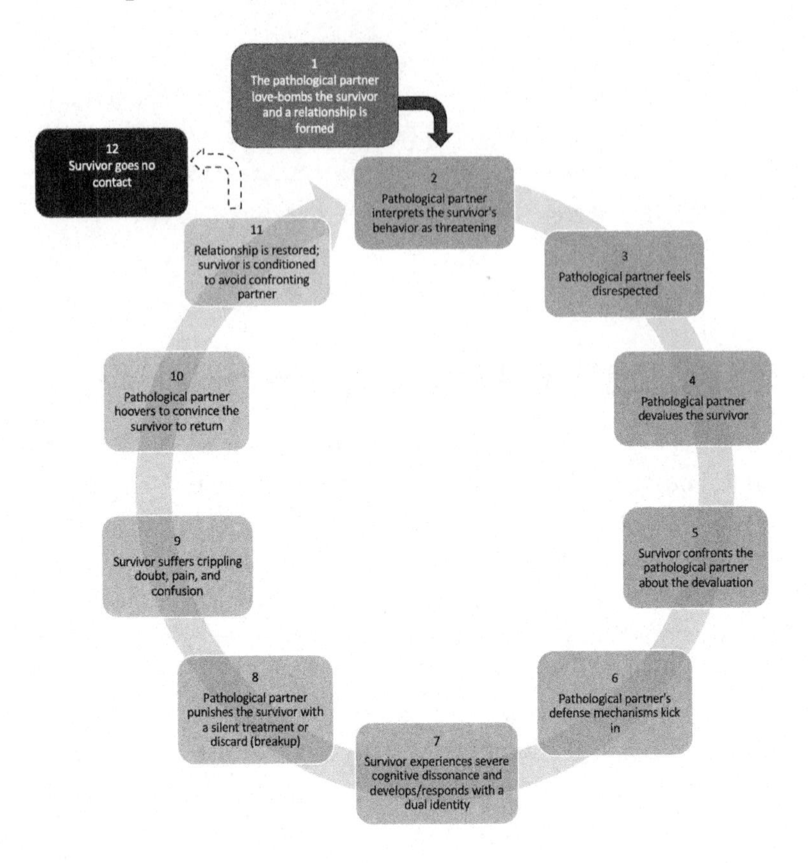

Stage 1. The Pathological Partner Love-Bombs the Survivor

We've discussed love-bombing extensively throughout the book. To review, love-bombing occurs when pathological partners put their targets on a pedestal, bombard them with attention and affection, and create an emotional "safe space." This safe space is a perfect reflection of everything you want to see and hear, based on what your partner learned about you. There is fast familiarity, accompanied by grandiose statements about destiny or a once-in-a-lifetime connection. For you, it induced positive feelings of love, trust, and vulnerability. For your partner, this period is what they crave most, as it is when you reflect to them the purest version of their own idealized view of themselves.

Stage 2. The Pathological Partner Interprets the Survivor's Behavior as Threatening

The idealization cannot be maintained because the relationship is not supported by principles that make up a healthy relationship, such as mutual trust, honesty, and commitment. Your partner has an interpretation of the world that causes them to put themselves at the center of the relationship. Pathological individuals often maintain double standards about what's acceptable in relationships. In *Stage 1*, they may disguise their control of your activities and time as concern. However, beginning in this stage, as cracks begin to show and you recognize their double standards, they begin to feel threatened by actions that don't conform to their unreasonable expectations. You may not even realize what you did or why it triggered them. Sometimes they simply become bored or annoyed when the inevitable problems of the real world begin to pierce the relationship fantasy.

Stage 3. The Pathological Partner Feels Disrespected

Regardless of the reason your partner now feels threatened, it triggers in them feelings of resentment, emptiness, shame, and disrespect. They never perceive the problem as their own interpretation of events but as something you have done. Your partner feels unappreciated and slighted because you have not made him or her feel special enough, which is a distraction from their feelings of inadequacy. In their minds, they gave you the fantasy—why didn't you just do as they said? It didn't matter that what they wanted from you was out of line. Maybe you even tried to do what they asked a few times, even though you knew it was wrong, just to keep the peace. However, the bar keeps moving. No matter what you do, it's never enough.

Stage 4. The Pathological Partner Devalues the Survivor

You fall off the pedestal. In your partner's mind, you aren't the person they thought you were. Individuals with these personality disorders can suffer from something called "object constancy." If you're not with them, you're against them. Once you are placed into the "bad" category, you are viewed as the enemy. This is when the abuse begins. The cruelty inflicted is limited only to the levels of sadism, self-control, and imagination of your partner. Their devaluations and punishments of you are viewed as justified.

Notably and even more damaging, as the cycle continues, they devalue you *to other people.* They turn the tables on you, sharing slivers of the moments you have questioned their behavior, requested for it to stop, or made inquiries into their actions. Yet they leave out the things they have done to you. By sharing these things, they try to use them as "proof" to others that you are the abusive one, or are "crazy," or harassing them, instead of what they are: reactions to abuse, attempts to uphold your boundaries and maintain your human rights.

Stage 5. The Survivor Confronts the Pathological Partner about the Devaluation

During this stage, your partner's new treatment of you is at complete odds with the soulmate persona portrayed at the beginning of the relationship. Your partner says and does things your enemy wouldn't even say and do and often seemingly without any reason. You have tried to make your partner as happy as they made you, but something is very "off," and you don't understand why your partner has changed. You are devastated but baffled because you can't see they are interpreting your behavior through a pathological, narcissistic filter in which they are the center. You question them about why things have changed, look for answers, maybe even demand to be treated with respect. These are all perfectly rational actions.

The longer the relationship lasts and the more times the cycle repeats, the less rational you become in your attempt to understand your partner's behavior. In later stages, your partner starts to gaslight you about events, telling you things you saw or heard didn't happen. They might even convince you that you are exaggerating the effects of their abuse, and they tell you your emotional responses are the problem. Because of this continued manipulation, your own words and behaviors are no longer consistent as you continue around the cycle with them and feed into their narrative that there is something wrong with you.

Stage 6. The Pathological Partner's Defense Mechanisms Kick In

Your partner's "object constancy" also applies to themselves. When you aren't idealizing them, they cannot see themselves as "good." They can't allow the focus in the relationship to shift to your emotions. If it does even for a moment, they cannot let that happen because of anything they did because of the deep feelings of shame and worthlessness it causes them to feel. They direct you to leave the past behind (but without having to earn back your trust and without changing behavior that caused you to lose trust). If you try to explain why that's difficult or talk about how you feel or what they did, the tactics they use to get you to stop become legendary: deflection, projection, gaslighting, blame-shifting, stonewalling, threats, further abuse, and degradation.

Stage 7. The Survivor Develops a Dual Identity

After the blaming, gaslighting, and refusal to discuss their behavior continues for months or years, you begin to lose touch with your intuition and judgment. Your partner seems to hate you and feels threatened by your behavior, and just as you feel you can't take it anymore, your partner comes back to express their undying love. You never get to resolve these two competing views because your partner's actions are unknowingly drawing you into their distorted, volatile reality. You also develop a trauma response to your partner's behavior, walking on eggshells, having panic attacks, and withdrawing from other activities. Your partner may try to isolate and control your behavior to keep you away from people who would help you see the relationship from an objective point of view.

Stage 8. The Pathological Partner Disappears Temporarily

Your partner becomes increasingly disillusioned, disgusted with your traumatic reactions to their behavior. Stages #2–7 form a mini-cycle within this larger cycle. They have created a looking glass in us in which they see themselves reflected and don't like the image they see. Your partner's cruelty increases as they fail to understand their role in the cycle. Finally, to avoid confronting the totality of what he or she has done, your partner will walk away for a long period of time, known as a "silent treatment" or sometimes even a "discard." He or she will disappear at this stage for days or weeks at a time—or even longer. Sometimes, they do not physically disappear; however, they may ignore you and treat you with contempt or as if you don't exist.

Stage 9. The Survivor Suffers Crippling Pain, Doubt, and Confusion

During silent treatments, you likely feel such extreme panic that your partner is gone that you may feel desperate for them to return. Sometimes, it's a feeling of something Hassan refers to as "floating," in which it feels as if the rest of the world has an "unreal" quality full of triggers that remind us of them and you don't exist without them.[169] You have come to view the entire world through their reality so nothing feels real when they suddenly depart. It's as if everything they ever did to hurt you when the two of you were together has disappeared. The acts you consider and the things you do at these moments to end the pain of their departure are things you never would have considered in any other circumstance. You only know you can't go on living like this.

Stage 10. The Pathological Partner Returns to Draw the Survivor Back In

You are extremely vulnerable to being drawn back into the relationship. Without outside intervention or connecting with your authentic self—the version of yourself who helps you overcome your partner's cognitive abuse—it's almost certainly inevitable. Even if you don't reach out to your partner first, they will usually reach out to you. Pathological partners contact you when they are sure you are ready to accept some version of what they said or did previously that seemed unthinkable to accept at the time.

Stage 11. The Relationship Is Restored Under an Increasingly False Reality

On the surface, the relationship has been restored to its early state of bliss. Yet the result of your partner's absence was to condition and coerce you into accepting his or her version of reality: *if you don't do what I want you to do, I will shut you out of my life.* You must forgive your partner and repress what happened or look the other way. They may even expect you to apologize for whatever they decide you did wrong and promise to "change." If you do these things, you will get the prize: you get your partner back. Yet you live with the cognitive dissonance that will splinter you into two identities. You know deep down all is not well, and the foundation was always rotten, so getting your partner back means there is a problem. For the moment, your partner has put the voice to sleep that has this knowledge. Yet it will be back when the cycle starts again.

The Never-Ending Cycle

How many times have you gone back to your partner? My own answer to that question is in the double digits. Maybe even in the triple digits. Yes, the triple digits. It may very well have been over a hundred times that I returned to my partner after trying to leave. So, don't worry if you're concerned about your answer to this question. I doubt you have me beat. There's no shame in your response to this question.

Have you ever told yourself the relationship was over, then found yourself going back, and you didn't even understand why? How many times did you keep it a secret?

Imagine yourself actually *in* the cycle. Physically in it. Imagine without judgment. Where are you? How did you get to the stage where you are right now—what incident occurred? What will happen next before you get to the next one? Can you predict it? Why does this cycle persist, and still we are unable to escape it even when there is that part of us that wants to?

As the cycle repeats, the stages remain the same each time; however, you and your partner both change as you rotate through it. Each time it starts over, you become weaker, and your partner grows stronger. You are being boxed in. This is why you feel as if you have lost yourself—you have! Every time you have given up more of yourself to try to repair the relationship, your partner takes even more from you and gives you even less in return.

The longer you are in the relationship, the more diminished you become. You may have begun to develop psychosomatic illnesses, which may be trying to force you to act on your behalf to take care of yourself or to send you a message about the danger of your environment.[170] Ironically, it is the most difficult for you to summon your strength to leave even as it is the most crucial for you to do so. Do you think that is an accident? The smaller your partner can make you, the less likely you are ever to escape. **Your partner is feeding you lies about yourself: That you don't deserve better. That you are to blame. That you can make things better if you just try a little harder. That no one else wants you. That *you* are bad. That you are <u>[fill in the blank]</u>.** You were always worthy. You always deserved more than the way your partner treats you.

If you are having difficulty leaving, there is nothing wrong with you. Your partner led you here to this point. But just as he or she manufactured fake problems until you ended up here, you can tear them all down until you lead yourself out and into the final stage of this cycle—the exit. *Your* exit.

If you can predict the next event, the next stage, you can take one small step to forge a new path.

It won't be easy. You will feel like you're crawling out of hell. But you will make it out. This is the secret your partner does not want you to know. You may not believe at this moment you'll ever be free, but for now, if you can glimpse the exit, that means you've found the door.

Stage 12. The Survivor Exits the Relationship

Once the dynamic in the cycle becomes clear, reflection on some level becomes possible. You gain the understanding that, as painful as it is to accept, there is nothing you can do that will ever change your relationship. There can never be a different outcome. This was never a great relationship where something just "went wrong," and if you could only do the right thing, it would go back to being great again. This was always the way things were going to go because of your partner's pathology. Note that healing from what happened and how you choose to feel about what your partner did is another, different path to walk down. First, however, you must decide to leave the relationship and go "no-contact" with your partner. Your true self recognizes that the cycle cannot be broken, and staying is killing you, if not literally, in other ways you can no longer bear.

One of the hardest things you may ever do is kill or weaken your false self, the part of you that loves your partner more than it loves you, so you can allow yourself to walk away.

The rest of this book is dedicated to helping you do that.

15

The Road Not (Yet) Taken

On an early morning in April 2003, Aron Ralston headed out to the Bluejohn Canyon in Utah to do some hiking and canyoneering alone. As he tried to scale down one wall of a narrow canyon out in the desert, he lost his grip. He knocked a boulder loose as he scrambled for safety, and as the rock slid down the wall with him, it pinned his right arm to the side of the canyon. For five days, he stayed down at the bottom of the canyon, becoming weaker as each one passed.

Then, on the sixth day, he escaped.[171]

Now is the part of the book where I must talk about some of the most difficult things you will have to face. Ralston's story can provide us with hope and inspiration for finding the mental courage to do the impossible.

When we reach this point in the relationship, like Ralston down in the canyon with the boulder on his arm, we are trapped and growing weaker with time. During those six days, Ralston didn't only sit there.

He tried to remove the boulder from his arm using tools from his backpack. The rock didn't even budge.

He tried to smash the boulder, but that was even more futile.

Ralston tried calling out for help, but there was no one around to hear him. He was isolated. He hadn't told anyone where he was going, so no one knew he needed help.

He rationed his food and water to try to stay alive long enough for someone to find him; however, he eventually ran out and prepared himself for the likelihood that he was going to die.

Yet on the final day Ralston was trapped in the canyon, he saved himself. To do it, however, he had to do something most of us could not fathom: he had to cut off a part of his arm.

But he did it. He lived.

Ralston reached a turning point where he knew he had to choose between dying and losing his arm. Yet it wasn't only that. He knew if he didn't act then, it would be too late. He couldn't change his mind later, as he would grow too weak to act at all even if he realized later he should have done it when he had the chance.

Once we realize that if we stay in the relationship something bad will happen, we have subconsciously recognized we are left with only two choices: live or die. The nuance in those choices smooths out over time as all our attempts to get our partners to stop abusing and hurting us have been in vain. What we want in our relationship, what we have always wanted, is the impossible dream: we want to be free of the pain our partners cause but without losing our partners. Staying in the relationship, however, means being trapped in the narcissistic abuse cycle indefinitely, absorbing their poison and accepting their blame.

Pathological Love Stories

Feeling Captured and On Edge

"[The most painful part of the relationship is] feeling trapped and the anxiety I feel anytime he is near, calls, texts . . . the gripping fear of what will happen, how he will behave and respond. Future repercussions of one innocent comment I might make—walking on eggshells and trying to reason with an unreasonable man."

"I felt weak, trapped, and suicidal. Suicide ended up being a comfort blanket. The thought that I could always end it all if it really got too much. I was in constant pain, stressed to the max, exhausted from sleep deprivation. My stomach was churning from the moment I woke up each day. All day, every day. I was a wreck, and I hated myself for it."

"I was afraid of him. When I heard his car, I went into a panic, heart pounding, not sure what to expect. . . . I was very lonely."

"The constant feeling of anxiety and game playing that messes with your head and your health. Had to get my heart checked due to the constant anxiety attacks and racing heart syndrome. Never had it before I met the narcissist."

"After her love-bombing phase, she started avoiding me. Hot and cold treatment, not replying to my texts, phone calls. Things [went] from 'I love you. Don't you ever leave me' to 'whatever is going on between us.' I wanted to get out of this but could not. I could not hurt her. Suddenly, she changed her entire attitude towards me."

"The relationship isn't a real one. It feels fake. I can't relax. Have to be on-guard, non-trusting at all times. I have to be analyzing what he is thinking and why he is doing what he is doing, saying what he is saying. I am always one step behind. It's so exhausting."

"[A] constant sense of imbalance and uncertainty . . . was engineered. Information was used as a weapon; he would keep it from me for control and punishment. And I was never sure of where I stood with him, what our level of commitment was, what our boundaries were. Every time I tried to set any, he would break them immediately and then make it my fault that he had. My life became a constant quest to seek his attention."

"The confusion of what was happening in the beginning. Later in the relationship, the walking on eggshells constantly, I would feel/sense the devaluation period coming. I was much weaker emotionally and mentally at this point, and all I could do was shut down. When I would try to fight back, she would say, 'Why are you so defensive?' There was no right response, sadly. I know that now."

"Trying to 'measure up' to the fantasies he spun around how my life should be and, at the same time, fighting the false interpretations he gave for who I was. Part of me knew I'd been captured and tricked. Probably knowing all that deep down and being unable to get free was the hardest part."

See Appendix A.

Every time you concede another millimeter of one of your boundaries or a basic human right because you try to avoid the cycle, another small part of you is erased. You may stop reacting to anything your partner does at all, and it won't even be by choice anymore. Eventually, you will become drained of your will to participate in life. You may stop feeling anything at all.

Or you can live. You can leave the relationship. To leave, you must accept what feels unthinkable right now. The truth we must face to save ourselves is that our partner is not separate from the abuse he or she inflicts. We must free ourselves from the relationship to be free of the exploitation.

We cannot stay in the relationship because our partners will never stop abusing us.

I understand what it feels like to deny this truth. When this dual choice began to form in my mind (live or die), I was not ready to face the initial truth of the false persona he had presented to me because I was not strong enough to let go of it and fully inhabit my authentic self again. It had been torn down and could not handle the pain of the truth yet.

Then one day, the cracks in what seemed genuine about his love for me grew so large it was as if my very reality had cracked open, and I could no longer deny the other one buried underneath. I finally saw through the mirror he held up, and something lived behind it on the other side. The dream they want you to see doesn't fall away all at once. It winks out in a slow fade, like a sunset tugging at your heart on a day you never wanted to end—but also like a bullet wound that should have killed you that scabs over instead.

Like Ralston, we try every other option before reaching our point of desperation and pain. We try reasoning with our partners. We try demanding our rights and to be treated with respect. We try just walking away. We may have tried reaching out to others, but no one really understands. No one else can protect us.

No one ever really leaves a relationship with a pathological partner. They escape one.

Our partners have made sure that when we leave them, we will have to rip out a piece of ourselves and leave it behind to do it.

The Narcissistic Abuse Cycle Is Not Your Destiny

Just as I escaped my relationship, you will too. With the new knowledge of how you got where you are and why you can't just walk away, you can use the stages of the narcissistic abuse cycle itself to get closer to the exit by changing how you react to your partner.

We know the cycle repeats each time because our partners always perceive something we do as disrespectful after they come back to draw us into the relationship. They will always feel victimized again when we fail to live up to their expectations. **Recognize this for what it is.**

This pattern is their default filter that constantly shifts people in and out of the categories of "good" and "bad" based on how they view the behavior of others. **You did nothing to jump-start the pattern.** It is their view that never lasts. They will always interpret actions they don't control as threatening. Each time the cycle starts again, they will find a new behavior to be threatened by. The verbal tactics our partners use to deny any responsibility for wrongdoing, however, do not allow us to see the truth. ***This is why things feel upside down and why we chase after the crumbs they offer—they have made themselves not only a source of love but the sole source of logic.*** The next time around, our box will be even smaller. This is it. This is what's behind the curtain. This is the core of pathological love relationships.

Once you put yourself in your partner's mind long enough and remember it was always them who had the twisted way of perceiving things, then other beliefs you have that trap you in the relationship start falling apart. You can start to replay in your mind the times when your partner tried to make you believe you did something wrong. He held up a funhouse mirror, but what was in it was his reflection—not yours!

Even though you are trapped in this cycle and feel as if you can't get out, there are four important opportunities for you to do something differently to change the pattern the next time it cycles. Each small act can eventually cause a major change, and these acts help put your authentic self back in control.

In the expanded cycle of narcissistic abuse, these opportunities to act are:

- ***When the cycle starts again after we are drawn back into the relationship (Stage 11)***
- ***When we confront our partners over their abuse (Stage 5)***
- ***When we consciously struggle with our dual identity (Stage 7)***
- ***When our partner disappears, and we are left alone (Stage 9)***

In the past, our behavior in each of these four stages was a reaction to what our partners had done. With a new understanding of why we behaved that way, we can do something different, even if the only thing we can do at first is reframe our partners' actions to view them in a different way.

1. Stage 11: When You Can't Stay Away, Work on Seeing What's in Front of You

We've broken down the pattern and what happens when they come back to you. If you're back on the pedestal, you know what they needed to see from you first. You made yourself smaller again so they could feel safer. Look forward. Can you see that the box you're in at this moment is going to break, too, no matter how sweet they're being to you right now? Now. If every box is going to break and if you can't predict when or what will break it, what might free you is to accept it's going to happen, then try to live without restricting yourself. Too difficult? Try just accepting it then.

"Accepting" does not mean you want it to happen. It doesn't mean you support it, or you're willingly saying to yourself, "Bring it on." You're not resigning yourself to misery or giving up in defeat. Instead, what you are doing is saying to yourself that you accept your partner has a filter that causes him or her to see the world this way, and *you* cannot control that. You accept your partner is inevitably going to view some of your normal behavior as a threat. You can't stop it.

As soon as you stop resisting that idea, you have released some of their control over you. That mental energy you expended trying to make yourself perfect can now be spent trying to figure out what you want to do. When you begin to change how you think, you begin to stop living in fear and doubting yourself.

2. **Stage 5: When You Want to Confront, Do Nothing**

In this stage, again, awareness is key. You no longer need to confront your partner because *now you know why they are behaving this way.* It doesn't have to be shocking, baffling, or surprising. Additionally, because you now know it is their view of themselves and the world causing them to put on such a big magic show, *you know it really doesn't have anything to do with you.*

Yes, the things they say and do still hurt, but it's easier to prepare yourself and block some of their attacks emotionally because you can see through them for what they really are. Try to view the abuse as if they are a child throwing a temper tantrum. Walk out when they do something to hurt you, no matter how painful it is. Say to yourself, "I don't need to take that seriously anymore." Imagine watching them from up above trying to pull you down into a pit with them. The important thing is to try to remain calm.

3. Stage 7: When You Feel Cognitive Dissonance, Strengthen Your Authentic Voice

You know now how your partner disconnected you from your own sources of trusting the world—by telling you your perception of reality was wrong, and you could not rely on your own thoughts or even your senses. You understand this has helped suppress your true self but also that it's still there. What are the ways your authentic self speaks to you? Think about that at this moment.

Because you're reading this book, you know it's speaking to you right now. What emotions and sensations in your body seem to be associated with the feeling of being called to pick it up and read it? Now, think about what other things you do that are in opposition to your relationship or that your partner wouldn't like. Those are the things you have been conditioned to reject and deny.

You can try to do at least two things to strengthen your authentic self. First, you can do more of the things that make you have those sensations and feelings in the first place, things like reading this book and keeping a journal to track your thoughts and feelings and to document events so you can stay firmly grounded in your own reality. Second, you can stop and really focus on those sensations and feelings when they arise spontaneously. Instead of letting them make you feel anxious because you don't know what to do with them or shoving them away in a corner, just sit with them and try to listen to what they have to say to you.

4. **Stage 9: When Your Partner Shuts You Out, Use the Break to Build Yourself Up**

It's probably impossible to eliminate the emotional suffering that occurs when they leave by sheer will alone, and I'm not suggesting that will happen. However, by starting to recognize you are not the real cause of why they left and there was nothing you could have done differently to stop it from happening, you can make it less personal.

Once you begin to accept this on some level, even if not fully, their ability to use their absence as a punishment is diminished. It doesn't mean you don't miss them. However, when you recognize they *falsely constructed the idea* for you that the reason they left was because of something you did, you also recognize they falsely constructed the idea that if you stop doing this "something," they will return.

This stage can actually be one of the most powerful in the cycle. When your partner is not around, he or she cannot keep feeding you these lies and stories, and your mind has the opportunity to start to clear if you take it. Is there anything your partner doesn't like you to do, forbids you to do, *hates* it when you do? Now is your chance to rebel and enjoy those things as a free woman or man. They are acts of rebellion, but also, they are just acts to remind yourself that you are a *person with your own dreams, desires, wishes, likes, thoughts*, and you don't have to feel guilty or ashamed for any of them. There are no thought police, and no one is going to shame you for what you want to eat or watch on TV.

I used to tell myself Amir was "teaching me how to live without him," and he was. This stage is a period of self-reflection and self-care. Do you feel that relief flooding in, however distant and buried? Part of you glimpses what life is like without him or her around. Slip inside that part of your mind for only a little while and enjoy that peace you're feeling without an iron grip around your throat.

Now, the next time you go through the cycle, something may be different. Or nothing may be different. But don't give up. Use the suggestions again. Keep working with them, adjusting them to your situation and personality. It took months or years for you to get to this point, so you may have to keep at it, getting closer and closer until your partner is no longer appealing or until something snaps and you break through. Repeat all of this as many times as it takes.

It is your partner, not you, who is the one truly trapped in the cycle of abuse. The difference between you and your partner is that he or she is doomed to repeat the pattern forever.

You are not. You can change it.

What Does Breaking Up with a Pathological Partner Mean?

The main thing to accept about breakups with pathological partners is that they don't. Break up, I mean. They may storm out, stonewall, give you a silent treatment, disappear for days or weeks at a time, stage a fight and say it's over, and give lip service to breaking up. Sometimes they even mean it.

But they don't move on because they lack the insight to learn from their experiences. They never gain any new wisdom that would foster outgrowing anything and leaving it behind.

Yet a breakup with a pathological partner doesn't end well. They end abruptly and with each person having a different narrative for what unfolded in the relationship. It shouldn't surprise us, given that pathological partners perceive our normal human behavior while we're in the relationship as criticism. When the relationship ends, they continue to reject and deny our version of events and blame us for why it ends. The refusal to validate our experience of abuse and lack of closure adds to the trauma.

Yet pathological partners have a strange quirk about keeping a permanent mental backburner of all their past partners.

No matter what happened the last time we interacted with our partners, they may not view it as an end. Under the right circumstances, they will pull out a shovel and try to resurrect your zombie relationship as if no time has passed. Almost everyone in a relationship with a pathological partner seesaws in and out of the relationship multiple times. This leaves us in a sort of relationship limbo, floating in a halfway in and halfway out status.

You may already be in that state right now. H.G. Tudor, a narcissistic sociopath who writes about narcissistic abuse on his website, writes:

> *You may see no action for weeks, months and even years as news reaches you that we are fighting on other fronts, seemingly content to leave you be. At least for the time being. Then out of nowhere you may reduce your vigilance and we are by your side, seeking to snake our tendrils around you once again. . . . How long will this final battle last? It will continue until one of us no longer lives.*[172]

In their eyes, we "belong" to them, and they will always feel entitled to reach out to us. Despite how long it's been, they may try to re-enter our lives if only for a few minutes or perhaps for longer. This appears to hold true in story after story from both survivors of pathological love relationships and from the pathological partners. Their lack of respect for boundaries and the inability to imagine how other people feel makes them believe they are entitled to come and go in the lives of their partners, regardless of how they treated their partners in the past.

You will have to end the relationship.

But how do you define the end?

The obvious answer to the question is that the end is when you walk away and mean it.

But how do we *know* it's the last time?

Pathological Love Stories

Realizing We're in Relationship Limbo

"I'm in no-contact with a narcissist right now because I have a protective order against him. I feel like I'm still in a relationship with him because he still controls my life. He has been stalking me, he still has keys to the house, and he comes and goes as he pleases. He has his flying monkeys checking up on me. I still feel his presence around me."

"I was discarded four years ago. Got back to together. He was still seeing the other person when I thought we were back together and got her pregnant. He continued to hoover. I eventually learned about NPD. But I was too weak and continued to see him (same cycle every time) for four years. It ended finally two months ago. I'm seeing a therapist and working very hard on my recovery. I've been extremely trauma bonded, and it's a very real thing I never knew existed."

"I have been out two years. It never breaks. For one year, I kept hoping. Now year two, I'm trying to build a bigger boat so he can't blow me over. I need a divorce. It'll be messy. I'm just planning and preparing."

"My narcissist is currently in jail, but he contacts me every day."

"I hope that I'm not in a relationship with him anymore; however, if the last nearly two years are anything to go by, my determination not to go back evaporates into nothing, and I find myself with him again. I don't tell family or friends anymore whether I'm with him or not. They've stopped believing me, that I really mean it when I say I'm not going back to him. I don't believe me either. But I don't want to be with him. . . .

I'm hiding out at my mum's twenty miles away. She doesn't know that I am trying to break the trauma bond. She thinks we broke up permanently three months ago when he nearly killed me. So, no, we're not together in my eyes, but oh crikey, I don't know. I don't want to be with him, but he always gets back in somehow."

"I would answer both yes and no, and I'm sure you could guess why. My narcissist hurt his back, and I just allowed him to begin staying in my home to help him out temporarily, but that was more than six months ago . . . and I honestly cannot believe that he got his claws gripped into me once again. I have been led blindly in the dark, trying to figure out what is happening once again. So, of course, it's unknown if I am in a relationship with him, probably, and probably not."

"We are married, haven't lived together in three years. I'm not 'supposed' to be seeing him, and nobody knows I do."

"Ex-wife keeps calling. Divorced thirty years ago."

"This is yes and no. Because I'm always in that state of 'what the fuck is going on?'"

"As of two days ago, I 'ended' the 'relationship' for the 100th time."

"I am not sure whether or not I am still in it. I hope not and have been trying to be 'out' out for years now. But we had sex last night, so it seems that I am still in it."

See Appendix A.

To others, we appear to be living our lives as if we are free, but in reality, there are invisible chains wrapped around our throats.

Keeping What's Real but Not True

Psychologist Martin Seligman's research in 1961 on "learned helplessness" explains the defeat that sets in. He performed experimental studies in which he confined dogs to boxes and gave some of them electric shocks (obviously, this was not a very humane study!). All the dogs tried to escape the boxes, but the dogs who received the shocks eventually gave up trying and instead backed themselves into a corner and stayed there, resigned to their fate. The experiment concluded when Seligman provided all the dogs their potential freedom. The dogs who had received the electric shocks, however, did not even try to escape the boxes when they had the chance.[173]

What Seligman's study demonstrates is that we can be conditioned to believe we are powerless and to give up. As our stories show, our partner's behavior puts us in a walking sleep-state of mental slavery to their whims that we don't understand. Tudor, once again, says it best:

> *Your heart will never accept that it was not real. That crack, that fracture, that tiny chink that remains from your frenetic and devastating time with me shall always remain. It is through it that I can return as I slip, shadow like into your heart through that unhealed wound. That is why we did what we did; so we always had a way back in.*[174]

Tudor's choice of words feels harsh to us as survivors. It helps to explain the emotional bond to the false persona we developed early in the relationship, however, so I chose to include it to demonstrate the importance of eliminating the false self our pathological partners implant in us.

Let's unpack what Tudor's words mean. He seems to be suggesting that, once we become involved with them, it's basically for life and at their whim. Pathological partners have a perpetual ability to subvert our free will and come and go as they please, whether it's now or at some future date.

However, this is very presumptuous! It pre-supposes that survivors can't overcome the psychological manipulation that implanted the false self that would let the pathological partner return to exploit us. He claims the way it would be done is through our lack of acceptance that what we experienced isn't real.

This is a key to understanding why it's so difficult to leave our relationship. The relationship feels special to us, and we cherish our good memories of the relationship. If we destroy the false self our pathological partners created, it may feel as if all we have left is a version of the relationship that was not real. The horror of the existential emptiness behind the idea that the love is "unreal" or false can sometimes feel even more painful than love that is real but puts us in danger. We know what to do and how to feel about dangerous love. It's understandable that we put ourselves in harm's way because we were coerced and conditioned to do so. It's more difficult to accept that we never even really loved anyone—that we were coerced and conditioned to do that too.

Is there a way to hold onto the idea that we feel something real that has brought us joy and made us feel alive *and* that we must eliminate a part of ourselves that is manufactured and will bring us harm if we don't? I think so, by reflecting on an idea taught by Buddhist teacher Tsoknyi Rinpoche: some things are real but not true.[175] In other words, the love we felt was real, and it was accompanied by real experiences, emotions, and thoughts; however, it could not be wholly representative of the reality around us when our partners were not their genuine selves. By holding both ideas in our minds at the same time, we can see more clearly what we can keep and what we should get rid of because it can still hurt us.

If a dog bites me, I might feel fearful around dogs, even when I have no evidence a new dog I meet will bite me. My feeling of fear is real, and I can acknowledge it, but each time I experience it with a new dog that has never hurt me, it isn't a "true" reaction to my experiences with the new dog. The love you feel for your partner is genuine; however, the relationship is not what it appears to be. The conditions under which you based your love weren't truthfully presented to you, and your love has been used against you. Your love isn't a true representation of the situational dynamic.

We can hold onto our love as part of our authentic selves and feel joy knowing we are capable of loving others that much. If we did it in this relationship, we can do it again. If that love had not come from our authentic self, it would not have been any use to our partners. Our partners may have manipulated the conditions under which we would fall in love, such as how quickly and how intensely; however, the love we felt was genuine.

We not only must leave the relationship for today, but we must psychologically leave all *future* versions of our partners as well. We must make a conscious choice that it doesn't matter when they ever come back or who they come back claiming to be. That door can never open again.

It's a pre-emptive rejection, for we know the relationship will never really fade into the past for them. If we have already considered their reappearance an inevitability, it won't matter if they do or not. Like Aron Ralston, we will have already decided that it's better to leave behind a piece of ourselves and live than to stay hidden at the bottom of a dark canyon, grow weaker, and fade away.

16

But . . . Does My Partner Love Me?

Reading about love-bombing can hurt because it seems calculated and inauthentic. The love you felt was real, and the memories you have are probably special and right now may be some of your most treasured. The idea that those memories aren't "real" may not only be scary, but it may not seem to fit your own experiences. Even though your partner has also put you through a nightmare, a nagging voice inside you may not believe what you're reading about love-bombing. It's saying to you something like this:

"I understand love-bombing is a manipulative tactic, and I also understand my partner has hurt me and a lot of this is hitting home for me, but there's no way everything my partner said and did during those early days was purely manipulative. I know at least some of it was real. He (or she) has to at least love me a little bit because I *felt* it."

Before we talk about anything else, I want to give space to a discussion about the love you share with your partner and, especially, to what you experienced at the beginning of the relationship so you know what to do with thoughts like these.

To adequately consider the question of whether our partners really love us or not, we must ask ourselves what love is. If we think love is only an emotion like any other, then we can ask ourselves if our partners are capable of feeling it. We know some people who exhibit narcissistic tendencies have the chemical reactions associated with love in their brains, and if you ask those individuals whether they are in love, the feeling itself is real to them.[176]

My guess, however, is that if I asked you to stop for a minute and think about the definition of love, it would not only consist of a feeling you have but a bond you share with another person. That bond may manifest itself in many ways, but it would ultimately be supported by acts that represented mutual support and loyalty, compassion and sensitivity, commitment, trust, and honest communication.

This is where we return once again to the idea of cooperative social actors and pathological social actors.

Figure 16.1: Traits of Cooperative and Pathological Social Actors

COOPERATIVE SOCIAL ACTORS:
-Experience guilt
-Feel empathy
-Make amends due to remorse
-Consider the consequences to others before taking action
-Make a genuine attempt to change or avoid behavior that hurts others

PATHOLOGICAL SOCIAL ACTORS:
-Conscience is impaired
-Lack empathy
-May make amends for self-serving reasons or not at all
-Do not factor in the consequences to others before taking action
-Unable or unwilling to change or avoid behavior that hurts others unless there's something in it for them

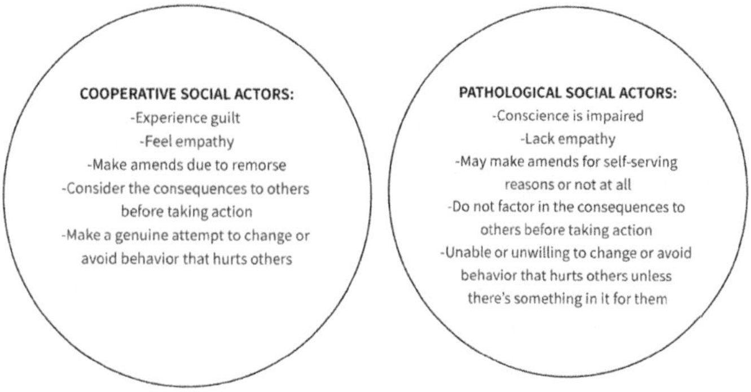

There is a gap between what pathological partners may *feel* and the way they act. Their brains are hypersensitive to rewards, and they constantly seek stimulation. After all the neurochemicals of love—norepinephrine, oxytocin, dopamine, and vasopressin—are released into the brain during the idealization stage of the relationship, our brains return to baseline. Normally, this is when the deeper stage of the relationship would take place. We have formed an attachment and are invested in the relationship, but our partners never attach to the relationship due to an empathy deficit. As their brains return to baseline, they may begin to see our flaws and resent us or see us as responsible for their boredom.[177]

We are left wondering why it sometimes feels as if our partners love us and other times as if our partners hate us or pretend as if we don't exist. It's not normal to shut love off and on like a light switch. Cooperative social actors care when they hurt someone and, as a general rule, try not to do it. Pathological partners, however, aren't biologically bound by a conscience that would restrict them from behaving in ways that would violate their relationships even with people they claim to love.

I can't tell you what your partner actually felt, and I don't know if this is relevant to your experience or not. Only you will be able to take this information and decide if it seems applicable to anything you went through or not. Some people may believe it's counterproductive and even dangerous to consider the idea that people without empathy can love you, that if survivors consider the possibility, it may provide them with false hope that the pathological partner can change.

Just because your partner may have felt a child's version of selfish love for you doesn't mean your partner is capable of participating in a relationship where you will ever be emotionally safe.

Yet understanding that some pathological partners experience love can provide us with *more* information we need to empower ourselves to leave and not less. The idea is not to consider whether pathological partners can love us so we can stay with them. The idea is to consider it so we can let go of obsessing over whether it was true or not. Just because your partner may have felt a child's version of selfish love for you doesn't mean your partner is capable of participating in a relationship where you will ever be emotionally safe.

Outside information about narcissism needs to ring true to our own experiences for us to figure out how to arm ourselves with it and apply it to our lives. When we read books or articles that explain pathological partners are incapable of love and it seems to contradict our own experience, it may discourage us from trusting our authentic voice. We need our authentic voice to break the psychological spell we're under and get out of the relationship.

What you should do with this knowledge about pathological partners and love is use it to empower yourself. Listen to your authentic voice. Perhaps your partner goes through the motions of love, says all the right words, appears to love you, and maybe even feels a neurochemical reaction in his or her brain, but what they are reacting to is not what you think it is. It's not the love you deserve. It's not even the same thing you mean when you say the word "love." As previously explained in Chapter 7, pathological partners have difficulty understanding and interpreting abstract concepts. "Love" to them, according to Sandra L. Brown, M.A., often means "compliance."[178] Compliance, as we reviewed earlier in the book, is about those subtle tactics they use to slowly erode our identity. When they can override our free will, they consider it love.

Once we can finally accept that, we can stop obsessing over which one is real: the version of our partner who loves us or the version who hates us.

They are two sides of the same coin that cannot be separated from one another.

QUESTION FIVE:

How Do I Get Out of Here?

Something powerful took hold of me, and the emotional and mental abuse I suffered at his hands became so apparent I finally realized I couldn't go another day living through it.

—*Hannah*, survey respondent

When you're in a pathological love relationship, you're almost always in emotional limbo. Either you leave, then find yourself somehow drawn back to them again, or they coldly shut you out after tormenting you, only to return after days or weeks to tell you they can't live without you.

You feel mysteriously bound to them in a way that is unbreakable, the bond a formless shape, ever-shifting and boundless, with no end in sight. It is a relationship, yet there seems to be no predictable relationship patterns or parameters.

Things would be perfect, you think, if only they would stop hurting you in ways that are fantastical in their inexplicable cruelty. It is hope and despair, both lost and found. It is a slow death by a poisoned will to act.

You've already known the truth, but they won't let you keep it—you must rip it away from them.

This fifth question is about pushing past the confusion and the pain to the point of no return. With this question, we realize we can no longer stay. The only thing left is to find the pathway out.

The pathway out may be illuminated just enough that we can tiptoe gingerly down it and slip out when our partner isn't looking. Or the exit may suddenly explode with a luminescence that blocks out all other objects in our vision so we can hurl ourselves toward it almost unthinkingly. Either way, we have a moment of clarity that comes from our authentic self: *I can do this.*

What having this final realization means is that we no longer only see the relationship as bad for us, but we see the end as imminent. We are more willing to accept the unknown than to accept the nightmare we have been living.

My Story

A picture of Amir and his wife loaded on the screen in front of me when I clicked on Amir's Facebook account. Under his new profile picture, one of his cousins had posted a comment that said, "That's the queen right there!"

He had responded, "The one and only!"

Contempt welled up inside me. Pure disgust and hatred. Only a few hours before, he'd questioned me for hours when he'd learned I had spent time with another man.

He had unleashed accusatory fury at me hundreds of times over the years when it wasn't true. I'd grown almost numb to it.

A defiant voice inside me had been speaking recently, one that whispered, If he treats you that way no matter what you do, then it doesn't matter what you do. Stop trying to be so careful not to enrage him because every action is equally offensive to him. *Those thoughts added more cracks in that box that had trapped me over the years. A careless indifference began to settle over me.* Oh? He's mad again? Another silent treatment? What a surprise!

That indifference turned into rebellion one night when I let it take over. I shut off my phone with a calmness that was abnormal, knowing Amir wouldn't be able to reach me. When I checked it the next day, Amir had sent me over a dozen messages, the tone ranging from contemptuous to worried. I finally responded to him after a little after noon.

"Something doesn't feel right. Did you go out on a date with someone?"

Then, I knew I had to tell him. I wanted to tell him. So, I told him the truth. "I did spend the night with someone, but I didn't have sex with him." I cringed at my need to tell him that much of my personal business, to preserve my purity status with him to avoid his verbal abuse.

"Wow. Then, what did you do?"

"Sleep," I said.

"But you kissed and did things other than sex. Are you really going to do this to me? Wow. I knew it. I had a feeling."

"I know you knew. That's why I told you."

"Wow, just wow. Oh, my God. Do you like him?"

"What do you mean when you say that? Do I want to be his girlfriend? No."

"You find him attractive?"

"Yes, he is conventionally attractive. A lot of women think so."

"Wow. Enjoy your life. I'm hurt."

"I'm sorry. I understand. I do know how it feels."

"So, you're taking your revenge?"

"No, I'm being my own person. You have your own life without me. Why can't I have one?"

"At least I'm not sharing my body with someone else when I'm with you."

"Amir, you're married. What are you talking about?"

"Supposedly, you love me, and then you go and sleep with other guys. Why did you do it? Never mind. You said you find him attractive. Anyway, enjoy your life. I love you."

"You have to ask me why? If you have to ask me how I can go kiss or sleep next to another man if I love you, first go stand in front of a mirror and then ask yourself that question. Then, you will have your answer, and you won't have to ask me."

"I think this is the end. Goodbye, Kristen. Please don't respond." I wondered what answer he had come up with in that thought experiment I had just given him that led him to give me that response.

"Of course, it is, because you can dish it out, but you can't take it. You betrayed and abandoned me so many times for other girls, and I was still there by your side. It broke my heart in pieces, but now all you want to do is just go silent like I don't even exist."

"I love you, but now you're just trying to hurt me and take your revenge, so I don't think you love me anymore. I don't think it's a good idea that we talk because you have moved on. Even though I am hurt, I wish you nothing but happiness, and I am glad you have moved on. I will always love you. Goodbye, Kristen."

"If I was trying to hurt you, I would be saying things that were meaner than this. Can't you see this isn't about you?"

"Okay. I'll leave you alone. I'm sorry. You don't want me no more. And I'll walk away. Oh, my God. I just can't believe this."

"When you chose someone else, when your energy went somewhere else, my heart and mind and body finally understood what that meant. I get it now. The part of me that loved you started dying. I didn't want it to. I wanted you so much."

"I think we should stop talking. I can't take it right now."

I didn't know how to explain that in my mind, nothing had changed. He was still married, and we were never going to be together. I was still grieving that, and I was still living my new life. It's just that I was finally getting to climb out of a box he wanted me to stay preserved in, a box that didn't allow me to feel anything or express anything.

"How do I know it won't happen again? What you did last night?"

My fingers hovered over the phone keyboard trying to understand the question. "Well, you don't, I guess. But your question implies that I did something wrong. Why do you expect or think I should be faithful to a relationship that doesn't exist? When you can't and don't even give me that? That's a serious question. I'm genuinely curious."

"I love you, and I can't have thoughts of other guys with you. That's all. That's the answer."

"We aren't in a relationship. You always wanted and expected that of me, but you never gave it back. If you want that from a person, generally, you have to give it back. That's pretty much the definition of a monogamous relationship."

He stopped responding.

The next morning, dissatisfied and uneasy with the way the conversation ended, I checked Facebook to see if I could find any insight into his state of mind, and that's when I'd seen he'd changed his Facebook photo to one of he and his wife.

I took a screenshot and texted it to him.

"You say the same thing to every woman. Every woman is your one and only. I hate you. You're disgusting."

"If someone says something about me or my wedding, I have to act like that and act like I'm happy."

I scoffed in disbelief, even as a part of me deep inside grasped at his excuse. I hated myself for it. At that moment, all I wanted was to tear it all down, stop feeling myself grasping for him when he offered up these non-reasons, non-responses as if I had no independent will.

"Do you ever think about what you do? Look at yourself in the mirror and think about how you're making a mess out of your life and everyone else's? You use the exact same words with every woman, and they have an effect on the women you say them to. Those words mean something. People believe you. They make life decisions because they believe you. Do you understand this?"

"Look, I'm really upset about what you did yesterday," he said. "I called off work. I can't go in like this. I can't argue, so please just let me be. You're turning all this around when you were doing what you did with that guy. Please don't message me again. I need my space, please."

"I don't want to talk to you anymore either. All I want is for you to admit you didn't really love me. I am ready to accept it, and it would finally make my world make sense, and I will be at peace."

"It shouldn't matter to you what I feel about you because you have moved on."

"It matters because I want things to make sense. I just want closure, and then I will go away."

"Well, I will always love you because you will always have a special place in my heart. If you're dying and you call for me on your deathbed, I would go to you. There you go. This is your closure. It's for you to believe or not believe."

Tears sprang to my eyes. No, no. That wasn't what I wanted at all.

Yet some part of me did. Would I never stop feeling that little shiver when he said he loved me? This was not love. This was not love!

"You will always love me! Well, you had a funny way of showing it."

All I wanted was for him to stop saying it was love, to just admit he'd used me, that he had never loved me and hadn't cared if he hurt me, that he'd knowingly lied to me all along about everything. Whatever hurtful, hateful, ugly words came out of him—as long as they were his truth—I needed to hear them. I knew it would be far less painful than these melodramatic outpourings that were the opposite of the way he'd treated me. I was ready to beg for them the next time he said something.

But one minute passed, and there was no response. Then five minutes. Then ten. His silence was deafening.

An hour went by. I waited for another text from him. One always came.

The next day, still there was nothing. I couldn't relax.

Two weeks passed, and I sent him a long email. In it, I did my begging and pleading. I laid it out line by line, numbering my evidence for why he could never have possibly loved me, no matter how many thousands of times and how intensely he'd declared it to be true, whispering it deep into my subconscious and embedding it where my rational mind couldn't touch it. I told him I forgave him, and I would never bother him again, but all I wanted was for him to set me free and tell me the truth. If he had ever cared for me even a little bit, I said, he would do this one last thing for me.

His response came back almost immediately: "I don't know why you care how I feel since you were with that guy. You've probably had sex with him by now, so I don't even want to hear from you. Goodbye, Kristen."

17

Letting Go of a Dream

I didn't realize it at the time, but I was trying desperately to leave the relationship without actually leaving it.

Having the realization that it is possible to leave your partner at all may seem to suggest you have a very purposeful change in conviction. It may imply that everything is suddenly crystal clear, and every move we make is with determination and a sense of self-awareness and direction.

It also implies there is some dramatic confrontation where we tell off our partners and walk out the door with all our belongings, never looking back, leaving them speechless and regretful for the way they treated us.

No.

This isn't like a movie, where the wrongs are suddenly righted, where the bully comes to his senses, and everyone gets a happy ending.

The end is an angst-ridden earthquake, a freefall into a future in which we no longer even know who we are. It's an emotional roller coaster. It's a death, fraught with loss and uncertainty. The end is a blind spot where we uproot our partners from where they implanted themselves in our psyche, leaving behind a gaping nothingness that aches for what was once there.

How much time do we spend going over and over the relationship in our minds, like a *Choose Your Own Adventure* story playing out endlessly, where there's that one path to the end that will give us our *happily ever after* if only we can find it?

Our *happily ever after* is behind the door we never wanted to open—the one where we walk out alone.

The thought of being without your partner and being happy at the same time may seem impossible right now—I promise you it's not! For now, I want you to know there is a beautiful place waiting for you that isn't filled with pain. There are many things you must do to get to it, but the first step, the very first one, is getting away from your partner.

When I say getting away, I don't just mean physically. I mean psychologically.

You will need to be far enough away psychologically to take the final step physically. You will also need to be far enough away physically to ever have the hope of breaking the rest of those psychological chains.

Because of this constant battle we fight after we have this realization, not everyone leaves in quite the same way.

Pathological Love Stories

The Moment We Escaped

"I ended the relationship by asking my sister to come to my house, and then I told my 'girlfriend' that she needed to leave if she did not want to be with me. I did that because I was

worried that if I did not have someone there, she would say that I did things that did not happen. It's sad really because I questioned myself once again and called my sister at the last minute just in case she had not left her house. I was going to tell her not to come. All I could think about was missing my daughter and my girlfriend, but my sister was already almost to my home when I called, so it felt as though I had no choice but to follow through."

"Being sucked back in over and over without understanding what I was dealing with caused so many physical, emotional, and legal traumatic injuries I just reached a breaking point and was trying to get away by leaving the state. He followed and did the whole confusing routine. . . . This took six years of marriage to escape. I almost lost my life."

"I kicked him out. It took a toll on my health, the lack of empathy and mask removed. He was creepy in the end, even got violent."

"I realized that he wanted to establish a short breakup of the relationship to punish me for not complying with his wishes, and when he asked me from the phone to take a little time apart, I stated my position. I told him that this was the last time that he was going to hurt me again, so I didn't give him the time, and I told him that it was over and goodbye."

"After I went no-contact, things got complicated. He harassed me at work, and I nearly lost my job. To protect myself, I have proceeded to go legal (court order)."

"I started therapy, which enabled me to see what was going on. When I started calling him out on his behavior, he would rage, give the silent treatment, or abuse me with name calling, using

my past as weapons and belittling me. I guess he got tired of being called out on his bad behavior and saw it wasn't working any longer, so he left."

"I ended the relationship in March, but it took me four more horrible months to get him to leave. We lived in my house, so moving out myself wasn't an option. He left on July first, and on that day, I went no contact."

"I ended up calling 9-1-1, and getting smuggled away when his craziness went far enough, I felt a threat for my life."

"Four years ago, I sought a divorce from my ex-husband. Because we had a then-minor child, I had to communicate with him but only when and as necessary according to court orders. I went no-contact when the child graduated from high school in June 2019."

"I finally couldn't take it anymore. He threatened to call the police. I eventually called his mother—that scared him away. He texted me and followed me to work the next day, harassing me. Then, I told him to get the rest of his things because I was throwing them away. He got pissed and blocked me on everything. I haven't spoken to him until two weeks ago when we bumped into each other. He wants to get back with me, and I said no."

"He ghosted me, ignored me, and discarded me for months. He then had roses with a 'Happy Valentine's Day' message. I texted him, asked why. He told me I deserved it. I took the roses and threw them in the trash. The next day, I called him and told him he wasn't worthy of me and that I deserved better than he was. I sent him a photo of the trashed roses and mailed him every cheap trinket he gave me (and they were cheap tin, while

I gave him gold and silver jewelry). I deleted everything from my phone and email and never looked back. It was the most painful thing I have ever endured."

See Appendix A.

Dr. Steven Hassan, author of *Combating Cult Mind Control*, writes that cult members leave cults in one of three ways: they walk out, get kicked out, or are counseled out.[179] Former cult members who had been successful at walking out had strong support systems outside the cult. Outsiders who support a cult member who walks out or who counsel them out can provide them with the alternative perspective they need to help them understand how they are being influenced through mind control to suppress their authentic selves. Many cult victims, no matter how they leave, often don't refer to the group they were in as a cult, even if they understand it was a negative situation.

It's unsurprising the same methods of leaving exist in pathological love relationships. For survivors of pathological relationships, however, this is where the *relationship dynamics* may create some differences. The equivalent to these three methods of exiting the relationship exist: the survivor leaves the relationship; the pathological partner discards the survivor; and others intervene until the survivor recognizes the peril in circumstances, and the spell is broken. The latter is the equivalent of "cult deprogramming."[180]

So little is known about pathological love relationships that intervention in its purest form is still a rare method of exit for them. Outsiders tend not to want to become involved. They may believe that when the survivor is ready, we will come to them for help. They may even engage in harmful victim-blaming or abandon us if it appears to them that we can't seem to get our act together and "make up our minds."

The lack of knowledge about the impact of pathological love relationship on survivors' cognitive and psychological functionating and of undue influence in general is a larger societal issue that is outside the scope of this book, but it's a serious issue that interferes with survivors getting the support we need. If you are a loved one reading this book and you want to help, resources and intervention services do exist! Please see Appendix C to learn more.

Often what all this means for survivors is that intervention is not available to us. We also may experience the other two options—"walking out" and "being kicked out"—differently than cult survivors because of the intense one-on-one interactions with the pathological partner and the relationship dynamics that our partner may use against us as the relationship comes to an "end." Yet it also means that there are other, creative ways that survivors have of leaving the relationship beyond these three identified in cults.

As you prepare to leave the relationship, it's important to recognize that leaving on good terms will never be an option. Pathological partners usually never let their partners walk out without trying to punish them for it, seeking vengeance, or trying to gain the control back. Pathological partners see independent action as threatening. They feel entitled to control you and to lose control makes them feel personally affronted. To pathological partners, leaving is "the nuclear option," and if they're going down, you're going down—it's mutually-assured destruction. With no conscience and limited ability to think through the consequences of their actions, this could be an especially high-risk time for stalking, harassment, damage to your reputation or career, harm to children or pets, destruction of your property, and physical abuse. They have always let us know that we are "theirs." The big question mark is what will happen when they learn it isn't true. The question mark may have instilled fear in us, both real and irrational: "Competent women who are CEOs of companies become paranoid and believe that the psychopath will know when she attempts to leave—even if he is out of town."[181] This can be one factor that stops us from acting. This is why "Walking Away" is not always the best option in a pathological love relationship, depending on the dynamics of your particular situation.

Even pathological partners who are not prone to violence will still likely never give you closure. They may instead just cut off contact and ignore you. Before they do it, they may try to do some psychological damage; for example, they may run out and find another partner immediately—even the same day!—and parade them around in your face. Yet everything you shared will suddenly be to them as if it meant nothing. They will turn you into a new story they can tell potential partners—another one who "did them wrong" by leaving just like all their other past partners. Remember Lifton's criterion for thought reform from Chapter 11, "Dispensing of Existence?" Anyone who leaves the cult is shunned, treated as if they no longer exist.

In the survey survivors completed for this book, their responses revealed seven ways that they leave relationships. Note that these are *end* states, not *limbo* states.

1. **Walking Away**

   Survivors reach a breaking point and finally realize they can't take anymore. This may seem like a spontaneous decision, but it often builds for a long time first, and the authentic self puts weight behind it. The decision to walk away spontaneously during moments of conflict with the pathological partner usually doesn't "take." Spontaneous walk outs, however, can potentially make survivors more resistant to their pathological partner's hoover attempts. The pathological partner may come to view their partner's strength as threatening, which hastens the cycle. When the pathological partner disappears, the survivor can use the time to build even more strength, as described in Chapter 15. For the survivor to successfully navigate walking away, a support system and access to some resources is helpful. Those who spent some time planning for their physical and psychological well-being before they leave are even better off.

2. **Disappearing**

   Because when survivors leave, the pathological partner's response is either extreme anger or intense hoovering or a combination of the two, some survivors feel they may never get away from the relationship for that reason and live in fear of how they will ever escape. Their response is to just disappear. They move away, change jobs, change phone numbers, delete their social media profiles, and other important methods of going anonymous to ensure the pathological partner can't contact them once their decision has been made.

3. **Outsider Assist (Healthy)**

   Survivors may work with therapists or friends to plan a safe escape, then use their support person or team as a lifeline to offer encouragement and distraction in the most crucial early days after the escape so they don't return to the relationship.

4. **Outsider Assist (Unhealthy)**

   Another method of leaving the relationship by involving others is by jumping straight into a new relationship. Exit affairs or exit relationships help survivors leave a pathological love relationship; however, ***I strongly recommend avoiding this as a strategy.*** I'm classifying this as unhealthy because many survivors report that this is how they end up in another pathological love relationship. In previous chapters, we discussed that the number one commonality of people who ended up in cults, relationships with pathological partners, or who had been victims of fraud: they were going through a major life change just as you're doing now by trying to break up with a pathological partner. I'm not suggesting everyone who wants to date you is pathological—just that when we're in this vulnerable position, it's a really bad time to try to assess someone's character.

5. **Life-Changing Events**

   Sometimes something happens unexpectedly or outside the survivor's control, and it upends daily life or causes a life-changing realization. Survivors may suffer a loss or find out about something new their partners did that has had a profound negative impact on their lives. The stakes change, as the shake-up gives survivors either less to lose or even more to lose. For example, the survivor may get pregnant and realize she doesn't want to raise a child with her abuser. Sometimes survivors use the fact that their pathological partner gets arrested as an opportunity they have been waiting for to break the tie while the pathological partner is incapacitated and cannot use the same methods of control.

6. **Voluntary Discard**

   If their pathological partners just won't leave them alone, sometimes survivors orchestrate situations or events to make pathological partners go away on their own. This may be a deliberate act, using a strategy called "gray rock," which is discussed in Chapter 18. However, often it's more of a subconscious act of desperation. Because pathological partners have rules for their partners to follow or they punish them with discards and silent treatments, survivors may break the rules, becoming careless about getting caught. Once the pathological partner realizes their partner is no longer under their control, if they already have other partners lined up, they may respond by rejecting the survivor who isn't responding the way the pathological partner expects or desires, switching over to a new partner who is more controllable and hasn't seen behind the mask yet. **NOTE: This is not always safe, as the pathological partner may instead respond with rage and attack or try to exert even more control, so proceed with caution before trying this method.**

7. **Involuntary Discard**

   In these situations, the pathological partner breaks up with the survivor when the survivor does not want it to happen. At the time the breakup occurs, the survivor's false self is in control, and the authentic self is not yet prepared for the end of the relationship. This is one of the most common endings to their pathological love relationships that survivors listed. Even if your pathological love relationship ends with your partner walking out, however, there's still work to do. The relationship hasn't truly ended until you decide it has ended. An involuntary discard is just the way a pathological partner has decided to leave things for the time being until he or she decides they want to come back (see Chapter 18). Because pathological partners only put relationships on pause, all the power is still in your hands whether your partner is in the picture now or not. You will have to walk away, metaphorically speaking. They don't have the right to come and go as they please whether it's ten days, ten weeks, or ten years from now. You still must choose to lock the door on them so they can never return. That is your power now.

The three strategies that are the most successful and that I recommend, *if they are feasible for your situation,* are **walking away, disappearing,** or **healthy outside assist.** I cannot choose a strategy for you, nor can I help you select the best strategy for your life. Everyone's plan will be based on factors, such as the level of support you already have, your access to resources, how dangerous your partner is, how much of your life is shared with your partner, and other factors only you know. Future chapters can help you think through factors you may want to consider, but only you can decide how you can best prepare to leave.

A Note about Voluntary and Involuntary Discard

My pathological love relationship ended because of a voluntary discard. It wasn't the first time. I'd tried exposing his secrets and lies to others—the fact that he was still reaching out to me to declare his love even after he had married someone else. It didn't work, however. He disappeared to clean up the mess, then returned to me with even more stories I couldn't reconcile. The incident that finally sent him away where he didn't come back was the one I included in this book. When I kissed another man and did not even try to hide the fact, Amir finally left me alone.

I did not consciously choose this strategy.

Amir discarded me only because of deliberate actions I took, and when I took them, I knew I was doing things that risked that happening. However, I did not do them *with the conscious intent* for him to discard me.

How is this possible?

I was being torn apart by Amir's incongruous words and actions. I became desperate to stop that pain. My dual identity, my cognitive dissonance, prevented me from taking the actions deliberately to push him away; however, it allowed me enough awareness that I had to stop the pain. I was constantly zig-zagging back and forth between "knowing" and needing to get out from under the nightmare and "not knowing" because the aware part of me would be pushed back into a pool of denial almost without my consent. Over and over and over again. That constant whipsaw was making me fall apart. I had reached a point to where one of the two had to "win." I could not make the choice. Amir had to make it. Even though I "knew" the truth, the other part of my brain would not let me completely hold onto it until he gave me that consistency, and my reality came together.

Let me be clear about this: **I do not recommend this strategy.** I am including it and writing honestly about my experience with it because I *don't* recommend it. What I did was unpredictable, dangerous, and reckless. Instead of pushing him away, it could have done the opposite. He had threatened to kill me if I cheated on him, and when he found out what I'd done, he could have tried to tighten his grip instead of letting go. Even though we were no longer together, he still claimed an ownership over me that was obviously difficult to unchain myself from. There had always been ambiguity in what he considered "cheating," and I had tried to stay within the lines to keep from inciting his anger and abuse.

By doing what I did, it shows how little I understood what had happened to me. By the time I reached this point, I had blocked out a part of myself that cared about the consequences of being blatant with my actions with someone else.

The pain of being trapped in the relationship was so bad I could not imagine anything worse.

I got lucky. He left me alone; however, it was not empowering. I still felt the pain of his rejection even though his leaving is what I (my authentic self) wanted all along. Up in smoke went years of my life and all his supposed undying Romeo-and-Juliet love for me. I was left questioning my value, scratching my head at that last little dart he'd thrown at me on his way out. *After all he put me through, and that's all I'm worth? I'm just nothing now?*

If I had had this information about psychological manipulation and the emergence of dual identities, I would not have had to come to such a place of desperation that I was willing to put myself in danger to escape. I also would not have suffered as much because I would have had a better understanding of why my emotions felt so out-of-control. I would have been able to take control of my own choices.

The months I wasted and the unnecessary pain I went through just figuring all of this out are at the center of why I wrote this book. A book cannot save you, but maybe it can plant a seed to bring you one step closer to saving yourself.

You don't have to do what I did. Let yourself look around and see things for what they really are, then use what's around you to make your life different one small step at a time and build your plan. You can do this.

The most important part of understanding these options for leaving the relationship, however, is recognizing that *there is a choice at all.* Sandra L. Brown, M.A., found in her research that women left when they reached a breaking point and were about to lose themselves completely. Read that again. "It is the destruction of the self that helps us understand the reason why women eventually leave," Brown writes. "It is not based on one particular behavior or another of his, but the outcome to herself and her identity. Women leave when their sense of self has been destroyed to a point that she is suffering the loss of her once congruent self."[182]

Knowing that, and knowing you're reading this book and have read the stories of other survivors, you are already ahead of the game. You have knowledge, you have some tools in your arsenal to try to get some of your power back, and you have some ways to try to plan so this doesn't take you by surprise.

Leaving is not something you have to do in the middle of the night when you are desperate and wonder if this time it will stick. It's not a "someday" wish in your mind. You can make a purposeful choice about the way that will best serve you and your circumstances. You can also consider avoiding the more dangerous methods of leaving and avoid the ones that may be unsuccessful for your situation.

The power is in your hands right now when you choose to take it. In fact, this is when you most have the power to shut him or her out forever—when they have let go of the chains long enough to show you how to live without them.

Prepare to have every last good memory wrenched away. You must accept that you will never receive closure from them.

The cage door is open. You may not know this, but you are already free. You have always been free.

Our partners' actions make us forget, but we have always been free.

18

When Pathological Partners Try to Come Back (And They Will)

Hoovering is serious business for pathological partners, and it's crucial to understand the relationship with them only ends when you decide it does because the possibility always exists for them to return.[183]

What makes a hoover a "hoover" is that it derives from our partner's fear that he or she has lost control of us. The desire for control makes their words insincere. If we fail to recognize that, we could be led to believe our partners have changed, or something could be different in the future if we stay or go back to the relationship. To have a hope of truly getting our lives back, we must finally accept that any promises or apologies pathological partners make when you aren't with them haven't been made because of genuine remorse. If they are hoovering, then they have decided there is still something to be gained from the relationship.

Hoovers can be as creative as the pathological partner you are with. These dramatic ways of reaching out are attempts to get their foot in the door so they can re-engage. They will use whichever method they deem is likely to be the most successful for whatever they want to accomplish at the time. Hoover attempts are always strong plays on deep emotions: Love. Hope. Sympathy. Guilt. Indignation or outrage. Fear. Shame. Obligation. An appeal to one of our core values.

25 Common Hoover Tactics

1. **Promise of Closure**

   "I have to talk to you. You must give me the chance to explain."

2. **Just One More Time**

   "I wish I could take you out just so I can see you one last time."

3. **Appeal to the Heartstrings**

   "I found these pictures of us. Ah, memories."

4. **False Accusations**

   "Someone told me you were on a dating app. I can't believe you. It's only been three days!"

5. **Remembering Important Dates**

   "How did your doctor's appointment go today?"

6. Passive Hoovers

Actions your partner knows you will see in which they don't actually say anything to encourage or provoke you into reaching out first, such as sending blank texts or putting random likes on your social media posts.

7. Romeo Hoover

"I just can't live without you."

8. Metamorphosis

"Please give me another chance. I know what I did was wrong, and I've changed. I won't do it again."

9. Physical Objects to Return

"I found your extra phone charger at my apartment. Can I bring it to you?"

10. Heard Some News

"Someone showed me a picture of you on Facebook with a guy. How dare you!"

11. The Apology

"I'm sorry. I was immature back then, but I just want to show you that I can be good to you."

12. Elaborate Promises

"Let me take you on a trip—anywhere you want to go."

13. Upcoming Events

"I got us tickets to the ballet. I know how much you love it."

14. Here If You Need Me

"Let me know if you need help moving."

15. Destiny Hoover

"We have a connection no one else can understand, and we can't let anything break it apart."

16. Alone in the World

"You're the only one I can talk to."

17. The Reverse Hoover

When you reach out to your partner for a specific non-romantic purpose out of necessity, he or she turns the conversation into their heartbrokenness, undying love, and request to rekindle the relationship.

18. Children

"Have you heard from our daughter? Have her call me immediately."

19. An Emergency

"I just found out I have cancer."

20. Bad Feeling

"I had a dream that something bad happened to you."

21. Hoover by Proxy

This occurs when your partner gets someone else to reach out to you on his or her behalf. That person may try to persuade you that your partner has changed, and you should give him or her another chance, or that you're being too hard on him or her.

22. Threats

"There's no reason for me to live if you won't be with me."

23. Religious Hoover

"I know it's God's will for us to be together."

24. Future-Faking

"I was going to buy you a ring and ask you to marry me."

25. Playing the Victim

"Everyone in my life leaves me."

It's important to prepare for and learn to navigate the hoover for no-contact to succeed. There are certain conditions when hoovering is more likely to happen and many of them are under your control.

(1) When you've stopped contacting them

(2) When they see you look happy on social media or hear through others you are moving on

(3) If they want to test you to see if they can still control you

(4) If they have reason to believe you would be easy to draw back into the fold

(5) If they have easy access to you

(6) If they don't have any other source of attention or distraction, and you were a particularly good one

(7) If they are bored

Sandra L. Brown, M.A., refers to hoovering as the Boomerang stage of the pathological love relationship, and her research reminds us that no matter how bad the end of the relationship was or how long it's been, there is always a possibility a pathological partner will return. They require multiple possible sources of attention. Because you have been a source of that attention at some point in their history, you will now always be in their ever-rotating carousel of potentialities until something happens to cause them to reach out to see if you can be drawn back into the cycle with them again.[184] You cannot know or control what a pathological partner is doing with other people, how occupied or fulfilled he or she feels by those other people, or whether he or she is bored. Therefore, you can never completely trust a pathological partner will not come back.

To prepare for hoovering, you must first accept your partner is going to try to hoover you. You should make every effort on your end to make yourself as difficult to contact as possible. Recognizing that a determined low-conscience individual can always find a way, imagine the type of hoover the pathological partner in your life is likely to use. What would he or she say?

Just by making the decision to go no-contact, taking the proper precautions, and sticking with your decision, you can decrease the likelihood your partner will ever return. If you have developed the attitude of indifference that it doesn't matter what is going on in the life of your partner after the relationship ends, you have removed almost all their power to hoover you at all.

If you receive one of these hoover attempts, do not respond. Not responding includes not telling them you aren't planning to respond. It definitely involves avoiding rehashing the past with them or telling them anything about what you are feeling. You should also not insult or attack them.

Brown highlights the fact that every contact is viewed as an opportunity for a psychopath:

> *When she answers his call five years later to "give him a piece of her mind" and proceeds to ream him, [the psychopath] is grinning because even anger or hate is attention, and what he perceives as the flip side of love. Rubbing his hands together, his go-go-now brain says, "She wants me. I just have to be contrite."' Any contact is a green light for him to resume pursuit.*[185]

Just. Don't. Respond. It's tempting, but there is nothing you could say that will make them feel worse than your absolute silence, and nothing they can say will make you feel better than theirs.

Do not take the hoover bait. Don't worry about being seen as cold by not responding.

Just remember: your partner wasn't worried about all those times he or she was cold to you.

What if I Can't Go No-Contact?

What if you can't physically go no contact because of practical reasons that extend beyond your psychological will? This section is for you, particularly if you are in one or more of the following circumstances.

1. You Work Together

If you work with your partner, you may fear he or she will try to sabotage you when you break it off. The idea of starting smear campaigns with people you know socially is bad enough, but the knowledge that they might try to destroy your career could be paralyzing. You might need time to figure out how to get another job and the logistics of doing it without your partner knowing. There may even be a lot of soul-searching to do over whether you even want to do that or not if you truly love your job. In a tight economy or market, leaving may not be an option at all.

2. You Live Together

If you've started building a life together with your partner, whether you're married or not, you can't just walk out overnight. It takes time to figure out what to do next. Finding somewhere new to live takes time, not to mention working out the legal details if you own property together or both of you signed a lease or you share assets or debts.

3. You Don't Have the Resources

Perhaps you are completely dependent on your partner for survival. He or she has isolated you from almost everyone, and you don't have financial resources. You may be ill or lack job skills and may feel unable to live on your own and have no one else to assist you. At the very least, it may take a long time to gather the financial and supportive resources, or you may decide it isn't a practical possibility in your situation. Pathological partners do a great job of convincing us that no matter how bad things are with them, it's worse without them to create fear and dependency. I actively encourage you to envision a life without your partner and explore what resources are available to help you.

4. You Have Children Together

Your partner may decide he or she doesn't want to be a part of the children's lives; however, as long as the court system has left his or her parental rights intact, he or she can always reappear at any time to exercise those rights, and you have no control over how or when that may happen.

5. There Are Other Legal Reasons You Have to Be in Contact

If your partner assaulted you and there are criminal proceedings or there are civil court issues, such as property division or other legal reasons why the two of you need to maintain regular contact, this could potentially drag out for months or years. You may not need to have direct contact, but true no-contact, by definition, requires not interacting with or seeing the pathological partner at all, including through third parties. No contact is not possible as long as a legal tie exists.

6. Your Partner Doesn't Respect Your Decision to Leave

Perhaps you can't leave because you're afraid of what they'll do when you walk out, or they just won't leave you alone. Whether it's relentless stalking, threats, and violence or lovesick pursuit—or a twisted, mind-bending combination of both—the emotional overwhelm of terror and love and perhaps the very real threat to your life keep you trapped in a bond with them.

Often pathological partners leverage a combined set of these circumstances to make it difficult or impossible for us to go no-contact. They use the law or our access to resources or the things we need to survive to torment us. This can allow them to walk in and out as they please while keeping us off balance and provoking us into reacting as we become more desperate for stability and control over our lives.

If you cannot go no-contact, there is an alternative you can use instead of no contact, known as "gray rock."[186] When you use gray rock, you are in contact with your partner because circumstances require it; however, it can be thought of as emotional no-contact.

Gray rock requires cutting off your partner psychologically just as no-contact does. We must make the decision in our minds that the relationship is over, and there is no going back. We must prepare our mines then close off our partners from having access to us emotionally and psychologically. This means that even though you must keep interacting with your partner, his or her actions will have no effect.

Instead of cutting off your partner physically (or ensuring the pathological partner cannot contact you) as with no-contact, gray rock requires that you modify how you interact with your partner. That may take many forms, including:

- flat affect
- monotone voice
- responding only when they reach out and only when it is necessary to respond, in other words, not reaching out first unless it is unavoidable
- short responses that provide no extraneous information
- neutral delivery of information
- making yourself appear less interesting in their presence so they feel bored
- providing them with no more attention than necessary (for example, no prolonged eye contact)
- remaining uninterested in what they say or do and cutting conversations short if they try to divert conversations into unnecessary topics

Gray rock is about the end of the relationship as both of you know it. It's important to keep in mind that gray rock is equivalent to no-contact. You use gray rock when you are ready to break up with your partner and take back control of your mind and your life. It's a boundary-setting mechanism you use for yourself and your peace of mind.

By using gray rock, you let your partner know they can no longer expect any emotional response or stimulation from you. There will be no more drama he or she can feed on. It avoids giving the pathological partner any new information that can allow him or her to take advantage of you or use to further harm you financially or destroy your reputation. It helps to protect you from future emotional harm since making a clean separation from them completely is not possible. It helps protect you from hoovering.

You are conditioning your partner with gray rock to finally respect your wishes and leave you alone. It's the equivalent of blocking your partner from contacting you or receiving hoovers after no-contact and deleting them. If nothing your partner tries ever changes the way you react to him or her, your partner should hopefully move on. He or she may reach out to see if you'll respond, as with hoovering, but don't take the bait. It's up to you to set your intention that this is your stance, and they need to understand the goal up front.

Gray rock is a method of no-contact, which means it is not a method of trying passively to "give your partner a taste of his or her own medicine," get your partner to change, or punish your partner. This is what you do when psychologically cut yourself off from your partner; there's no going back, as with no-contact.

You should not feel guilty for using gray rock. You are not cruel for setting a boundary. Using gray rock is also not equivalent to the abuse your partner has inflicted on you throughout the relationship. It's all about motive. Pathological partners stonewall, walk out, ignore, and dismiss your feelings because they are manipulating you into suppressing your normal human emotions, needs, and reactions to suit them so they can exploit you. In contrast, you are implementing gray rock as a response to their behavior as a result of that manipulation only because they don't respect your boundaries and may be dangerous. Sadly, sometimes a pathological partner will further try to manipulate us into believing our healthy boundaries are equivalent to their attempts to exploit us. This is not the case!

If you find yourself unable to escape the death grip of the pathological partner, gray rock may cause your partner to release that grip on you.

19

Developing a Game Plan

Regardless of the strategy you're using to leave, it's always best not to do it spontaneously or by letting your authentic self do it for you subconsciously. It's better to try to make a plan to ensure you can be safe and have access to what you need during and after the process. Because of the nature of these types of relationships, there are external and environmental considerations you should factor in ahead of time to ensure your breakup can have the best chance to succeed.

Making a plan beforehand is about three things:

(1) planning for the things you know will happen rather than deciding as they come up

(2) preparing for things that might happen so you aren't caught off guard

(3) establishing an environment that will set you up to be successful

You should try to incorporate these things into your plan to assist you as you psychologically prepare to go no-contact.

The Actual Act of Going No-Contact

Make this a conscious, deliberate act, if possible. Or at least have as much about this sorted out as possible. What you want to try to avoid is breaking up spontaneously and ending up in danger or walking out without all your possessions and having them end up in a fire pit. "Winging it" is not a good idea. Questions to consider: *How* will you break up with your partner? In person? Over the phone? In a letter or email? Will you move away and simply cut off all contact? Will you just use gray rock, as described in the previous chapter? ***What other considerations and precautions do you need to take first? Is your partner likely to take revenge? How and what can you do right now to mitigate damage?***

If you decide to tell your partner you are leaving, consider carefully factors such as the reasons you will provide and how much detail you will offer. No matter what reason you provide or what tone you take, you should expect and be prepared for a variety of hoovering tactics immediately: promises to change, appeals to destiny, accusations, full on rage, appeals to your values, threats, victim ploys, finger-pointing at your past wrongs, future-faking, and others. You may want to meet in public or bring someone else with you if you decide to do it in person.

Access to Possessions/Information

Does your partner have keys, passwords, codes, or other access abilities that would allow him or her to take charge of possessions or accounts or to learn or gain private information about you? Is his or her name on any of your accounts? Take precautions to change these so he or she will no longer have access.

Contact Methods

Make a list of all the ways your partner can currently contact you. You will need to find a way to block or remove as many of them as possible either before or after the breakup, whichever you believe is the safer thing to do. Out of rage, your partner may do you the favor of doing this for you. If you must communicate, use methods that can be documented and keep it short.

Unexpected Contact

Visualize receiving unexpected contact from your partner after the breakup. What would it say? How does your partner typically use language to reel you in? Imagine yourself deleting it or throwing it away, then how you will distract and take care of yourself afterward.

Social Media

Review the people with whom you have made friends or who can view your profiles on social media. If possible, you should not remain in contact with anyone who will inadvertently give you news about your partner or report back to him or her about what you are doing.

Self-care

Your emotions are likely to fluctuate. You will doubt yourself, and you will feel guilty and lost. How will you manage these emotions? How will you fill your time now that your partner isn't dominating it? Who can you rely on for social support? Develop a support and self-care plan for yourself.

Physical Environment

If securing temporary housing is necessary until you can find something longer term, make sure you've talked to someone about having a place to go once you leave. If leaving your home is not an issue, think about your surroundings. What about your home reminds you of your partner? Is it arranged to his or her liking? Do you have mementos or gifts from your relationship lying around? If you can change or get rid of these items prior to the breakup, do so. If you are unable to do that now, make a plan for doing so as soon as you go no-contact.

Routines and Habits

Are there daily routines and habits you've established because of your partner or that remind you of your partner? Start dismantling them and replace them with pleasant routines that make you feel good about yourself before the relationship ends. For example, do you and your partner tell each other good morning each day by phone or text messages? Can you start your day by greeting someone else, too, when that stops so you won't feel the absence of that greeting with your partner as strongly? Is there a new way you can drive to work so you don't have to pass by your partner's house, one where you can maybe reward yourself with a cup of coffee at your favorite coffee shop? Or if you are unable to do that, maybe pass through a favorite park or stop by once a week and say hello to someone you care about?

There will also likely be other things specific to your relationship you will need to consider that pertain to the life you and your partner have established together or perhaps your partner's personality. These questions pertain to your safety, your living arrangements, your health, and your legal and financial situation. Although it is outside the scope of this book to consider the level to which these may affect you or all the factors that could apply, here are some of the most important questions you should ask yourself when developing your plan.

- Is your partner violent, or has your partner threatened you with violence?
- Do you fear your partner or have reason to believe your partner will take revenge on you or your loved ones?
- Do you currently live with or share a home with your partner?
- Will you need to divorce your partner? Do you have children with your partner?
- Are there currently any civil or criminal proceedings pending?
- Do you co-mingle finances with your partner or share debts or assets?
- To what degree are you isolated from social support, or does your partner have the ability to isolate you from your social support?
- Do you have any health conditions that require medication or access to doctors, and will you continue to have access to these after no-contact?
- Do you have financial resources you can rely on?

If any of these situations pertain to you, I would encourage you to consult the resources in **Appendix C** in this book for information on where to go for help. Please be safe and don't let your partner convince you that you are unworthy of a life without them, free of fear and pain.

In the event you are experiencing an emergency, however, please stop working on a plan to exit the relationship and dial 9-1-1 within the U.S. for immediate assistance.

20

But . . . How Will I Survive without My Partner?

Here you stand at the edge of the abyss.

You envision the days ahead, and you cannot imagine a future in which your partner is not there. The thought may even make you feel panicked.

I know because I was there.

Relationships with pathological partners keep us in a walking sleep-state. They hold us captive, tethered to them by the competing emotions inside us and the death grip they have on our hearts.

The big blank question mark in front of you exists because love-bombing is indoctrination. You were pulled under before you knew you were drowning, then swept to safety by the one who quietly put their hand over your mouth to keep you from asking why.

You are the only one who can know when it's time to take that leap. I know that however ready you are, you are already grieving the loss of your partner.

No one can tell you when you're ready, but to save yourself, you will one day have to let him or her go and make it to the other side of that decision, then keep going so you aren't frozen in a relationship that made you into a shadow of the person you once were.

I may not know exactly where you are along that path, but I understand the paralysis. Although there are many stops, the ways I got sidetracked along the path were always the same. There were times when my ex-boyfriend would come back to me with grandiose promises, and all the knowledge about narcissistic abuse I had gained would slip into the back of my mind as if I had never read any of it. I would tell myself none of it applied to him or us, that we were different or special. I would even block out a lot of what he had done to me. It was as if a part of me was asleep—and in a way, it was.

This sleep state is what this book is about.

No matter where you are now, no matter what your path looks like at this very moment—take what you know, what your mind will now let you accept, and just start walking and keep going. Your authentic voice knows what needs to be done, and it will guide you if you keep listening to it.

Do you feel more awake now? Are the answers to your unanswered questions any clearer?

The big blank question mark in front of you exists because love-bombing is indoctrination.

I know how painful all of this is. But I promise that if I can make it out, you can too.

If you're not there yet, it's okay. It takes time to break yourself out of this. But you can, and you must. I did it when my authentic self was wide awake and screaming at me to pay attention because I was slowly dying inside.

The fact that you are reading this means that voice inside of you is alive and trying to get you to pay attention.

I'm not going to lie to you. It's not easy at first on the other side either. But there are millions of us here on the other side waiting for you.

You may think you'll never get out of the relationship, however, rest assured in your heart that you can because your partner can never completely override your authentic self, as much as he or she may want to. Your authentic self is growing stronger, and you can help that happen—one day, one hour, one minute at a time.

If you doubt it, open the book to page one and start reading it again.

You will escape. You will take your life back.

Coda

April 12, 2018

Was that you trying to contact me?

September 25, 2018

Are you fucking Jordan?

February 22, 2020

Hey, I'm at Rocket Bar by your apartment. Reminded me of you. Come through if you get this.

In the immediate months after Amir and I broke up, I had wondered when I would accept that the relationship was over. I eventually did. I doubt Amir ever will.

As a tactic to get me to stop talking about one of the many destructive things he had done to me, he used to say, "Nothing I do is ever good enough for you."

He distracted me from what was behind the mask for a long time, but he could never get me to forget he was wearing one. That's what they'd truly like to distract you from: the mask itself. However, they can't once you recognize something is not what it appears to be because the mask is part of the pathology. It's like covering a scar with makeup. Their pathological behavior leads back to more pathology every time, even if we don't know what we're looking at.

When you start a relationship with a pathological partner, your relationship is already dying and you with it—you just don't know it yet. It's a multiple hit that would take anyone down:

1. First, they deceive you into forming an intimate bond.
2. Then, they violate, exploit, and degrade you in every way they feel entitled—sexually, financially, professionally, psychologically, and physically.
3. Next, they claim they are the real victims of your insistence on your autonomy, boundaries, and human rights. They will twist the story line until they make you believe it too.
4. Then, they shame you—even publicly—and strip you of dignity if you don't accept the responsibility for your own degradation and exploitation.
5. They then deprive you of your sanity by putting this program on repeat and sharing your meltdown with others so they can control the narrative to make the problem you and your instability (*and conveniently leave out the fact that they violated your human rights!*).

6. Finally, as you grow weaker, they drain everything left of you right out in the open where they now have everyone's support until they feel you're no longer of any use to them.

Amir sent me so many love songs over the years, songs I heard again and again until the words stitched themselves into my narrative of us and worked their way into my dreams.

One day, however, near the end, he played a different type of song for me. The song was titled "Thief" by Ansel Elgort, and the chorus repeated the singer's description of "stealing" a woman's heart, destroying it, and being unremorseful.

I waited for the sappy, dramatic arc that would weave its way into our love story. There wasn't one, however.

"Why are you playing this for me?" I asked.

He shrugged. "Because I know I did you wrong."

I didn't like it. I knew what he wanted to appear to say to me with the song, which was that he was acknowledging the damage he had caused me. Yet it seemed more like he was making a confession. The tone of the song didn't exactly convey its message with pride, but it didn't convey it with regret either. There were other lyrical references to the futility of redemption.

It wasn't until later that I realized why the song bothered me so much. I realized the song wasn't really about the acts committed in the lyrics at all but about the man committing them.

Turns out, Amir was right all along. Nothing he did was ever good enough. Because he wasn't capable of that.

Close your eyes, warrior.

Imagine it's a year from now. Imagine that someone knocks at your door and delivers you a box. When you open it, there are a dozen roses inside. There's a card with them that reads, "You'll always be the love of my life," along with your partner's signature.

Now. Imagine yourself throwing them in the trash.

Stay strong.

Cheat Sheet

Q. Why am I reading this book?

A. Some part of you recognizes that your partner is seriously harming you and that part of you wants to help you escape the relationship.

Q. What's wrong with my partner?

A. Your partner likely has an impaired conscience, which suppresses their ability to identify with your pain or care about the harm they cause you and factor it into their decision-making before they act.

Q. Is my partner really pathological?

A. If your partner demonstrates a lack of empathy toward your pain and a lack of remorse toward the harm they cause you—and they do this consistently and repeatedly even after you have told them that their actions hurt you—your partner may be pathological. However, it's less important what your partner is than what your partner does. Your partner's actions toward you are not normal or acceptable. Take that in. No label is needed for you to be justified in saying to yourself that you are being violated and treated unjustly.

Q. Can my partner change?

A. Philosophically speaking, no one can say with any certainty whether any one individual has the capacity to change or will change. However, if you have determined that your partner is likely pathological or is exhibiting pathological behavior, then the answer is almost certainly "no." Conscience-impaired individuals are often unwilling, and may be biologically incapable, of doing things it takes a conscience to do, like consider the impact of their behavior on others before acting.

Q. Is my partner "good" or "bad?"

A. This is a "false choice" question. It's a set-up, a question we ask ourselves because we can't resolve our cognitive dissonance when presented with their behavioral extremes. They do "bad" things because they don't take you into consideration when making choices or because they enjoy hurting you. Then, they do "good" things to try to convince you they actually do love you. The truth is that your partner has an impaired conscience. They can only be as "good" as the worst thing they are willing to do.

Q. Does my partner mean to hurt me?

A. When they want to get back at you for something or just want to watch you suffer, then yes. Sometimes, however, they aren't intending to hurt you. It's just that they don't care if something they do is hurting you or not. Their behavior is often not calculated. What's causing you so much added pain is the callousness. They didn't consider you or care that what they did hurt you.

Q. Why can't I just leave?

A. You were discouraged from resolving your cognitive dissonance using your own judgment and observation. You developed a pseudo-identity on top of your authentic self that suppresses the conclusions you've drawn about your partner's harmful behavior. The pseudo-identity identifies with your partner, defends your partner, takes the blame and feels guilty, and tries to please your partner. When your authentic self tries to speak up or get you to walk out, your pseudo-identity keeps you chained to your partner because of the psychological manipulation your partner uses to ensure the pseudo-identity stays active.

Q. Does my partner love me?

A. Your partner may feel some of the chemicals in the brain we associate with infatuation, such as dopamine and oxytocin, and may even say they love you because they feel the release of these chemicals. However, the way they express love is superficial and conditional. Their behavior doesn't reinforce their words, and when they use that word, they do not associate it with other important concepts usually tied to love, such as fidelity, trust, self-sacrifice, commitment, and honesty because they are not forming an attachment.

Q. Where did *I* go?

A. The pseudo-identity has taken over and your authentic self is being suppressed. This is a form of dissociation. You're constantly flipping back and forth between the two views of your partner, and it has caused a sense of fragility because you can no longer figure out what's real. You're still in there, though.

Q. What if the problem is me?

A. If the problem was you, you would always have felt this way. All your other relationships would be like this one. You would feel like this when you interacted with people in relationships other than your romantic ones. Plus, your partner would never have needed to manipulate you to make you compliant—and you know you've changed, that you've been manipulated because of the way you feel now.

Q. How do I get out of here?

A. Devote time to strengthening your authentic self and weakening the pseudo-identity before you leave. Plan your exit strategy carefully. Psychologically prepare yourself for your partner to try to continue to keep you trapped in the relationship and take small steps, using your awareness of what's going on and your authentic self, to interact with your partner differently.

Q. How will I survive without my partner?

A. It's impossible to believe when you're in the relationship, but after it's over, despite the agony, there is also relief. The relief you will feel occurs because the painful invisible chains wrapped around you break almost immediately. Your authentic self wants to be free, even though it will hurt at first when you let go. Though the agony starts to fade, the relief never does. You eventually don't just survive—you thrive.

Appendix A—Survey Description

The survivor experiences included in this book were collected from responses to a website survey between October and December 2019. The complete survey consisted of sixteen total questions, which are collapsed in the appendix into fourteen questions based on the number of responses. The total number of questions each respondent had the opportunity to answer was dependent on the responses received to key questions, a method of survey delivery known as conditional branch logic. The questions were designed using narcissistic abuse terminology, which often uses the term "narcissist" to refer to all pathological partners.

Voluntary responses were solicited by emails sent to the readers of Fairy Tale Shadows, a website aimed at providing research and resources to survivors of narcissistic abuse. There were a total of 605 respondents. Where **N** appears beside each question below, it designates the number of respondents who provided an answer to the question.

The open-ended questions in the survey were as follows:

Q1. Please briefly describe the moment you realized something was wrong in your relationship or how you came to recognize that your partner was a narcissist. What happened to cause you to have this understanding? ***(N=514)***

Q2. What do you feel was or is the most painful part of being in a relationship with a narcissist? ***(N=553)***

Q3. What do you believe has helped you maintain "no-contact" the most? ***(N=169)****; Respondents who answered "I went no contact" to Q8. (Who ended the relationship?) were provided with the opportunity to respond to this question.*

In addition, the following closed-ended questions also included comment sections that provided an opportunity for qualitative analysis:

Q6. Are you currently in a relationship with a narcissist?

Q8. Who ended the relationship?

Q14. How long ago did you come to the realization that something was wrong or that your partner was a narcissist?

These six questions provided a total of 1,902 responses. I used grounded theory to identify the major concepts in the comments and to group the concepts into larger categories.[187] These concepts and categories formed the major themes of the book, particularly the five major questions on which this book is based. Survivor experiences are used throughout the book in the ***Pathological Love Stories*** feature based on these questions, as well as other themes.

The remaining closed-ended questions and their responses are shown below to provide more information on the relationship situations of the respondents.

Relationship Background

Q4. What was or is your relationship to the narcissist—in other words, what was your role in the relationship?

Table A-1

N=573		
Wife	*190*	*33.2%*
Girlfriend	*181*	*31.6%*
Boyfriend	*72*	*12.6%*
Husband	*66*	*11.5%*
Other	*64*	*11.2%*

Q5. Have you had more than one adult-to-adult relationship with a narcissist?

Table A-2

N=514		
No	*260*	*50.6%*
Yes	*254*	*49.4%*

Relationship Status

Q6. Are you currently in a relationship with a narcissist?

Table A-3

N=605		
No	*421*	*69.6%*
Yes	*184*	*30.4%*

Q7. How long were you previously in a relationship with the narcissist?

Table A-4

*N=404**		
More than 10 years	*152*	*37.6%*
4–10 years	*123*	*30.5%*
2–3 years	*79*	*19.6%*
7 months - 1 year	*35*	*8.7%*
0–6 months	*15*	*3.7%*

*Respondents in Q6 who answered "No."

Survivors Not Currently in a Pathological Love Relationship

Q8. Who ended the relationship?

Table A-5

N=404*		
I went no contact	*174*	*43.1%*
It's complicated	*147*	*36.4%*
The narcissist left the relationship	*83*	*20.6%*

*Respondents in Q6 who answered "No."

Q9. How long have you been "no contact" with the narcissist?

Table A- 6

N=169*		
0-6 months	*83*	*49.1%*
7 months–1 year	*46*	*27.2%*
2-3 years	*31*	*18.3%*
4-10 years	*7*	*4.1%*
More than 10 years	*2*	*1.9%*

*Respondents in Q8 who answered, "I went no contact."

Q10. How long has it been since you had contact with the narcissist?

Table A- 7

N=169*		
0-6 months	*104*	*61.6%*
7 months–1 year	*38*	*22.5%*
2-3 years	*21*	*12.4%*
4-10 years	*4*	*2.4%*
More than 10 years	*2*	*1.9%*

*Respondents in Q8 who answered, "I went no contact."

Survivors Currently in a Pathological Love Relationship

Q11. Has the narcissist tried to reach out to you since you implemented "no contact?"

Table A- 8

N=169*		
Yes	*119*	*70.4%*
No	*50*	*29.6%*

*Respondents in Q8 who answered, "I went no contact."

Q12. How long have you been involved with the narcissist?

Table A- 9

N=170*		
More than 10 years	*95*	*55.9%*
4-10 years	*49*	*28.8%*
2-3 years	*22*	*12.9%*
7 months–1 year	*4*	*2.4%*

*Respondents in Q6 who answered "Yes."

Q13. What is the most difficult part of the relationship to explain to others?

Table A- 10

N=451*		
Why I stay(ed) as long as I have or did	*118*	*26.2%*
What narcissistic abuse is/what happened to me in the relationship	*111*	*24.6%*
Why the relationship is so traumatic/ why it takes so long to recover	*108*	*23.9%*
Why I miss the narcissist even though they hurt me so much	*53*	*11.8%*
Why I was unable to see or heed the red flags	*31*	*6.9%*
How difficult it was/is to break up	*20*	*4.4%*
My own motivations for being in the relationship	*10*	*2.2%*
Other(partner's behavior, respondent's behavior)*	*4*	*0.9%*

*Written comments stating "All of the above" are excluded from the analysis.

Q14. How long ago did you come to the realization that something was wrong or that your partner was a narcissist?

Table A- 11

N=514		
More than one year ago	*369*	*71.8%*
Between one month ago and one year ago	*138*	*26.8%*
More than a week ago but less than a month ago	*6*	*1.2%*
Within the last week	*1*	*0.2%*

Appendix B—Pathological Love Relationship Glossary

For a comprehensive glossary of terms related to pathological relationships, narcissistic abuse, and recovery, please review the one on my website, Fairy Tale Shadows, at https://fairytaleshadows.com/narcissist-dictionary-terms/

Anti-Social Personality Disorder (ASPD): A personality disorder in which someone shows a strong disregard for norms, morals, and the law, and often the rights and safety of others. A typical person with the disorder has a willingness to manipulate and exploit others, behaves impulsively and irresponsibly to get what they want, and is unconcerned with what anyone else thinks. Lack of remorse and empathy are key characteristics.

Ambient Abuse: Atmospheric abuse created through persistent gaslighting, isolation, information control, instability, covert manipulation of events, and other psychologically abusive tactics. It results in an erosion of the victim's confidence, perception of reality, and independence so the abuser can control and exploit the victim in other ways.

Abuse Amnesia: Involuntary denial in which the survivor of a pathological relationship suppresses awareness of the abuse during periods of love-bombing to avoid psychological conflict or anxiety. This develops subconsciously over time as an adaptation to extreme cognitive dissonance after suffering through multiple rounds of the narcissistic cycle of abuse to continue to function while surviving a relationship that feels impossible to escape.

BITE model: A model developed by cult expert Dr. Steven Hassan, it consists of four components that a person or group can use to psychologically manipulate someone if successfully controlled: **B**ehaviors, **I**nformation, **T**houghts, and **E**motions.

Brainwashing: A term used to explain the most repressive forms of mind control in which individuals know they are under a coercive influence, such as totalitarian societies and prisoners of war. Because of this, they may be subjected to the most overt and some of the most physically harsh methods of thought reform.

Coercive Control: A term for excessive monitoring and covert or overt dominance over one or more areas of a partner's life, such as finances, career, friendships, clothing choices, hobbies, or communication. It usually begins as concern for the partner, starts slowly, and can be subtle, when it can be cloaked and hidden in many seemingly loving behaviors. These include criticizing in an off-handed way the partner's body, clothing, accomplishments, or friends; invading privacy by reading private messages or listening in on phone calls; accusing the partner of cheating when no evidence exists; insisting the partner remain in constant contact; and making it very unpleasant for the partner to do things that don't involve the abuser. The results of these behaviors are to cause doubt and lower the self-esteem of the partner and to isolate him or her from others and give the pathological partner more control.

Cognitive Dissonance: The uncomfortable feeling of anxiety that results when our actions, beliefs, or emotions conflict with one another or when we hold two contradictory beliefs. The greater the dissonance, the stronger the urge to resolve it.

Cult: A group in which deceptive practices are used to recruit members, the members express very strong or absolute devotion to an idea or a person, and a leader or leaders exploit and manipulate the devotion of the group members to their own detriment.

Dissociation: The state of feeling disconnected to what is happening around oneself, as if it has an unreal quality to it or is happening to someone else. This state is an adaptation to the trauma of the narcissistic abuse cycle. There are two types of dissociation: compartmentalization and detachment. Compartmentalization is the dissociated type most relevant to the trauma described in this book.

Dual Identity: After a person has been in a repressive environment that restricts his or her thoughts and actions, including a relationship with a low-conscience individual, he or she may develop dual thoughts and motivations that stem from the "authentic self" that recognizes the partner's behavior as abusive and the "false self" that has adapted to the abuse and emerged due to the partner's manipulation. This results in survivors of pathological love relationships developing a dual identity as a survival mechanism to avoid being absorbed by the partner. It allows them to protect their true self while also resolving cognitive dissonance and avoiding further punishment.

Final Discard. Pathological partners follow a relationship pattern (see **Idealize-Devaluation-Discard**), but they often return and keep their ex-partners in a rotation for months or even years (see **Hoovering**). A final discard is considered the moment when some pathological partners decide to discontinue the cycle on their own and leave the partner forever, sometimes in the most damaging way possible. Yet, with a pathological partner, partners can never know if the cycle is over or he or she is putting it on pause—even a long one. Therefore, an argument can be made that the "final discard" is theoretical.

FOG: The mental state of confusion generated by the psychological and emotional abuse perpetrated by pathological partners. It stands for Fear, Obligation, and Guilt, some of the primary manufactured emotions pathological partners use to try to keep their partners bound to them.

Future-Faking: Grandiose promises to survivors that pathological partners make about highly desirable events or tangible items the pathological partner knows are meaningful to their partner, but the pathological partner has no intention of following through on—unless it is beneficial and convenient to the pathological partner. The promises are made to fake intimacy and familiarity so the pathological partner can gain something in the moment.

Gaslighting: Providing conflicting information or lying to someone in direct contradiction to what that person blatantly perceives for himself or herself. Over time, people subjected to repeated gaslighting can start to doubt their perceptions of reality. The term comes from a 1944 play turned film, in which a man purposely tries to drive his wife insane by making the gaslights flicker, then telling her she is imagining it when she points it out.

Gray Rock: When there are barriers that prevent a partner from ending contact with their narcissistic partner entirely (see **No-Contact**), this is an alternative in which the partner remains in technical contact with the pathological partner out of necessity, however, has emotionally detached from him or her. The contact occurs only when necessary, is devoid of emotion, and does not provide the pathological partner with any information beyond what is essential to convey.

Grooming: The process of slowly combining negative behavior with positive behavior in a relationship to erode a partner's boundaries so he or she will accept abusive treatment. Sometimes a metaphor of "boiling the frog" is used to explain how this can happen, in which the heat is turned up slowly, and the frog doesn't know it's being boiled until it's too late.

Hoovering: A "hoover," named after a brand of vacuum cleaner, is a tactic used by pathological partners to "suck" a survivor back into the narcissistic abuse cycle. It happens after a period of silence (a "discard") during which the survivor and the pathological partner are not in contact with each other. During a hoover, the pathological partner reaches out to the survivor again to make contact using a predictable method that eventually consolidates in declarations of (undying) love. What characterizes a hoover is that it is insincere. Its purpose is to bring the survivor back under control, and despite any promises otherwise, no lasting change in behavior from the pathological partner will have occurred.

Hypnosis: A trance state in which a person's mental focus turns inward, and he or she disconnects from the external environment. This results in the body being able to perform acts without mental attention.

Idealize-Devaluation-Discard: The stages of the narcissistic cycle of abuse. In the **idealization stage** at the beginning of the relationship, the pathological partner puts his or her partner on a pedestal and showers them with excessive praise and attention. At some point, the pathological partner will begin to see his or her partner as flawed or even grow bored, and the **devaluation stage** begins. The pathological partner begins to abuse the partner but sees himself or herself as the victim because the partner is not providing attention or not bending to his or her will. Finally, when the pathological partner no longer sees any value in the partner, perhaps if the partner has asked one too many times for an explanation of why something has changed or demanded to be treated with respect, the pathological partner **discards** the partner for a new partner. The cycle often repeats many times before the relationship ends.

Identity Erosion: During all stages of the narcissistic cycle of abuse, narcissistic abusers use emotional control, behavioral control, information control, and thought control to reward and punish their partners. As a result, the partner adopts a perspective that identifies and protects the partner and his or her personality changes. This identity erosion is not "total" and, in other contexts, is referred to as a "dual identity" or "doubling" because partners may often feel as if they are in conflict with themselves over their own desires.

Intermittent Reinforcement: A pattern of behavior in which the pathological partner randomly intersperses kindness between acts of cruelty. Psychological research demonstrates this is an especially powerful method of influencing behavior. Because the partner never knows when the pathological partner will show kindness, the randomness is one of the most critical forces that keeps the partner tied to the relationship, hoping it could come at any moment, and that each time, the cruelty has come to an end.

Learned Helplessness: A psychological attitude the survivor of a pathological love relationship may develop in which he or she feels powerless to leave or escape the relationship despite having a desire to be free of it. It can result from traumatic or ineffective attempts to leave due to dramatic or aggressive responses by the pathological partner. As pathological partners repeatedly draw survivors back into the cycle, survivors begin to feel as if they have no control over their own lives.

Love-Bombing: A period of intense, positive domination of the time, attention, and/or space of either a new partner or a partner who has been hoovered back into a relationship. The pathological partner bombards the partner with excessive flattery, over-the-top declarations of love and romantic gestures, gifts, sex, and many psychologically manipulative tactics to elicit fast-tracked familiarity and intimacy (see **Mirroring, Future-Faking**). As a result, partners form (and later strengthen) a powerful bond with the pathological partner. The pathological partner's behavior elicits trust, vulnerability, and dependence, which makes the survivor easier to exploit.

Malignant Narcissist: A special sub-type of narcissist who shares some of the characteristics of those with ASPD, such as aggressiveness, deceitfulness, and remorselessness. They are often sadistic and gain pleasure from hurting others.

Mind Control: The use of tactics or behaviors to influence a person's autonomy and identity. They may be forcible or deceptive, known or subtle. The goal is to replace the person's authentic self with a different identity that will act in ways that serve the interests of the controller. The mind control is usually not total when the environment is non-immersive, thus the dual identity emerges (See **Dual Identity**).

Mirroring: One of the tactics used during love-bombing. It can be physical, such as when the pathological partner mimics the partner's body language, behaviors, and actions. Mirroring may also be verbal/psychological. For example, the pathological partner could claim to enjoy the same activities or to have had similar experiences as a partner to make it appear as if the two have a lot in common.

Narcissistic Personality Disorder (NPD): A type of personality disorder in which a person has fantasies of self-importance and grandiosity that they believe entitle them to expect deference and special treatment from others. They lack self-insight and often claim they are being victimized when deference from others is not forthcoming. Their lack of emotional empathy leads them to exploit others to benefit themselves.

No-Contact: The deliberate physical and psychological act by a partner of leaving a relationship with a pathological partner or, if the pathological partner is not currently in the picture, of ensuring the relationship will never rekindle. No-contact includes taking steps in the material world to ensure the pathological partner cannot make contact with the partner and mentally preparing psychologically for not interacting with the pathological partner again.

Pathological Love Relationship: A relationship in which a person experiences "inevitable harm" as a result of their partner's low-conscience disorder.

Pathological Lying: Known to be a common behavior of narcissists and sociopaths, this type of lying is done compulsively out of habit. Often pathological liars tell lies to establish control. The lies may not always seem to personally benefit the liar; however, some lies may be told simply for enjoyment in what is known as "duper's delight."

Projection: A defense mechanism in which someone accuses others of their own wrongful actions to avoid shame. Pathological partners also project because they often see other people as extensions and reflections of themselves, so they often have an unfounded belief that others are exploiting them as much as they are exploiting others.

Reactive Abuse. A method of entrapment in which pathological partners manipulate their partners through hidden violence, manufactured emotions, coercive control, and other tactics over a long period of time until a partner responds aggressively, saying or doing things they wouldn't have done under ordinary circumstances. Also known as violent resistance, a coping mechanism for intimate terrorism.[189] Pathological partners use the reactions to justify their own abuse or claim to be the true victim in the relationship.

Silent Treatment: A period of non-responsiveness used as a punishment by pathological partners, in which they disappear and cut off their partners, treating them as if they don't exist. It can be used for any behavior the pathological partner doesn't like or arbitrarily when the pathological partner perceives a fault in the relationship.

Smear Campaign: A covert operation on behalf of the pathological partner to attack the credibility of the survivor by spreading gossip or telling half-truths and lies to those in both their own social circle and the survivor's social circle. The pathological partner does this to isolate the survivor from social support and to guard against their own exposure if the survivor decides to discuss the abuse. They may also do it to prepare for their exit from the relationship or to gain sympathy from others.

Stockholm Syndrome: A phenomenon in which victims of trauma who are subject to horrific conditions or threats to their safety identify with their tormentors due to moments of kindness the victims are shown during the event. Those moments of humanity enable them to develop positive feelings toward the tormentors as an unconscious defense mechanism to survive the trauma.

Stonewalling: Refusal to engage in a conversation or provide information or other resources as a form of punishment when the survivor expresses thoughts or emotions the pathological partner doesn't like.

Trauma Bond: A loyalty bond that forms between two or more people who experience the same traumatic event together. When it is based on power and control, it's a negative trauma bond because at least one of the people is exploiting the loyalty of the other(s).

Triangulation: A tactic used by pathological partners in which a third party is brought into a conflict either literally or abstractly to make the pathological partner appear in high demand, pit two people against one another, or to manufacture emotions, such as jealousy.

Undue Influence: A legal term for deceptive influence used to manipulate someone into doing something against their own best interests, it has only recently been argued for use as a legal defense against deceptive forms of mind control.

Walking on Eggshells: A metaphorical term for the emotional anxiety the survivor of a pathological love relationship often feels, due to not knowing what might set off an emotional tirade from their pathological partner. The survivor begins watching everything he or she says or does and curbing his or her behavior to avoid upsetting the pathological partner.

Word Salad: Circular language tactics pathological partners use that disable attempts by survivors to discuss their concerns. Word salad conversations can include rage, projection, stonewalling, blame-shifting, gaslighting, twisting words the survivor used to have a different meaning, using false equivalencies, playing the victim, covert put-downs for bringing up the issue, bringing up unrelated issues, accusing the partner of starting arguments, and others. These tactics absolve the pathological partner of responsibility for harm, instill fear and exhaustion in the survivor, create an atmosphere of "walking on eggshells," and result in a lack of closure and resolution. They condition the survivor to avoid or to stop talking about anything the pathological partner finds unpleasant or offensive to avoid these verbal punishments.

Appendix C—Resources

As of the time of writing, all websites and contact numbers in this Appendix were active. Please note that this list does not seek to be a comprehensive list of resources about the dynamics of pathological relationships, narcissistic abuse, or low-conscience disorders. The resources below may help you more specifically learn about the hidden manipulation described in this book. For a broader list of resources that is kept updated, please visit my website, Fairy Tale Shadows: https://fairytaleshadows.com/the-best-resources-for-narcissistic-abuse-recovery/

If You Need Immediate Assistance

- U.S. or Canada: Call 9-1-1
- U.K. or Ireland: Call 112/999

- Australia: Call 000
- India: Call 112
- China: Call 110
- South Africa: Call 10 111 for police or 10 177 for an ambulance
- New Zealand: Call 111
- Germany: Call 112

If You Need Crisis Assistance

- U.S. Crisis Text Number: #741741
- Canada Crisis Text Number: #686868
- Lifeline Crisis Chat (online live messaging): http://www.crisischat.org/
- **U.S. National Domestic Violence Hotline:** *For any victims and survivors who need support, call **1-800-799-7233** or **1-800-799-7233** for TTY, or if you're unable to speak safely, you can log onto http://thehotline.org or text **LOVEIS** to **22522**.*
- **U.K. National Domestic Violence Hotline: 0808 2000 247**
- **Canada—Go to this website to find resources within your province:** https://www.sheltersafe.ca/
- **Australia Domestic Violence Hotline: 1-800-737-732**—https://www.1800respect.org.au/ (live chat 24/7)
- **South Africa Stop Gender Violence Helpline: 0800-150-150**

- **The Trevor Project:** *Call 1-866-488-7386 or text* ***START*** *to* ***678678****. A national 24-hour, toll free confidential suicide hotline for LGBTQ youth.*
- **Trans Lifeline:** *Dial* ***877-565-8860*** *for US and* ***877-330-6366*** *for Canada. Trans Lifeline's Hotline is a peer-support service run by trans people, for trans and questioning callers.*
- **The National Sexual Assault Telephone Hotline:** *Call* ***800-656-HOPE (4673)*** *to be connected with a trained staff member from a sexual assault service provider in your area.*

Resources to Leave the Relationship Safely

Get help with . . .

- Emergency shelters and/or transitional housing: https://www.thehotline.org/2012/07/09/finding-resources-in-your-area/
- Making a safety plan: http://www.thehotline.org/help/path-to-safety/
- Restraining orders: http://www.loveisrespect.org/legal-help/restraining-orders/
- Documenting abuse: https://www.loveisrespect.org/legal-help/documenting-abuse/
- Finding legal assistance: https://narcissistabusesupport.com/legal-aid/
- Court information and assistance for divorcing pathological partners, particularly with relevance to custody: https://onemomsbattle.com

- Effectively going "gray rock" when you have children with a pathological partner: https://talkingparents.com/home/
- Finding a narcissistic abuse support group: https://narcissistabusesupport.com/narcissist-abuse-support-groups/
- Finding a therapist who specializes in narcissistic abuse: https://narcissistabusesupport.com/practitioners-page/

Learn More about Undue Influence, Mind Control, and Pathological Love Relationships

- *Bounded Choice: True Believers and Charismatic Cults* by Dr. Janja Lalich
- *Coercive Control: How Men Entrap Women in Personal Life* by Evan Stark
- *Combating Cult Mind Control: The Guide to Protection, Rescue and Recovery from Destructive Cults* by Steven Hassan
- *Cracking the Cult Code for Therapists: What Every Cult Victim Wants Their Therapist to Know* by Bonnie Zieman
- *Freedom of Mind: Helping Loved Ones Leave Controlling People, Cults and Beliefs* by Steven Hassan
- *Invisible Chains: Overcoming Coercive Control in Your Relationship* by Dr. Lisa Aronson Fontes
- *Shunned: A Survival Guide* by Bonnie Zieman

- *Take Back Your Life: Recovering from Cults and Abusive Relationships* by Dr. Janja Lalich and Madeleine Tobias
- *Terror, Love and Brainwashing: Attachment in Cults and Totalitarian Systems* by Alexandra Stein
- *Thought Reform and the Psychology of Totalism* by Robert Jay Lifton
- *Visible Bruises: What We Don't Know About Domestic Violence Can Kill Us* by Rachel Louise Snyder
- *Women Who Love Psychopaths* by Sandra L. Brown, M.A.
- **Coercive Control Collective**: https://coercivecontrolcollective.org/
- **Freedom of Mind Resource Center**: https://freedomofmind.com/
- **The Institute for Relational Harm Reduction** and Safe Relationships Magazine: https://saferelationshipsmagazine.com/
- **Lovefraud** (videos, courses, blog, and forum): https://lovefraud.com/
- **Open Minds Foundation**: https://www.openmindsfoundation.org/
- World Narcissistic Abuse Awareness Day: June 1
    - o Every year since founding World Narcissistic Abuse Awareness Day on June 1, 2016, Psychotherapist Bree Bonchay gathers together the world's leading narcissistic abuse experts and trauma therapists for a free virtual summit to empower survivors and raise awareness. You can sign up for notifications about the new one each year at https://wnaad.com/.

Acknowledgments

No one who leaves a pathological love relationship comes out of it the same person they were before they entered it. I don't take for granted how fortunate I am to have been able to take advantage of some of the best mental health resources and trauma therapy in the world. Without it, I would not have the coping skills and emotional strength I do today. I will always be thankful to Dr. Andrew Radu, Victoria Leonard, Lisa Sherper, Lenni Synder, Kim Wolfe, and everyone at Wake-Kendall. They have each had a permanent, positive impact on my life and have inspired and enabled me to give back. This book would not exist without them.

In addition to therapy, writing and research are two other important things that helped to bring me back from the land of the lost. I offer special gratitude to all the teachers who encouraged me to write with passion and all the professors who taught me how to think without judgment. I learned from you that almost nothing is what it seems, that it's okay not to have the final answer, that everything should be examined from multiple angles, and that we all have a story. Thank you for broadening my world Carolyn Wade, Dr. Susan Sharp, Dr. Trina Hope, Dr. Loretta Bass, Dr. Alan Brown, Dr. Craig St. John, Dr. Ann Beutel, Dr. Kelly Damphousse, Dr. Tom Burns, Dr. Wil Scott, and the late Dr. Harold Grasmick, who taught me one of the secrets of the universe—that linear algebra can be fun when you realize that the *x* and the *y* can be used to help explain why people do things.

To my friend and editor, Tina Morlock, thank you for encouraging me to keep taking the next steps forward all these years. You were with me as I lived through this nightmare relationship almost from the beginning even when you didn't know it because I was keeping so much hidden, and you have been my biggest supporter as I wrote my way to recovery. It was you who inspired me to keep going on this book when I wanted to give up. If not for you, I'm sure the book would still be unfinished. You pushed me to reach for more than what I believed I could accomplish and gave me the confidence to share it with the world. I don't even deserve you. Thank you for your love, friendship, advice, and support.

To two of my oldest and dearest friends, Dianeme Weidner and Amber Scott, thank you for always loving and treating me nonjudgmentally and for all the ways, great and small, you've offered your support, especially over these last few years. I treasure our friendship and look forward to making new memories with you. Love you, ladies.

The strangest things can save us in small but important ways. I want to thank the first District Karaoke team I ever joined. I'd also like to thank #teamnosleep, with whom I shared some positive and life-altering moments. Those moments helped me see myself from a different perspective and envision a life beyond the one I was presently living that didn't have my ex-boyfriend in it. Also, a big shoutout to

RevEx, one of the most openhearted groups of people I've ever met. Finally, thank you to Gen Kelsang Demo, whose teachings have had a profound impact on my life.

To Greg and Ayreen: you changed everything, and I will always be grateful for your kindness and support. Thank you for being such amazing human beings.

To Charles: During the longest and most stressful period of writing this book, you provided me with crucial emotional support. You're really the only person other than my editor who knows how much anxiety and pain I went through writing it. You listened to all my secret fears and never made me feel judged, and your steadfast confidence in me helped me finally reach the finish line. It takes a special person to deal so patiently and empathetically with someone else's obsessive quest to finish a project like this one. Thank you for restoring my hope and my ability to trust and love just by being exactly who you are.

Thank you to my mom and dad, Susan and Jim, for instilling in me the value of knowledge and the power of the mind and for their love and support. Thank you to my sister, Kim, for your kindness and generosity. Your strength is an inspiration to me. I'd especially like to thank my brother, Ian, who was there for me during freefall, those first few hours after I left the relationship when I had no idea who I was or what had just happened. You were always the one with whom I could share anything and thank you for being there at that time in my life.

To my son, Ash: Every action I take to try to make anything about the world better is always at its heart for you. You have always been the best thing that has ever happened to me. Without you, nothing else I do would mean anything. I'm so lucky to be your mom.

I owe Dana and Shannon my sanity and my freedom. Thank you for your honesty.

Finally—thank you to all the readers of Fairy Tale Shadows—especially Vesta and Hugh. You were witnesses to my pain, and your validation was crucial to my recovery. I think about many of you with whom I had conversations often, and I hope your darkness has turned to light as mine has.

Notes

Chapter 1

[1] I will often use singular gender pronouns and plural pronouns interchangeably throughout the objective sections of this book to represent pathological partners of all genders. Passages written about my subjective experiences will use the gender pronouns that reflect my personal experiences. As you read, please substitute the pronouns that fit your situation as appropriate and that you are most comfortable using.

[2] Christopher W. Tyler and Maureen B. Clarke, "Autostereogram," *Stereoscopic Displays and Applications* 1256 (September 1, 1990), Proc. SPIE, https://doi.org/10.1117/12.19904. For examples of stereograms, visit https://www.magiceye.com/ and http://www.colorstereo.com/gal-his/dir-gal-his.html.

[3] As described in Chapter 2, there are problems with the language commonly used to explain and describe pathological love relationships, including a lack of clarity. The survey conducted for this book used terminology with which many survivors are often most familiar due to the terminology used in most mainstream

resources available. These terms include "narcissist," "narcissism," and "narcissistic abuse." One primary limitation of using these terms is that the responses provided were assumed applicable to the term used to describe this type of relationship abuse in this book, "pathological love relationship," which was not used in the survey. However, a premise of this book is that the partner's diagnosis and how the abuse or relationship is labeled is less important than the behavior of the partner. Because a convenience sample of respondents who visited a website for narcissistic abuse survivors was used and the descriptions of the abuse on the website were similar to the descriptions used in this book, there is little risk of including respondents whose experiences were not representative of a pathological love relationship as described. For a description of the survey and the results, see Appendix A, "Narcissistic Abuse Survey Description."

Chapter 2

4 Sandra L. Brown, M.A.,"60 Million Persons in the U.S. Negatively Affected by Someone Else's Pathology," *Psychology Today,* August 8, 2010, https://www.psychologytoday.com/us/blog/pathological-relationships/201008/60-million-people-in-the-us-negatively-affected-someone-elses. This figure does not include survivors of all relationship types, such as parent-child. Note that Brown's writing has focused on women because she reports that almost all her clients who sought treatment at the Institute for Relational Harm Reduction have been women. She states, however, that her conclusions about the effects of pathological love relationships on partners hold for everyone.

5 American Psychiatric Association, *Diagnostic and Statistical Manual of Mental Disorders*, Fifth Ed. (Arlington, VA: American Psychiatric Association, 2013), 659–72.

6 Sandra L. Brown, M.A. and Jennifer R. Young, *Women Who Love Psychopaths: Inside the Relationships of Inevitable Harm with Narcissists, Sociopaths, and Psychopaths,* 3rd ed. (Balsam Grove, NC: Mask Publishing, 2018), p. 62–63.

7 Brown and Young, *Psychopaths*, 3rd ed., 119–126.

8 Sandra L. Brown, M.A., "The History of the Narcissistic & Psychopathic Abuse and Relationship Field." *Association for NPD/ Psychopathy Survivor Treatment, Research & Education,* accessed March 29, 2021, https://survivortreatment.com/history-of-the-field/.

9 Mary Jo Fay, "Narcissism Victim Syndrome, A New Diagnosis?" *Medical News Today,* July 17, 2004, https://www.medicalnewstoday.com/articles/10872#1.

[10] Christine Louis de Canonville, "Narcissistic Victim Syndrome: What the Heck is That?" *Narcissistic Behavior,* accessed December 17, 2020, https://narcissisticbehavior.net/narcissistic-victim-syndrome-what-the-heck-is-that/

[11] Louis de Canonville, "Narcissistic Victim Syndrome."

[12] The National Domestic Violence Hotline, "Understanding Relationship Abuse," *thehotline.org,* accessed March 1, 2021, https://www.thehotline.org/identify-abuse/understand-relationship-abuse/. The Hotline recognizes several distinct types of abuse and coercion, such as physical abuse, emotional abuse, sexual abuse, and financial abuse, and includes forcible coercion; however, it does not name narcissistic abuse as its own type.

[13] Barbara Brody, "Narcissistic Abuse is the Scary New Kind of Abuse You Need to Know About," *Health.com,* November 16, 2018, https://www.health.com/relationships/narcissistic-abuse.
Claire Jack, "The Day You Discover You're a Victim of Narcissistic Abuse," *Psychology Today,* May 25, 2020, https://www.psychologytoday.com/us/blog/women-autism-spectrum-disorder/202003/the-day-you-discover-youre-victim-narcissistic-abuse.

[14] Marie-France Hirigoyen, *Stalking the Soul: Emotional Abuse and the Erosion of Identity*, (New York: Helen Marx Books, 1998), 106–112. Hirigoyen describes the erosion of identity as emotional abuse that strips out the victim's emotional stability through irrational and confusing behavior so the victim is unable to defend oneself against exploitation.

[15] Brown and Young also include borderline personality disorder (BPD) in the list of low-conscience disorders because, as stated on p. 64, "it is listed in the DSM5 . . . (and the disorder is often notably damaging to relationships)." The DSM-V includes antisocial personality disorder (ASPD), borderline personality disorder (BPD), histrionic personality disorder (HPD), and narcissistic personality disorder (NPD) as cluster-B personality disorders, which it explains are "dramatic, emotional, or erratic" (p. 646). Brown does not include HPD in her list of low-conscience disorders. For the purposes of the pathology described in this book, I distinguish both BPD and HPD from the other cluster-B personality disorders because they do not appear to have the qualities that lead to a "relationship of inevitable harm." Those qualities include low empathy, lack of remorse, and an inability to change. Lack of empathy or remorse are not criteria for the diagnoses of either HPD or BPD. In addition, there is evidence to suggest that some types of treatment, such as dialectical-behavioral

therapy, can reduce or eliminate symptoms leading to a diagnosis for a large percentage of BPD patients who enter treatment, indicating that it may not be a pervasive disorder. Please note that their exclusion is not intended as a comment that harm or poor relationship quality is absent in relationships where a partner has BPD or HPD.

[16] Otto Kernberg, *Borderline Conditions and Pathological Narcissism* (New York: Jason, 1975), 115–117.
Heinz Kohut, *The Analysis of the Self: A Systematic Approach to the Psychoanalytic Treatment of Narcissistic Personality Disorders* (New York: International University Press, 1971), 107–110.

[17] Otto Kernberg, "A Psychoanalytic Classification of Character Pathology," *Journal of the American Psychoanalytical Association*, 222 (1970): 255–267, https://doi.org/10.1177/000306517001800403.

[18] Kernberg, *Borderline Conditions, 187.*
Kohut, *Analysis of the Self, 125.*
Eddie Brummelman, Sander Thomaes, Stefanie A. Nelemans, Bram Orobio de Castro, Geertjan Overbeek, and Brad J. Bushman, "Origins of Narcissism in Children," *Proceedings of the National Academy of Sciences*, 112, no. 12 (March 24, 2015): 3659–3662.
John W. Livesley, Kerry L. Jang, Douglas N. Jackson, and Phillip A. Vernon, "Genetic and Environmental Contributions to Dimensions of Personality Disorder," *American Journal of Psychiatry,* 150, no. 12 (1993): 1826–1831.

[19] *DSM*-V, 645.

[20] Michael B. First, Carl C. Bell, Bruce Cuthbert, John H. Krystal, Robert Malison, David R. Offord, David Reiss, Shea, Tracie M., Shea, Tom Widiger, and Katherine L. Wisner, "Personality disorders and relational disorders: A research agenda for addressing crucial gaps in DSM," in *A research agenda for DSM—V,* ed. David J. Kupfer, Michael. B. First, & Darrel A. Regier (Washington, DC: American Psychiatric Association, 2002), 123–199. Retrieved from http://citeseerx.ist.psu.edu/viewdoc/download?doi=10.1.1.454.966&rep=rep1&type=pdf. The issues with personality disorder diagnoses identified by the authors included the fact that many patients with pathological personality traits met some criteria for multiple disorders but couldn't meet the criteria of any single disorder. Other patients met the criteria for multiple personality disorders. The authors argued that multi-dimensional criteria for diagnosing personality disorders to examine how individuals function across many areas of their lives would help to eliminate these problems.

[21] *DSM*-V, 761.

[22] *DSM*-V, 669.

[23] Eve Caligor, Kenneth N. Levy and Frank E. Yeomans, "Narcissistic Personality Disorder: Diagnostic and Clinical Challenges," *American Journal of Psychiatry*, 172, no. 5 (2015): 415–422.

[24] Kernberg, "Psychoanalytic Classification," 255-267. Stephen Diamond, "Is it Narcissism or Sociopathy?" *Psychology Today*, July 18, 2017, https://www.psychologytoday.com/us/blog/evil-deeds/201707/is-it-narcissism-or-sociopathy.

[25] John G. Gunderson and Elsa Ronningstam, "Differentiating Narcissistic and Antisocial Personality Disorders," *Journal of Personality Disorders*, 15, no. 2 (2001): 103–109.

[26] *DSM*-V, 768.

[27] The description of the psychopathy variant of ASPD can be found in the DSM-V on p. 765. On the terms, sociopath and psychopath, Robert D. Hare, Ph.D., who is considered a world-renowned expert on psychopaths, states in his book *Without Conscience*, "Most clinicians, writers, and researchers use the terms, *psychopath* and *sociopath* interchangeably. . . . Thus, some clinicians and researchers, as well as most sociologists and criminologists, who believe the syndrome is mostly forged entirely by social forces and early experiences use the term *socio*path, whereas those . . . who believe that psychological, biological, and genetic factors also contribute to the development of the syndrome generally use the term *psycho*path. The same individual could therefore be diagnosed as a sociopath by one individual and a psychopath by another" (New York: The Guilford Press, 1993), 23. The *DSM-V* equates psychopathy and sociopathy in the traditional model of ASPD (p. 659) but in the multi-dimensional model of ASPD describes psychopathy as a variant of ASPD and does not mention sociopathy (p. 765). Because there is no clear observable distinction between a sociopath or psychopath and experts do not agree on the meanings of the terms, this book will not attempt to distinguish between them.

[28] Brown and Young, *Psychopaths*, 3rd ed., 61–4.

Chapter 3

[29] William Hart, Gregory K. Tortoriello, and Kyle Richardson, "Are Personality Disorder Traits Ego-syntonic or Ego-dystonic? Revisiting the Issue by Considering Functionality," *Journal of Research in Personality*, 76 (2018): 124–8.

[30] Martha Stout, *The Sociopath Next Door* (New York: Harmony Books, 2005), 52–3.

[31] Brown and Young, *Psychopaths*, 3rd ed., 63.

Chapter 4

[32] Lawrence Gelder, "At the Movies," *The New York Times,* September 13, 1991, https://www.nytimes.com/1991/09/13/movies/at-the-movies.html.

[33] The memoirs mentioned in this paragraph are Mary Turner Thomson, *The Bigamist,* (Self-Published: WhiteWater Publishing Ltd., 2017); MrsXNoMore, *The Secret Life with Captain X: My Life with a Psychopathic Pilot,* (Self-Published: Telemachus Press, LLC, 2014); and Abbie Ellin, *Duped: Double Lives, False Identities, and the Con Man I Almost Married,* (New York: Public Affairs Books, 2019). Thomson published a sequel/retelling of her experience in a pathological love relationship titled *The Psychopath* in 2021. There is currently an explosion of memoirs about individuals who have been married to pathological partners.

[34] Dateline, "Deborah Newell Opens Up about Dirty John," *NBCNews.com,* January 9, 2018, https://www.nbcnews.com/dateline/video/debra-newell-opens-up-on-dirty-john-1133156419736?v=raila&.

[35] Dennis Publishing Limited, "Women's Aid Issues Gaslighting Warning Over Love Island," *The Week,* June 21, 2018, https://www.theweek.co.uk/94456/women-s-aid-issues-gaslighting-warning-over-love-island.

[36] Natasha Jokic, "Need Proof That Hannah Should RUN from Luke P? Check Out These 6 Warning Signs," *Cosmopolitan,* June 25, 2019, https://www.cosmopolitan.com/entertainment/tv/a28183611/luke-p-gaslight-hannah-the-bachelorette/.
Jordyn Taylor, "Luke P. Moves to Gaslight America After Failing to Gaslight Hannah B. During *Bachelorette* Fight," *Men's Health,* July 17, 2019, https://www.menshealth.com/entertainment/a28421959/luke-p-gaslighting-hannah-b-fight-the-bachelorette/.

[37] Press Association, "MP's Daughter in 'Toxic' Relationship Before She Died, Inquest Hears," *The Guardian,* April 12, 2018, https://www.theguardian.com/uk-news/2018/apr/12/deputy-speaker-daughter-natalie-lewis-hoyle-inquest-toxic-relationship.
Diane Apen-Sadler, "Heartbroken Mother Tells How Her Daughter, 28, Committed Suicide while in a 'Toxic' Relationship and Blasts 'Gaslighting' Social Media Trend of Psychological Manipulation," *Daily Mail,* April 17, 2018, https://www.dailymail.co.uk/news/article-5626877/Mother-Deputy-Commons-Speakers-daughter-warns-gaslighting-committed-suicide.html.

[38] Katie Scott, "Pamela Anderson Posts Hospital Video, Photos Alleging Abuse by Ex-boyfriend," *Global News,* July 3, 2019, https://globalnews.ca/news/5455480/pamela-anderson-alleges-abuse-by-ex-boyfriend/.

Chapter 5

[39] Harry Velten, "The Influences of Charles Perrault's Contes de ma Mère L'oie on German Folklore" in *The Great Fairy Tale Tradition: From Straparola and Basile to the Brothers Grimm,* Jack Zipes, ed. (New York: W.W. Norton & Company, 2000), 966.

[40] Hervey Cleckley, *The Mask of Sanity,* 1st Ed. (St. Louis, MO: The C.V. Mosby Company, 1941), 286-7.

[41] Kristen Milstead, "Defining Narcissistic Abuse: The Case for Deception as Abuse," *PsychCentral,* July 11, 2018, https://psychcentral.com/lib/defining-narcissistic-abuse-the-case-for-deception-as-abuse/.

[42] Brown and Young, *Psychopaths,* 3rd ed., 129.

[43] The original source of the abbreviated idealize-devalue-discard version of Sandra L. Brown, M.A.'s five-stage cycle of pathological love relationships is unclear. One of the earliest resources appears to be a YouTube video posted by Sam Vaknin in 2011 (https://www.youtube.com/watch?v=KvEc0ojAWqU). As early as 2015, books and articles for narcissistic abuse survivors began to include the idealize-devalue-discard model. See, for example, Jackson Mackenzie, *Psychopath Free,* (Berkeley: Penguin Random House, 2015), 57–62 and Andrea Schneider, (2015), "Idealize, Devalue, Discard: The Dizzying Cycle of Narcissism," *GoodTherapy,* https://www.goodtherapy.org/blog/idealize-devalue-discard-the-dizzying-cycle-of-narcissism-0325154 In a phone conversation the author had with Brown on March 16, 2021, Brown hypothesized that the five-stage model may have been condensed into three stages by other writers to correspond with the more well-known cycle of violence developed by Lenore Walker to explain domestic violence generally. This model consists of three stages: Stage 1—Tension Builds, Stage 2—Violent Episode, Stage 3—Honeymoon/Remorseful Phase. (See https://www.womenscenteryfs.org/index.php/get-info/prevention/education/14-cycle-of-violence). Note that these stages do not correspond in their meaning with the stages in the narcissistic cycle of abuse. The motivations of the abuser are also not the same. For example, the pathological partner is not remorseful for his or her

actions. The idealization stage starts again only when the *partner* "falls in line." This is discussed more in Chapters 14 and 15.

[44] Shahida Arabi, "Love Bombing is Crack Cocaine," *Thought Catalog,* August 3, 2018, https://thoughtcatalog.com/shahida-arabi/2018/01/love-bombing-is-crack-cocaine-the-addictive-cycle-of-narcissistic-abuse/.

Chapter 6

[45] Elinor Greenberg, "What Type of Narcissist Does Well in Therapy?" *Psychology Today*, February 3, 2019, https://www.psychologytoday.com/us/blog/understanding-narcissism/201902/what-type-narcissist-does-well-in-therapy.

[46] Brown and Young, *Psychopaths*, 3rd ed., 92–4.

[47] Rebecca Umbach, Coleen M. Berryessa, and Adrian Raine, "Brain Imaging Research on Psychopathy: Implications for Punishment, Prediction, and Treatment in Youth and Adults," *Journal of Criminal Justice,* 43, no. 4 (2015): 295–306, https://doi.org/10.1016/j.jcrimjus.2015.04.003.

[48] Hare, author of *Without Conscience*, and Brown, founder of the Institute for Relational Harm Reduction, both suggest that more education and for mental health professionals, police, courts, and lawyers and the use of valid and reliable personality instruments that measure psychopathy could better separate those who would benefit from rehabilitation and reduced sentences from those who could not. However, these suggestions can only be helpful with individuals who are already involved with the legal or criminal justice system and have no benefit for men and women in relationships with pathological partners who have not violated the law and/or agreed to mental health treatment.

[49] As quoted in Sandra L. Brown, M.A., *Psychopaths, 2nd ed.*, 94.

Chapter 7

[50] Oprah Winfrey, "When People Show You Who They Are, Believe Them," *Oprah Lifeclass,* October 26, 2011, http://www.oprah.com/oprahs-lifeclass/when-people-show-you-who-they-are-believe-them-video.

[51] Sun Myung Moon, "We Who Have Been Called to Do God's Work." Speech, London, England, July 23, 1978, https://www.unification.net/1978/780723.html.

[52] Steven Hassan, *Combating Cult Mind Control* (Newton, MA: Freedom of Mind Press, 1988), 88–9.

[53] Claire Strutzenberg, Jacquelyn Wiersma-Mosley, Kristen Jacquelyn & Jennifer Becnel, "Love-Bombing: A Narcissistic Approach to Relationship Formation," *Discovery Journal*, 18, no. 1 (2017): 81-89, https://scholarworks.uark.edu/discoverymag/vol18/iss1/14.

[54] Dale Archer, "The Danger of Manipulative Love-Bombing in a Relationship," *Psychology Today*, March 6, 2017, https://www.psychologytoday.com/us/blog/reading-between-the-headlines/201703/the-danger-manipulative-love-bombing-in-relationship.

[55] Brown and Young, *Psychopaths*, 3rd ed., 144–151 (twinship tactics, including mirroring) and 187-191 (mimicking and parroting).

[56] Marvin Galper, "The Cult Indoctrines: Behavioral Science Perspectives Applied to Therapy," 1976, Paper presented to the Tampa-St. Petersburg Psychiatric Society, Tampa. See also Brown and Young, *Women Who Love Psychopaths* and Hassan, *Combating Cult Mind Control.*

[57] Hassan describes trance states as those where attention is focused internally in *Combating Cult Mind Control*, 111. Stronger gamma and theta brainwave activity correlated to these regions is found in studies published by Guiliana Mazzoni, Annalena Venneri, William McGeown, and Irving Kirsch, "Neuroimaging resolution of the altered state hypothesis," *Cortex; A Journal Devoted to the Study of the Nervous System and Behavior (Review)*, 49, no. 2, (2012): 400–10, DOI: 10.1016/j.cortex.2012.08.005 and *Raz M. Landry*, "Hypnosis and imaging of the living human brain," *The American Journal of Clinical Hypnosis (Review)*, 57, no. 3 (2015): 285–313, DOI: 10.1080/00029157.2014.978496.

[58] Clark Leonard Hull, *Hypnosis and Suggestibility: An Experimental Approach* (D. Appleton-Century Company, 1933).

[59] Brown and Young, *Psychopaths*, 3rd ed., 159.

[60] Bonnie Zieman, Cracking the Cult Code for Therapists: What Every Cult Victim Wants Their Therapist to Know (North Charleston, SC: Createspace, 2017), 56.

[61] Helen Fisher, *Why We Love: The Nature and Chemistry of Romantic Love*, (New York: Henry Holt, 2004).

[62] Preston Ni, "8 Signs That Someone is in a Relationship with a Gaslighter," *Psychology Today*, February 15, 2018, https://www.psychologytoday.com/us/blog/communication-success/201702/8-signs-someone-is-in-relationship-gaslighter.

[63] Mackenzie, *Psychopath Free*, 47-51.

[64] Shannon Thomas, *Healing from Hidden Abuse,* (Tempe, AZ: MAST Publishing House, 2016), 45.

[65] Hare, *Without Conscience,* 128.

[66] Brown and Young, *Psychopaths,* 3rd ed., 176–187.
Hare, *Without Conscience,* 129–130.

[67] B.F. Skinner, *The Behavior of Organisms: An Experimental Analysis,* (New York: Appleton-Century-Crofts, 1938).
Raymond Miltenberger, *Behavioral Modification: Principles and Procedures,* (Boston, MA: Thomson/Wadsworth, 2012).

[68] Shahida Arabi, *Your Brain on Love, Sex and the Narcissist: The Biochemical Bonds That Keep Us Addicted to Our Abusers* (Self-Published: Self-Care Haven, 2016). Also published online here: https://self-care-haven.com/2015/04/27/your-brain-on-love-and-the-narcissist-the-addiction-to-bonding-with-our-abusers/.

Chapter 8

[69] Leon Festinger, Henry Riecken, and Stanley Schachter, *When Prophecy Fails,* (Minneapolis, MN: University of Minnesota Press, 1956).

[70] Maria Konnikova, *The Confidence Game,* (New York: Penguin Books, 2016), 237.

[71] Leon Festinger and James M. Carlsmith, "Cognitive Consequences of Forced Compliance," *The Journal of Abnormal and Social Psychology, 58, no.* 2 (1959): 203–210.
https://doi.org/10.1037/h0041593.
Joel Cooper and Stephen Worchel, "The Role of Undesired Consequences in the Arousal and Cognitive Dissonance," *Journal of Personality and Social Psychology*, 16, no. 2 (1970): 312–320, https://doi.org/10.1037/h0029830.

[72] Leon Festinger, A Theory of Cognitive Dissonance, (Evanston, IL: Row-Peterson, 1957).

[73] Vincent van Veen, Marie K. Krug, Jonathan W. Schooler, and Cameron S. Carter, "Neural Activity Predicts Attitude Change in Cognitive Dissonance," *Nature Neuroscience,* 12 (2009): 1469–1474, https://doi.org/10.1038/nn.2413.

[74] Darwyn E. Linder, Joel Cooper, and Edward E. Jones, "Decision Freedom as a Determinant of the Role of Incentive Magnitude in Attitude Change," *Journal of Personality and Social Psychology,* 6, no. 3 (1967): 245–254, https://doi.org/10.1037/h0021220.

[75] Ashley A. Murray, James M. Wood, Scott O. Lilienfeld, "Psychopathic Personality Traits and Cognitive Dissonance: Individual Differences in Attitude Change," *Journal of Research in*

Personality, 46, no. 5 (2012): 525–536, https://doi.org/10.1016/j.jrp.2012.05.011.

[76] Joel Cooper and Russel H. Fazio, "A New Look at Dissonance Theory," *Advances in Experimental Psychology*, 17 (1984): 229–262, https://doi.org/10.1016/S0065-2601(08)60121-5.

[77] Ruth Thibodeau and Elliot Aronson, "Taking a Closer Look: Reasserting the Role of the Self-Concept in Dissonance Theory," *Personality and Social Psychology Bulletin*, 18 (1992): 591–602, https://doi.org/10.1177/0146167292185010.

[78] Brown and Young, *Psychopaths,* 3rd ed., 320.

Chapter 9

[79] Thomas, *Hidden Abuse,* 45.

[80] M.E. Thomas, *Confessions of a Sociopath,* (New York: Broadway Books, 2013), 140–1.

[81] Hare, Robert, Without Conscience, 49–56.

[82] Scott, Marvin B., and Stanford M. Lyman, "Accounts," *American Sociological Review,* 33, no. 1 (1968): 46–62, https://doi.org/10.2307/2092239.

Chapter 10

[83] Jim DeRogatis, "Inside the Pied Piper of R. Kelly's 'Cult.'" *Buzzfeed,* January 6, 2019, https://www.buzzfeednews.com/article/jimderogatis/parents-told-police-r-kelly-is-keeping-women-in-a-cult.

[84] Ruth Ingram, "Supporting People with Social Care Needs Who Are Experiencing Coercive Control," (2016): 1–17, Department of Health, Women's Aid, https://coercivecontrol.ripfa.org.uk/wp-content/uploads/Guidance-sheet-four-the-experience-of-people-with-care-and-support-needs....pdf.

[85] Evan Stark, *Coercive Control: The Entrapment of Women in Everyday Life. (Oxford: Oxford University Press, 2007).* Note that though Stark's original concept of coercive control conceptualized it as a type of abuse that men perpetrated on women due to the unequal power dynamics embedded in both gender roles and the larger economic division of labor, it is now recognized that any gender can be a perpetrator or a victim of coercive control and that it exists in relationships other than heterosexual ones.

[86] Stark, *Coercive Control.* See also Ingram, "Supporting people with social care needs who are experiencing coercive control."
[87] Sam Vaknin, *Malignant Self-Love: Narcissism Revisited,* 1st Ed. (Skopje, Macedonia: Narcissus Publications, 2015), 641.
[88] Daniel Lang, "The Bank Drama," *The New Yorker*, November 18, 1974, https://www.newyorker.com/magazine/1974/11/25/the-bank-drama.
[89] G. Dwayne Fuselier, "Placing the Stockholm Syndrome in Perspective," *FBI Law Enforcement Bulletin*, 68 (July 1999): 22.
[90] This phenomenon has been observed, documented, and reported in prisoners of war, cult survivors, pathological love relationship survivors, sex trafficking, and Nazi doctors. See Hassan, *Combating Cult Mind Control* and Brown and Young, *Women Who Love Psychopaths* 3rd ed. Also Robert Jay Lifton, *The Nazi Doctors: Medical Killing and the Psychology of Genocide,* (New York: Basic Books, 1986) and Alexandra Stein, *Terror, Love and Brainwashing: Attachment in Cults and Totalitarian Systems,* (New York: Routledge, 2017).
[91] Sandra L. Brown, M.A., "Cognitive Dissonance Perceived as Traumatic in Pathological Love Relationships," unpublished study conducted for The Institute for Relational Harm Reduction, as cited in *Women Who Love Psychopaths,* 2nd Ed. (2007), 321–2.
[92] Brown and Young, *Psychopaths,* 3rd ed., 333.
[93] Brown and Young, *Psychopaths,* 3rd ed., 334.
[94] Bertram Gawronski, "Back to the future of dissonance theory: Cognitive consistency as a core motive," *Social Cognition*, 30 (2012): 652–668, https://doi.org/10.1521/soco.2012.30.6.652.
[95] Brown and Young, *Psychopaths,* 3rd ed., 157.
[96] Sandra L. Brown, M.A., *Women Who Love Psychopaths,* 2nd ed.(Penrose, NC: Mask Publishing, 2009), 207–8.
[97] Bree Bonchay, "Getting Over A Relationship with A Narcissist," Free from Toxic, December 19, 2015, www.freefromtoxic.com/2015/12/19/getting-over-a-narcissist-by-dissolving-the-stranglehold-of-cognitive-dissonance-2/.
[98] Arabi, *Your Brain.*
[99] Patrick Carnes, *The Betrayal Bond,* (Deerfield Beach, FL: Health Communications, Inc., 1997), 32-36.

Chapter 11

[100] Brown, *Psychopaths*, 2nd Ed., 227–8.
[101] International Cultic Studies Association, *What Is a Cult?* Accessed June 22, 2020, https://www.icsahome.com/articles/what-is-a-cult.
[102] Zieman, *Cult Code.*

[103] Paul LaRosa, "How to Identify a Cult: Six Tips from an Expert," CBSNews.com, February 25, 2018, https://www.cbsnews.com/news/how-to-identify-a-cult-six-expert-tips/.

[104] The Jonestown Institute, "Alternative Considerations of Jonestown and Peoples Temple," Transcript, by Fielding M. McGehee III, *The San Diego State University, accessed July 7, 2020,* https://jonestown.sdsu.edu/?page_id=29079.

[105] Barry Meier, "Inside a Secretive Group Where Women Are Branded," *New York Times,* October 17, 2017, https://www.nytimes.com/2017/10/17/nyregion/nxivm-women-branded-albany.html?pagewanted=all.

[106] See for example Steven Hassan, "Controlling Relationships," *Freedom of Mind,* accessed February 22, 2021, https://freedomofmind.com/controlling-relationships.
Stein, *Terror, Love and Brainwashing.*
Zieman, *Cult Code.*

[107] Derron Brown, *The Push,* 2018, https://netflix.com. We should not take Brown's show to be a random experiment; he does not select individuals for the show at random but intentionally selects those who met criteria during the "interview process" he believes make them more compliant.

[108] Randy J. Larsen and David M. Buss, *Personality Psychology: Domains of Knowledge about Human Nature*, (New York: McGraw-Hill Higher Education, 2010).

[109] Solomon Asch, "Effects of Group Pressure on the Modification and Distortion of Judgments," in *Groups, Leadership and Men*, ed. Harold Guetzkow (Pittsburgh, PA: Carnegie Press, 1951), 177–190.

[110] Stanley Milgram, *Obedience to Authority,* (New York: Harper & Row, 1974).

[111] Philip Zimbardo, "The power and pathology of imprisonment," *Congressional Record*, Serial No. 15 (1971): 10–25. Hearings before Subcommittee No. 3, of the United States House Committee on the Judiciary, Ninety-Second Congress, *First Session on Corrections, Part II, Prisons, Prison Reform and Prisoner's Rights: California.* Washington, DC: U.S. Government Printing Office. Zimbardo's study has recently come under increased scrutiny and criticism due to its methodology, notably that a review of additional study documentation showed that Zimbardo had provided direction to the guards in his study about how they should treat the prisoners, in contrast to the information published with his results. Originally, the results of his study appeared to demonstrate the importance of social roles in the dynamic between the guards and prisoners and that the effects on the prisoners of the

guards' behavior arose spontaneously. However, the new knowledge that Zimbardo provided instructions to the guards casts doubt on these study conclusions, instead emphasizing the role of obedience and compliance with instructions from an authority figure in creating the conditions under which the guards would inflict harm and indignities on the prisoners.

[112] Brittney Rigby writes in an article about the immorality of putting contestants through the trauma of believing they murdered someone (https://junkee.com/the-push-netflix/151177). Olivia Truffaut-Wong asks, "Is *The Push* on Netflix real? Or is it just an elaborate prank on the audience?" (https://www.bustle.com/p/is-the-push-real-netflixs-creepy-new-special-is-simply-unbelievable-8343345). Another article by Stewart Perrie quotes viewers from across the Internet as they weigh in on the contestants: https://www.ladbible.com/entertainment/film-and-tv-people-are-calling-for-the-push-contestants-to-be-arrested-20180302.

[113] Andrea Wolfson, "A Hoax Most Cruel: Caller Coaxed McDonald's Managers into Strip-Searching a Worker," *Courier Journal,* October 9, 2005, https://www.courier-journal.com/story/news/local/2005/10/09/a-hoax-most-cruel-caller-coaxed-mcdonalds-managers-/28936597/.

[114] In his seminal book, *The Science of Social Influence: An Index of Tactics,* Anthony R. Pratkanis argues that all species have methods of influencing each other in efforts to try to gain resources and identified and described over a hundred techniques that have been used to influence people through advertising to subconsciously change their behavior. Beyond the Foot in the Door approach, these techniques include Ingratiation, Love-Bombing and Grooming (described in this book), Help Me Help You, Everyone is Doing It, Door in the Face, and This May Be Your Only Chance (Milton Park-Abdington, UK: Taylor and Francis, 2007).

[115] Edward E. Jones, *Ingratiation: A Social Psychological Analysis,* 1st Ed. (New York: Appleton-Century-Crofts, Inc., 1964).

[116] Janja A. Lalich, *Bounded Choice: True Believers and Charismatic Cults* (Oakland, CA: University of California Press, 2004).

[117] See, for example, Hassan, *Combating Cult Mind Control;* Robert Jay Lifton, *Thought Reform and the Psychology of Totalism* (Chapel Hill, NC: University of North Carolina Press, 2012); Alan W. Scheflin, "Supporting Human Rights by Testifying Against Human Wrongs," *International Journal of Cultic Studies*, 6, no. 1 (2015): 69–82, https://www.icsahome.com/articles/supporting-human-rights; Edgar

H. Schein, Inge Schneier, and Curtis H. Barker, *Coercive Persuasion: A Socio-Psychological Analysis of the "Brainwashing" of American Civilian Prisoners by the Chinese Communists*, (New York: W. W. Norton & Company, 1961); Margaret T. Singer and Janja Lalich, *Cults in Our Midst: The Continuing Fight Against Their Hidden Menace*, (San Francisco, CA: Jossey-Bass, 2003).

[118] Brown and Young, *Psychopaths,* 3rd ed., 343.

[119] Steven Hassan, The BITE Model of Authoritarian Control: Undue Influence, Thought Reform, Brainwashing, Mind Control, Trafficking and the Law, (Ph.D. Diss., Fielding Graduate University, 2021), 15, https://www.researchgate.net/profile/Steven-Hassan/publication/348419785_THE_BITE_MODEL_OF_AUTHORITARIAN_CONTROL_UNDUE_INFLUENCE_THOUGHT_REFORM_BRAINWASHING_MIND_CONTROL_TRAFFICKING_AND_THE_LAW_A_dissertation_submitted/links/5ffe37f3a6fdccdcb84d7270/THE-BITE-MODEL-OF-AUTHORITARIAN-CONTROL-UNDUE-INFLUENCE-THOUGHT-REFORM-BRAINWASHING-MIND-CONTROL-TRAFFICKING-AND-THE-LAW-A-dissertation-submitted.pdf.

[120] Edward Hunter. "Brain Washing Tactics Force Chinese into Ranks of the Communist Party," *Miami News,* (1950).

[121] Robert Jay Lifton, "Cults: Religious Totalism and Civil Liberties," in *Combating Cult Mind Control*, Steven Hassan, (Newton, MA: Freedom of Mind Press, 2018), 327.

[122] Margaret T. Singer, "Psychological Thought Reform Exists: Organized, Programmatic Influence," The Cult Observer, 11, no. 6 (1994): 3-4, accessed online April 22, 2021 https://www.cultrecover.com/sites/default/files/pdfs/CONTINUUM_INFLUENCE.pdf.

[123] Singer, "Psychological Thought Reform," 3.

[124] Margaret T. Singer, Maurice K. Temerlin, and Michael D. Langone, "Psychological Cults," *Margaret T. Singer Collection,* Carol Giambalvo & Rosanne Henry, eds. (1990): 118–145, http://www.prem-rawat-bio.org/academic/singer.html.

[125] Steven Hassan, "Controlling Relationships," Freedom of Mind Resource Center, accessed January 2, 2021, https://freedomofmind.com/cult-mind-control/controlling-relationships/.

[126] Hassan, *BITE Model of Authoritarian Control*, 48–62. A copy of the BITE model can be found online on Dr. Hassan's website, Freedom of Mind: https://freedomofmind.com/cult-mind-control/bite-model/.

[127] Hassan, "Controlling Relationships."

[128] Scheflin, "Supporting Human Rights," 69–82.
[129] Hassan, *BITE Model of Authoritarian Control,* 65.
[130] Scheflin, "Supporting Human Rights," 81–2.
[131] Tom F. D. Farrow, Michael D. Hunter, Iain D. Wilkinson, Camal Gouneea, Dianne Fawbert, Roger Smith, Kwang-Hyuk Lee, Suzanne Mason, Sean A. Spence, and Peter W. R. Woodruff, "Quantifiable Change in Functional Brain Response to Empathic and Forgivability Judgments with Resolution of Posttraumatic Stress Disorder," *Psychiatry Research: Neuroimaging,* 140 (2005): 45–53, https://doi.org/10.1016/j.pscychresns.2005.05.012.
[132] Singer, "Psychological Thought Reform," 3.
[133] Hassan, *Cult Mind Control,* 91–3.

Chapter 12

[134] Brown, *Psychopaths,* 2nd Ed., 238–241.
[135] Sandra L. Brown, M.A., Zoom call with the author, March 16, 2021. Brown and Young, *Psychopaths,* 3rd ed., 332.
[136] Lisa K. Fazio, David G. Rand & Gordon Pennycook, "Repetition Increases Perceived Truth Equally for Plausible and Implausible Statements," *Psychonomic Bulletin & Review,* 26, (2019): 1705–1710, https://doi.org/10.3758/s13423-019-01651-4.
Lisa K. Fazio, Nadia M. Brashier, Keith B. Payne, Elizabeth J. Marsh, "Knowledge Does Not Protect Against Illusory Truth," *Journal of Experimental Psychology: General,* 144, no. 5 (2015): 993–1002, https://www.apa.org/pubs/journals/features/xge-0000098.pdf.
[137] Brown and Young, *Psychopaths,* 3rd ed., 336–44.
[138] Brown and Young, *Psychopaths,* 3rd ed., 350–4.
[139] Zawn Villines, "What to Know about Executive Function Disorder," *Medical News Today,* June 6, 2019, https://www.medicalnewstoday.com/articles/325402.
[140] Brown and Young, *Psychopaths,* 3rd ed., 352.
[141] Janja Lalich, *Bounded Choice,* (Oakland, CA: University of California Press, 2004), 16.
[142] Sandra L. Brown and Jennifer R. Young, "Self-Perceptual Injuries from Pathological Love Relationships," unpublished study conducted for The Institute for Relational Harm Reduction, as cited in *Women Who Love Psychopaths,* 3rd Ed. (2018), 363.
[143] Hassan, *Cult Mind Control,*132.
Robert Jay Lifton, *The Nazi Doctors: Medical Killing and the Psychology of Genocide,* (New York: Basic Books, 1986).
Stein, *Terror, Love and Brainwashing.*

[144] Ginnie Jenkinson, "An Investigation into Cult Pseudo-Personality: What Is It and How Does It Form?" *Cultic Studies Review,* 7, no. 3, (2008), 199–224.

[145] Hassan discusses his views on this diagnosis in Combating Cult Mind Control (p. 300) and in his dissertation (p.7). The diagnosis can be found in the *DSM-V* on p. 305.

[146] Steven A. Hassan and Mansi J. Shah, "The Anatomy of Undue Influence Used by Terrorist Cults and Traffickers to Induce Helplessness and Trauma, So Creating False Identities." *Ethics, Medicine and Public Health* 8 (2019): 100, https://doi.org/10.1016/j.jemep.2019.03.002.

[147] Richard J. Brown, "Different Types of 'Dissociation' Have Different Psychological Mechanisms," *Journal of Trauma & Dissociation*, 7, no. 4 (2006): 7–28, DOI: 10.1300/J229v07n04_02.
Louis J. West and Paul R. Martin, "Pseudo-Identity and the Treatment of Personality Change in Victims of Captivity and Cults," *Cultic Studies Journal*, 13, no. 2, (1996), 125–152. Also accessed online April 24, 2021 here: https://sites.google.com/site/mcrais/pseudo.

[148] Carston Spitzer, Sven Barnow, Harald J. Freyberger, and Hans Joergen Grabe, "Recent Developments in the Theory of Dissociation," *World Psychiatry: Official Journal of the World Psychiatric Association (WPA), 5, no.* 2, (2006): 82–86, https://www.ncbi.nlm.nih.gov/pmc/articles/PMC1525127/.

[149] Brown, "Different Types of 'Dissociation'" 7–28.

[150] Brown and Young, *Psychopaths,* 3rd ed., 348–352.

[151] Brown and Young, *Psychopaths,* 3rd ed., 350.

[152] Lifton, *The Nazi Doctors.*

[153] Jenkinson, "Investigation into Cult Pseudo-Personality," 215–217.

[154] Hassan and Shah, "Anatomy of Undue Influence," 100.

[155] As quoted from "Cults: Religious Totalism and Civil Liberties," in Steve Hassan, *Combating Mind Control* (Newton, MA: Freedom of Mind Press: 2018), 329.

[156] Hassan and Shah, "Anatomy of Undue Influence," 100. Note that Hassan and others do point out that the identity disturbance remains after the cult influence (or other high-control influence) is gone and must be rooted out in therapy.

[157] Stein, *Terror, Love and Brainwashing*, 194.

[158] Brown and Young, *Psychopaths*, 3rd ed., 269–327.

Chapter 13

[159] Milstead, *Defining Narcissistic Abuse*, 2018.
[160] Zimbardo, "Mind Control."
[161] Martin C. Melchers, Mei Li, Brian W. Haas, Martin Reuter, Lena Bischoff, and Christian Montag, "Similar Personality Patterns Associated with Empathy in Four Different Countries." *Frontiers in Psychology* 7 (2016): 290, https://doi.org/10.3389/fpsyg.2016.00290.
[162] Brown and Young, *Psychopaths*, 3rd ed., 271–290.
[163] Brown and Young, *Psychopaths*, 3rd ed., 136.
[164] Hassan, *Cult Mind Control*,100-1.
Tom Buchanan & Monica T. Whitty, "The Online Dating Romance Scam: Causes and Consequences of Victimhood," *Psychology, Crime & Law*, 20, no. 3 (2014): 261–283, https://doi.org/10.1080/10683 16X.2013.772180.
Joan Reid, "Entrapment and Enmeshment Schemes Used by Sex Traffickers," *Sexual Abuse*, 28, no. 6 (2014): 491-511, https://doi.org/10.1177/1079063214544334.
Brown and Young, *Psychopaths*, 3rd ed., 136–7.
[165] Konnikova, *The Confidence Game*, 123.
Hassan, *Cult Mind Control*, 105.
[166] DSM-V, 774-779.
[167] Christine Hammond, "The Narcissistic Cycle of Abuse," *Psych Central*, May 4, 2015, https://pro.psychcentral.com/exhausted-woman/2015/05/the-narcissistic-cycle-of-abuse/.
[168] Brown and Young, *Psychopaths*, 3rd ed., 196–9.
[169] Mackenzie, *Psychopath Free*, 75.
[170] Hassan, *Cult Mind Control*, 277.
[171] Hassan, *Cult Mind Control*, 134.

Chapter 15

[172] Aron Ralston, *Between a Rock and a Hard Place* (New York: Atria Books, 2004).
[173] H.G. Tudor, "The Post Discard Battle Pt. 3.," *Knowing the Narcissist*, accessed July 11, 2020, https://narcsite.com/the-post-discard-battle-pt-3/.
[174] Martin Seligman, "Learned Helplessness," *Annual Review of Medicine*, 23, no. 1 (1972): 407–412, https://www.annualreviews.org/doi/pdf/10.1146/annurev.me.23.020172.002203.

[175] H.G. Tudor, "The Devastation of the Illusion," *Knowing the Narcissist,* accessed July 11, 2020, https://narcsite.com/httpnarcsite-com20161011the-devastation-of-the-illusion/.
[176] Tsoknyi Rinpoche and Eric Swanson, *Open Heart, Open Mind: Awaking the Power of Essence Love* (New York: Harmony Books, 2012).

Chapter 16

[177] Elinor Greenberg, "Narcissistic Love Patterns: The Romantic," *Psychology Today,* May 4, 2017, www.psychologytoday.com/us/blog/understanding-narcissism/201705/narcissistic-love-patterns-the-romantic.
Ross Rosenberg, *The Human Magnet Syndrome: Why We Love People Who Hurt Us,* (Eau Claire, WI: PESI Publishing and Media, 2013).
Ross Rosenberg, "Narcissists Can Love-- But You Should Still Run!" *The Good Men Project,* September 3, 2015, https://goodmenproject.com/featured-content/narcissists-can-love-but-you-should-still-run-fiff/.
[178] Rhonda Freeman, "Neuroscience Behind Idealize, Devalue, and Discard," *Neuroinstincts,* September 19, 2018, https://neuroinstincts.com/neuroscience-behind-idealize-devalue-and-discard-rhonda-freeman/.
[179] Brown and Young, *Psychopaths,* 3rd ed., 180–1.

Chapter 17

[180] Hassan, *Cult Mind Control,* 270.
[181] Hassan, *Cult Mind Control,* 202–226.
[182] Brown, *Psychopaths,* 2nd ed., 224.
[183] Brown and Young, *Psychopaths,* 3rd ed., 345–6.

Chapter 18

[184] Kristen Milstead, "How to Know if a Narcissist is Finished with You," *Fairy Tale Shadows,* January 19. 2019, https://fairytaleshadows.com/how-to-know-if-the-narcissist-is-finished-with-you/.
[185] Brown, and Young, *Psychopaths,* 3rd ed., 227–9.
[186] Brown and Young, *Psychopaths,* 3rd ed., 229.

[187] Skylar, "The Gray Rock Method for Dealing with Psychopaths," *Psychopaths, Girardian Theory & The 180 Rule*, accessed July 9, 2020 from https://180rule.com/the-gray-rock-method-of-dealing-with-psychopaths/. In the article, the author tells a story of how a stranger told her to be boring when her malignant narcissist partner is abusing her, and as a result, she came up with the term and approach "gray rocking" because gray rocks and pebbles are everywhere but no one takes notice. She has written a subsequent article about gray rock called "Gray Rock is a Mental Model" explaining further what she meant by the concept: https://180rule.com/the-gray-rock-method-is-a-mental-model/.

Appendix A

[188] Anselm Strauss and Julet Corbin, *Basics of Qualitative Research: Grounded Theory Procedures and Techniques* (Beverly Hills, CA: Sage Publications, 1990).

Appendix B

[189] Michael P. Johnson, *A Typology of Domestic Violence: Intimate Terrorism, Violent Resistance, and Situational Couple Violence* (Boston: Northeastern University Press, 2008).

Index

K

L

M

N

W

Z

About the Author

Kristen Milstead is a writer, researcher, and activist who is passionate about helping individuals with a history of trauma find their voices and overcome limiting beliefs imposed on them by others and about raising awareness about invisible exploitation and abuse. She worked in a homeless shelter for teens and taught classes at her own under-resourced high school before completing her Ph.D. in Sociology from the University of Oklahoma, where she focused on social norms and deviance, gender and sexuality, criminology, and sexual assault. After her experience in a pathological love relationship, she started a website for narcissistic abuse survivors, Fairy Tale Shadows (http://fairytaleshadows.com), which has reached millions of people from over 180 countries. She is currently an academic member of the Association for NPD/Psychopathy Survivor Treatment, Research & Education, and her writing has been featured on *PsychCentral*, *HealthyPlace*,

Your Tango, and *Thought Catalog*. She lives in Washington, D.C., with her Arabian Mau rescue cats from Kuwait, Bo and Chewbacca, and occasionally embarrasses herself by singing in a karaoke league.

Your pathological love relationship is over, but the emotional roller coaster is just beginning.
Coming soon!
Why Can't I Just Move On?
by Kristen Milstead, Ph.D.